The Foreign Policies of Lyndon Johnson

NUMBER ONE:
Foreign Relations and the Presidency
H. W. Brands, General Editor

In association with
The Center for Presidential Studies
George Bush School of Government and Public Service

The Foreign Policies of Lyndon Johnson

BEYOND VIETNAM

EDITED BY H. W. BRANDS

Texas A&M University Press
College Station

The paper used in this book meets the minimum requirements
of the American National Standard for Permanence
of Paper for Printed Library Materials, z39.48-1984.
Binding materials have been chosen for durability.

Library of Congress Cataloging-in-Publication Data

The foreign policies of Lyndon Johnson : beyond Vietnam / edited by
    H.W. Brands. — 1st ed.
        p.   cm. — (Foreign relations and the presidency ; no. 1)
    Includes bibliographical references and index.
    ISBN 0-89096-873-X
    1. Johnson, Lyndon B. (Lyndon Baines), 1908–1973.   2. United
States—Foreign relations—1963–1969.   I. Brands, H.W.
II. Series.
E846.F59   1999
327.73'009'046—dc21   98-46981
                                                           CIP

Contents

Publisher's Acknowledgment

Texas A&M University Press gratefully acknowledges the support and cooperation of the Center for Presidential Studies, George Bush School of Government and Public Service, Texas A&M University, in making possible publications of distinction on the presidency. The Center and its director, George C. Edwards III, have brought energy and prestige that make possible this book and others in this and related Press series. This contribution helps both the Press and the University accomplish their missions of promoting and disseminating the highest-quality scholarly research, analysis, and reflection.

The Foreign Policies of Lyndon Johnson

Introduction

H. W. BRANDS

In the study of every presidency, there comes a time when scholars turn from the issues that drew all the contemporary attention, to other matters, those that were less dramatic, less telegenic perhaps, sometimes less easily characterized (or caricatured) in terms of individuals and interpersonal conflicts. This is especially true regarding the foreign policies of postwar presidents. Studies of Truman administration foreign policy eventually moved beyond arguments about who started the Cold War; scholars of the Eisenhower administration got past debates about whether Dwight Eisenhower or John Foster Dulles wore the foreign policy pants in that Republican administration.

To some degree, the shift from the lead stories to those below the fold reflects a desire on the part of scholars to say something new; to some degree it reflects the availability of new things to say. The first wave of scholars to hit the archives tends to demand information on the issues that generated the greatest contemporary interest; this information feeds the second generation of writing (with contemporary reportage being the first). But by the time the second wave reaches the research rooms, the archivists have caught their breath and begun to make available a broader slice of the documentary record. This provides material for a third generation of writing.

The study of the foreign policy of Lyndon Johnson has reached this third generation. For obvious reasons, the Vietnam War dominated contemporary coverage of Johnson's foreign policy, and for most of those same reasons, as well as a couple just cited, it dominated the early histories of the Johnson years. But recently scholars have moved beyond Vietnam to examine other aspects of American dealings with the world during the Johnson years. The volume at hand presents the work of several of the best of these scholars. Robert Dallek, a distinguished diplomatic historian and biographer of Lyndon Johnson, evaluates the president as a world leader. Thomas A. Schwartz and John Prados examine Johnson's policies toward the North Atlantic Treaty Organization (NATO) and the Soviet Union. William O. Walker III and Peter Felten recount

American relations with the countries of the Caribbean, especially Cuba and the Dominican Republic. Douglas Little treats the principal Middle Eastern crisis of the Johnson years, the Six-Day War. Robert J. McMahon investigates American relations with three Asian allies: Pakistan, Thailand, and the Philippines.[1]

Two sets of questions come to mind in assessing the foreign policies of any president. First, who made the policies? Was the president an initiator of policy, or merely the overseer of policies conceived by others? Were the policies *his* policies, or simply policies of his administration? Second, how good were the policies? Did they manifest an insightful reading of the various elements impinging on policy? Did they appropriately match means to ends? Did they achieve their objectives?

Regarding the first question—as to who made Johnson's foreign policies—the authors here generally agree that Johnson did. All concede that the president preferred domestic affairs to foreign, and that domestic matters often influenced Johnson's responses to events overseas. On this point, received wisdom holds up well. But where some earlier writers have assumed that Vietnam so obsessed the president as to leave little room for other issues of foreign policy, the present authors perceive Johnson as firmly in control of his policies. Johnson was "a forceful foreign policy leader," in the words of Robert Dallek. John Prados discerns "a man actively engaged, grasping issues, exerting leadership." Douglas Little describes a president who took a very personal—albeit negative—interest in the activities of Egyptian president Gamal Abdel Nasser, to the extent of adopting an unspoken motto, "Nasser delenda est."

To be sure, Johnson's interest wasn't uniform across the globe of foreign relations. In the Caribbean, as William Walker and Peter Felten make clear, it waxed and waned depending on what Fidel Castro appeared to be up to. Robert McMahon sees something similar in Asia: a war between Pakistan and India could capture Johnson's attention, as could the connection to Vietnam of Thailand and the Philippines, but otherwise the president was only sporadically involved. What this demonstrates is not that Johnson didn't care for foreign policy, but that he was president rather than secretary of state.

As to the second question—whether Johnson's foreign policies were good ones—the authors deliver a mixed message. Peter Felten finds that presidential interest in the affairs of the Dominican Republic could be counterproductive. "When Johnson took the lead, he tended to bungle badly," Felten writes. On the other hand, when Johnson let others take the lead, Dominican policy proved more successful. Thomas Schwartz asserts an opposite view. Describing the Johnson administration's policies toward Western Europe as "impressive," Schwartz characterizes the president as a leader "capable of mastering the essentials of foreign policy as effectively as he had domestic affairs."

This said, some events transcended Johnson's control. As much as he distrusted Pakistan's growing ties to China, there wasn't much, as Robert McMahon explains, that he could reasonably do to keep this increasingly reluctant ally from essentially jumping camps. The Lyndon Johnson whom Douglas Little describes says, on the eve of the June War of 1967, that Israel is about to attack, and "there's nothing we can do about it." But, again, this is less a comment on Johnson than on the limits of power of any president, none of whom have been omnipotent.

If a single message emerges from the seven studies here, it is that the record of Johnson's foreign policy is more complicated than has generally been known. Johnson could be wise, and he could be foolish; his efforts to secure American interests in various parts of the world sometimes succeeded, and sometimes failed. Vietnam was an important influence on American foreign policy, but it wasn't always determinative. Domestic affairs shaped foreign affairs, but not to the exclusion of other influences. Robert Dallek cites the Dutch historian Peter Geyl: "History is argument without end." The authors here extend previous arguments about the foreign policies of Lyndon Johnson and ensure that those arguments won't end soon.

NOTES

1. At the cutting edge of Johnson scholarship during the last decade and a half (and covering domestic matters as well as foreign policy) have been three volumes edited by Robert A. Divine: *Exploring the Johnson Years: Foreign Policy, the Great Society, and the White House* (Austin: University of Texas Press, 1981); *The Johnson Years, Volume Two: Vietnam, the Environment, and Science* (Lawrence: University Press of Kansas, 1987); and *The Johnson Years, Volume Three: LBJ at Home and Abroad* (Lawrence: University Press of Kansas, 1994). Besides the contributions on specific topics by distinguished historians, these works display the masterful historiographical touch of the editor.

    Other volumes that examine Johnson foreign policy in the large are Diane B. Kunz, ed., *The Diplomacy of the Crucial Decade: American Foreign Policy during the 1960s* (New York: Columbia University Press, 1994), which also treats John Kennedy's foreign policy; Warren I. Cohen and Nancy B. Tucker, eds., *Lyndon Johnson Confronts the World: American Foreign Policy, 1963–1968* (New York: Cambridge University Press, 1994); and H. W. Brands, *The Wages of Globalism: Lyndon Johnson and the Limits of American Power* (New York: Oxford University Press, 1995).

1

Lyndon Johnson As a World Leader

ROBERT DALLEK

Lyndon Johnson's foreign policy leadership is synonymous with Vietnam. However, any rounded assessment of LBJ as president, and particularly as a world leader, requires us to look beyond Vietnam to other overseas' initiatives and reactions to foreign challenges and crises.

We have already made a good start on the study of Lyndon Johnson as a world leader with the appearance of Warren Cohen and Nancy Tucker's 1994 book, *Lyndon Johnson Confronts the World: American Foreign Policy, 1963–1968,* and H. W. Brands's 1995 volume, *The Wages of Globalism: Lyndon Johnson and the Limits of American Power.*

Both these volumes demonstrate that no study of Lyndon Johnson's foreign policy can leave aside Vietnam. The Johnson foreign policy, like all historical experience, is a seamless web. The LBJ policies toward the rest of Asia, toward Europe, the Middle East, and Latin America, were, to one degree or another, bound up with the war in Vietnam. This is not to suggest that historians shouldn't focus on other regions of the world, but in doing so they will need to remember that the war in Southeast Asia was the most compelling concern of the administration's foreign policy and national security leaders, including, of course, Johnson himself. As Nancy Tucker said in the concluding essay in *Johnson Confronts the World,* "the importance of southeast Asia for LBJ need hardly be emphasized, but the essays in this volume show clearly for the first time the enormous toll that their fixation took, dominating all other foreign policy discussions."[1]

My book, *Flawed Giant,* 90 percent of which focuses on Johnson's presidency, underscores Tucker's point by the emphasis I see the administration giving Vietnam compared to other parts of the world. To paraphrase the familiar adage that "war kills domestic reform," I think it is also fair to say that war destroys or at the very least substantially limits a president's freedom to focus on other foreign policy issues. Nevertheless, Johnson faced other world difficulties in Latin America, Europe, Asia, and the Middle East, and they deserve historical attention.

A greater understanding of Johnson as a world leader must begin with the man himself and the existing picture of his foreign policy leadership. The current portrait is of a domestic politician who had little patience with and understanding of external affairs. "Foreigners are not like the folks I'm used to," White House intellectual Eric Goldman quoted LBJ as saying. In his book, *The Tragedy of Lyndon Johnson,* Goldman cited the remark of another presidential aide that Johnson "wishes the rest of the world would go away and we could get ahead with the real needs of Americans." Goldman also pointed to Mrs. Johnson's mid-1965 wish that "foreign problems do not keep mounting. They do not represent Lyndon's kind of presidency." Johnson, Goldman said, thought of foreign policy as "something you had, like measles, and got over with as quickly as possible." The journalist Philip Geyelin described Johnson in his 1966 book on LBJ and the world as "King of the river," but a "stranger to the open sea."[2]

This picture of Johnson describes him as not only having limited interest in overseas affairs, but also as operating by reductionist clichés—the Alamo and Munich were his favorite historical analogies for how America should meet any and all difficulties abroad. Historian Waldo Heinrichs says in his 1994 essay in *Johnson Confronts the World* that "his appreciation of foreign nations was shallow, circumstantial, and dominated by the personalities of heads of state he had met. Lacking a detached critical perspective, he was culture-bound and vulnerable to clichés and stereotypes about world affairs."[3]

This unflattering portrait of Johnson as a generally uninformed and stumbling foreign policy leader hardly squares with H. W. Brands's observation that, apart from Vietnam, Johnson acquitted himself quite well in his handling of foreign policy matters. Johnson, Brands says,

> did better managing other aspects of the transition to a world no longer dominated by the United States. He dealt prudently and gracefully with de Gaulle. He negotiated a satisfactory solution to economic and political problems with West Germany. He prevented Turkey and Greece from going to war. He helped keep the third Arab-Israeli war short and localized. He held back from the second India-Pakistan war and did a fair job sweeping up the shards of his predecessors' policies afterward. He got out of trouble's way in Indonesia and positioned the United States to capitalize on the bad luck that befell Sukarno and the Indonesian left. He contained Castro in the Caribbean, if only by blunderbuss means.[4]

And, I would add to this list, the considerable success Johnson had in negotiating a nuclear nonproliferation treaty and a series of other agreements with the Soviets on outer space, consular relations, civil air transport, and the beginnings of strategic arms limitations that would blossom into SALT I during the Nixon presidency.

The point I wish to make is that the jury is still out on Johnson as a foreign policy leader. This is hardly surprising. As the great Dutch historian Peter Geyl said, "History is argument without end." The problem, I would suggest, is that until the Cohen-Tucker and Brands books we didn't even have an argument. I hope my paper may stimulate fresh debate and encourage further work on a subject of historical importance.

Let me begin by stating the proposition that, as in everything he did, Lyndon Johnson was a forceful foreign policy leader who consulted, listened to differing opinions, made up his own mind, and acted upon his conclusions with confidence that, all things considered, he was doing the best he could for the national interest. Moreover, I think it is simplistic to argue that Lyndon Johnson had limited interest in external affairs throughout his five-year term. We need a more dynamic picture of how LBJ's attention to outside events had its peaks and valleys. He knew that no modern American president could simply make domestic life the focus of what he did; he accepted the proposition that overseas matters were a vital part of his daily work as the chief executive of the world's greatest power.

Nor were clichés and stereotypes the principal ingredients of Johnson's foreign policy making. The historian's problem in getting at what Johnson intended in foreign affairs is the same one his associates confronted and biographers will always confront. Johnson, as Francis Bator, his National Security deputy for European affairs, says, "hated to be understood." Like Franklin Roosevelt, from whom he learned his primary political lessons, Johnson liked to keep his intentions hidden until he was ready to act. McGeorge Bundy echoed the point at the LBJ Library's 1991 conference on Vietnam. "This is not the easiest great man to understand in American history. . . ." Bundy said. "I think what we have to say to our friends the historians is, bear in mind the extraordinary complexity of Lyndon Johnson, how little we can agree on when he decided anything, and how much he would be delighted at our confusion."

Johnson's technique for obscuring his intentions was through rhetorical bombast, jokes, role playing, and a folksy sentimentalism that encouraged lots of people to misjudge his intelligence and shrewdness as a senator, president, and foreign policy maker in particular. Like all effective politicians, Johnson was a superb actor who used his talents to fill the stage and dominate an audience. He was an octagonal figure, in the words of one associate; a paradoxical character, in the view of another. And, this aide says, you never knew which qualities in the man were real and which were assumed. You simply couldn't tell.

A former LBJ aide told Ernest May and Richard Neustadt that "Johnson believed that what other people didn't know could hurt *him*. He guarded his thoughts from everyone except possibly his wife, Lady Bird. It was his custom, the same aide says, to reach a decision inwardly and *then* organize the process for making that decision appear the result of consultation and debate."[5]

None of this suggests that Johnson's leadership in foreign affairs was always wise or effective; to the contrary, there are plenty of instances in which historians can and will fault his judgments on overseas matters and his way of presenting policies to the public. But these limitations should not translate into clichés or glib assertions about Johnson's ignorance and parochialism. To date, commentators on LBJ's foreign policies have been more guilty of superficial analysis than Johnson was.

Simple analogs about World War II or Truman and Korea, for example, were not the principal stuff of Johnson's foreign policy decisions. He was attentive to current developments, recognizing that past actions were not surefire prescriptions for current problems.

Despite what military chiefs told him about the virtues of strategic bombing in World War II, for instance, Johnson himself doubted that such bombing would be sufficient to deter Hanoi from seeking control of South Vietnam. But once he had signed on to Rolling Thunder, he was reluctant to abandon the military action, thinking that would encourage the Communists to believe that the United States lacked the resolve to fight on in Vietnam. Consequently, his public statements on bombing and exchanges with advisers in Tuesday lunches, cabinet meetings, National Security Council discussions, and sessions with foreign policy advisers left the impression that bombing was an indispensable tool for fighting the war. Believing that some of his private comments would leak to the press, he adopted a consistent posture of faith in bombing. Nevertheless, there are plenty of instances in these many discussions about Vietnam in which his skepticism clearly comes through.

No one who wants to understand LBJ's foreign policy making can assume much from the record of any one conversation or even several. To decipher Lyndon Johnson's views, there is no substitute for reading the massive record over the course of his five-year presidency. It forcefully demonstrates the extent to which LBJ kept foreign policy making in his own hands and made judgments based on more than clichés and historical analogs.

Let me give you another example drawn from my research on Johnson's policy making toward Vietnam during the last fifteen months of his term. If you read Clark Clifford's memoirs, *Counsel to the President,* you will get a picture of Clifford and some of his associates leading LBJ toward a peaceful resolution of the Vietnam conflict. In Clifford's account, Johnson remained the captive of unrealistic thinking, encouraged particularly by Dean Rusk and Walt Rostow, about "winning" the war. Clifford later said that "despite his overwhelming personality and unique understanding of political power, Lyndon Johnson during this period often acted more like a legislative leader, seeking a consensus among people who were often irreconcilably opposed to each other, rather than a decisive Commander in Chief giving his subordinates orders." Clifford doubts that Johnson had a clear idea of his objective in Vietnam after his March 31, 1968, speech. He sees Johnson as "torn between an honorable exit and his desire not to be the first President to lose a foreign war."[6]

To Johnson, these were not mutually exclusive goals. Indeed, the key to his peacemaking was to arrange a settlement that both preserved South Vietnam as an independent state for the foreseeable future and the quickest possible American exit from a war the country by 1968 no longer wished to fight. Johnson, contrary to Clifford's belief, knew what he wanted. His problem was finding the means to get there, including the means to satisfy competing domestic factions urging different strategies for ending the war and the means to reach a settlement with Hanoi and an accommodation with Saigon.

My reading of the archival record has led me to a substantially different conclusion from Clifford's. It is true that both in public speeches and private discussions with his foreign policy advisers, Johnson spoke strongly about staying the course and assuring national self-determination for South Vietnam. No one should conclude that Johnson was indifferent to the fate of the South Vietnamese; he was greatly concerned to assure Saigon's survival in any postwar arrangement made with the Communists, which was one benefit he saw flowing from the U.S. sacrifice of blood and treasure in the war.

Nevertheless, the overall record demonstrates that by late 1967 Johnson believed that the American people wanted a prompt exit from Vietnam, and his every action was toward that end. Take the recently opened conversation Johnson had with Pope Paul VI in December, 1967. During their meeting he pressed the Holy Father to persuade President Nguyen Van Thieu, a Catholic, "to begin informal talks with some of those associated with the NLF [National Liberation Front]." Because Hanoi would not negotiate, the president hoped "that South Vietnam and representatives of the NLF can talk and settle their differences locally. . . . If South Vietnam's government would more or less leave us and talk informally with the NLF—and thereby the NLF leave Hanoi—this could be a way for South Vietnam to settle its own fate and have Hanoi and the U.S. pull away. . . . This would be one effective way of disengaging the NLF from Hanoi—and South Vietnam from us." When the pope replied evasively to the request, Johnson pressed harder for a commitment. "My motto now," he said, "is ' Peace in South Vietnam for South Vietnam and by South Vietnamese.'" He urged the pope to tell Thieu to talk to the NLF. "I strongly believe it would offer some chance of peace." The pope thought he could do something.[7]

By March, 1968, Johnson was desperately eager for an honorable way out of the war. He would not commit himself to a straightforward plan for ending U.S. involvement lest it look too much like an acknowledgment of defeat. Nor would he say anything in public that suggested that he was giving up on the possibility of an American victory. In speeches to the National Alliance of Businessmen on March 16 and the National Farmer's Union on March 18, he took a hard line. The contest in Southeast Asia, he said, was between Communist aggression and the forces of freedom trying to preserve the independence of South Vietnam. "We must meet our commitments in the world and in Vietnam," he declared. "We shall and we are going to win. . . . Make no mistake about it—I don't want a man in here to go back home thinking otherwise—we are going to win." It was time for all Americans "to unite . . . to stand up and be counted, . . . to support our leaders, our Government, our men, and our allies until aggression is stopped. . . ." The United States would not "surrender" or "pull out." We would not "tuck our tail and violate our commitments."[8]

Johnson's speeches were largely meant to intimidate Hanoi. Convinced that the Communists had taken a beating in the Tet offensive and might now be ready to talk, he wanted them to think that, despite growing opposition in the United States to the war, there was no likelihood of a U.S. pull back. He wished Hanoi to believe that its only hope for a settlement was through negotiations.

To give Hanoi an added incentive to talk, Johnson now signed on to a Rusk proposal for reduced bombing. On March 4, when Rusk suggested that we could stop bombing most of North Vietnam during the coming rainy season, a time of diminished air raids anyway, Johnson jumped at the proposal. "Dean," he responded, "I want you to *really* get on your horse on that one—right away." At a meeting the next day, Rusk urged the president to include a statement in a forthcoming speech on Vietnam directing "that U.S. bombing attacks on North Vietnam [would] be limited to those areas which are integrally related to the battlefield. No reasonable person could expect us to fail to provide maximum support to our men in combat. Whether this step I have taken can be a step toward peace is for Hanoi to determine. We shall watch the situation carefully."[9]

Johnson was eager to accept Rusk's suggestion. But he believed it could only succeed if Hanoi saw a new peace overture coming not from weakness but strength. During the second half of March, as he moved toward a major speech on Vietnam, Johnson played a double game. While he consulted and developed ideas about another try at negotiations, he did all he could to encourage the belief that the United States remained committed to South Vietnam's independence, even if it meant a long war.

To advance along the peace track, the president agreed to further discussions with the Wise Men, several of whom, including, most prominently, Dean Acheson, now saw the war as impossible to win and urged a withdrawal strategy. Clifford himself described the war as "a loser" and proposed to "cut losses & get out." The "ground war [was] wrong for us militarily," while the "air strikes [were] wrong politically." On March 16, Rostow gave Johnson a memo that "translated Acheson['s] idea" about withdrawing into a draft directive for a "team leader," who was to define "a policy of gradual reduction of U.S. forces in Vietnam: in the balance of 1968; 1969; 1970." When should the United States put forth a negotiating initiative? What should be its character? the memo asked. Additional evidence of Johnson's plans were in conversations he, Rusk, and Clifford now had with South Vietnam Ambassador Bui Diem. They all emphasized that Americans were "sick and tired of this war" and that Saigon faced "the loss of American support" unless it "broaden[ed] the government, clean[ed] up the corruption," and demonstrated a capacity to fight more effectively.[10]

At the same time, Johnson did all he could to hide his interest in de-escalation and a rising sense of urgency about peace talks. On March 14, Johnson told Clifford that he believed in consultation but did not want to bring too many people into the discussion for fear that Hanoi would learn about his "new policy." Johnson also worried that the head of the group studying Acheson's idea not reveal that he was "doing a Vietnam review job." During the two weeks before his speech on Vietnam Johnson emphasized that he intended to make his talk a justification for sending more troops and calling up the reserves. On March 20, eleven days before he was to speak, he told Harry McPherson to "get 'peace' out of the speech except [to say] that we're ready to talk. We are mixing up two different things when we include peace initiatives in this speech. Let's just make it troops and war. . . . Later on we can revive and extend our peace initiative."[11]

But Johnson's hard-line talk was a smoke screen for the peace initiative he was about to make. There has been much discussion of the idea that a Johnson meeting with the Wise Men on March 26 turned him away from escalation toward de-escalation. Though the majority of the advisers in that meeting expressed disillusionment and counseled a measured withdrawal from the war, several of them continued to urge a sustained commitment to the fighting.

Johnson himself encouraged the picture of a president startled by what the briefers had told the Wise Men and their change in perspective. He angrily asked Clifford and Rusk, "Who poisoned the well with these guys? I want to hear those briefings myself." But it is inconceivable that Johnson had casually allowed the Wise Men to receive objectionable briefings. Johnson, the master manipulator who never left preparations to chance, knew that the Wise Men would receive mixed messages from any honest briefing. As Mac Bundy told him after his meeting with the Wise Men, "We did *not* receive an unduly gloomy briefing. . . . I think your people gave us a clear, fair picture, and one which matched with what many of us have learned from all sources over recent weeks." Johnson's "outrage" over the briefings was feigned; it was part of his continuing effort to present himself as an unreformed hawk.[12]

Johnson's shift to a slow withdrawal strategy came not from what the briefers said and argued or what some of the Wise Men counseled. Instead, it came from a recognition of the reality that the war was stalemated and unable to be won without an escalation that would risk a domestic and international crisis unwarranted by the country's national security.

On March 20 he told his closest White House advisers, "I want war like I want polio. What you want and what your image is are two different things." As for his forthcoming speech, he wanted it to "meet emergency needs in strength" and to make "a reasonable offer on peace." On the 22nd, he told most of the same group that when the weather turned bad, "we should take advantage of possibilities for changes in bombing." Clifford endorsed the need for a change. The people "do not see victory ahead. . . . The military has not come up with a plan for victory. . . . The people were discouraged as more men go in and are chewed up in a bottomless pit. . . . The President asked for opinions on how to proceed on more peace moves." At a meeting with the chiefs on the 26th, Johnson gave what Clifford saw as a "painfully sad speech about his own difficulties." Johnson said: "We need more money in an election year, more taxes in an election year, more troops in an election year and more [budget] cuts in an election year. As yet I cannot tell them [the people] what they expect to get in return. We have no support for the war." The president's comments suggested to Clifford that Johnson "understood the need for a dramatic change in policy."[13]

When Johnson finally spoke to the nation on March 31, his speech was not a discussion of escalation or troop additions but of "Steps to Limit the War in Vietnam." The address began: "Tonight I want to speak to you of peace in Vietnam and Southeast Asia." He then reminded Americans that for years representatives of the U.S. government had unsuccessfully traveled the world seeking a basis for talks. His latest attempt at San Antonio last September to launch discussions had been rejected and the Tet offensive, which had "failed," had produced only more suffering in a country already burdened by twenty years of war. Now he wanted to renew the offer to stop bombing North Vietnam as a spur to negotiations, during which he assumed Hanoi would not take advantage of our restraint. He then announced an immediate unilateral halt to the bombing of North Vietnam, except in the area north of the Demilitarized Zone, where a continuing buildup threatened "allied forward positions." He named Averell Harriman as his personal representative, who would go anywhere, any time to talk peace. Reviewing the growing effectiveness of the South Vietnamese in their own defense and the need for a tax increase in the United States to meet expenditures in the war and at home, Johnson expressed the "fervent hope" that the North Vietnamese would cease their efforts to achieve a military victory and agree to join us at the peace table.[14]

My discussion here on Johnson and Vietnam in 1968 is meant to demonstrate how manipulative Johnson could be in behalf of a foreign policy end. This was not a man confused about goals or operating out of superficial assumptions about foreign affairs, but, in this instance, a tough-minded realist who rowed toward his objective, as was said of Lincoln, with muffled oars.

What the Vietnam examples also illustrate is the extent to which Lyndon Johnson aimed to assure his control of policy making. I think commentators have had it right when they have said that LBJ could not tolerate losing control over policy decisions and events either at home or abroad. No one who knows anything about Lyndon Johnson's leadership from his first days in the House of Representatives to his last hours in the presidency would disagree. Johnson had to be top dog, the master of the game. A large part of being a prominent public figure was setting the agenda or leading the Senate and then the nation along paths Lyndon Johnson believed they should go. Anyone who doubts this assertion need only read accounts of Johnson's service as vice president, when he suffered miserably as a nonleader consigned to the ceremonial chores that are the traditional norms of the office.[15]

There is a striking irony in Johnson's determined control of policy making and the realities he faced during his five-year presidency in overseas affairs. For someone who put such a premium on controlling events, it is almost painful to note how much foreign relations were beyond his control or were more the product of historical and contemporary influences than of what Lyndon Johnson said and did. Like Lincoln, who said privately of the Emancipation Proclamation, "I claim not to have controlled events, but confess plainly that events have controlled me," Johnson found himself forced to accommodate to international circumstances predating and surrounding his days in the White House.

Could Johnson have acted differently than he did in dealing with Cuba,

Panama, the Dominican Republic, de Gaulle, and the Six-Day War? Could he have avoided wider involvement in Vietnam? Possibly. Indeed, no one would want to argue that a president is bound hand and foot by what had come before or that current circumstances did not leave him with some options in responding to the major foreign policy questions of his term. In his dealings with Panama in 1964, for example, Johnson in fact showed a significant measure of flexibility and a readiness to open the way to negotiations that would culminate in the major treaty agreements during Jimmy Carter's presidency.

But most of Johnson's Latin American foreign policy was preordained by the specter of Castro's Cuba. As H. W. Brands says, "During his five years as president, Johnson pursued one objective in Latin America above all others: to prevent another Cuba. Strategic factors entered into the president's calculations," especially a concern to forestall the rise of another Soviet ally in the region and to assure the security of the Panama Canal. "But more than anything else," Brands believes, "the fear of political fallout from another successful communist revolution in the Americas motivated Johnson to take whatever measures were required to prevent it."

Latin American expert Joseph S. Tulchin agrees. "No matter how much time and energy Johnson and his advisers might devote . . . to the Alliance for Progress or to careful and considered reflection on how the U.S. might improve its relations with Latin America," Tulchin says, "U.S. policy was driven by spasmodic reactions to crises in the Caribbean Basin . . . and by an overpowering fear that instability would lead to 'another Cuba' in the hemisphere. That fear . . . inexorably reduce[d] the options Johnson was willing to consider in U.S. relations with the hemisphere."[16]

In the summer of 1967, during an off-the-record interview with a journalist inquiring about the president's plans for the forthcoming Punta del Este conference, Johnson declared that "failure of the United States to act in the Dominican Republic would have resulted in another Castro, and that the threat of communist aggression and of subversions exists throughout Latin America. He said that 12 countries were in danger in 1963, and the total is down to 4 or 5 now, but there are still many problems." In sum, Johnson measured U.S. gains in the hemisphere by how effectively his administration had blunted the communist threat. And in doing so, Johnson reflected what the Congress, much of the media, and most of the people believed was essential to the national interest in Latin America. Johnson, like most Americans in the sixties, saw hemisphere policy as primarily aimed at forestalling the rise of other Castro anti-American, pro-Soviet regimes.[17]

Was Johnson any freer to alter the course of events in the Middle East, particularly the Arab-Israeli Six-Day War of 1967? I think not. Despite applying what pressure he could to convince Cairo to reopen the Strait of Tiran and inhibit Israel from launching an attack, telling Israeli Foreign Minister Abba Eban, "Israel will not be alone unless it decides to go alone," Johnson lacked the wherewithal to prevent a war. He had little hold on Nasser and what influence he had on the Israeli government was weakened by his understanding that a preemptive strike by Tel Aviv would enjoy considerable support in the U.S. Congress and with the mass of Americans. Nor once the war began did the president find himself with enough influence to deter the Israelis from an attack on Syria. And when the Israelis attacked the intelligence-gathering USS *Liberty,* an apparently preconceived strike to keep Washington from knowing Tel Aviv's next moves against Syria, Johnson, despite his anger toward the Israelis, largely buried the issue. Only after Israel had made substantial strategic gains and the Soviets made threatening noises did the Israelis agree to a cease fire. Johnson, it seems fair to say, was more an observer than a shaper of events during the Middle East crisis of 1967.[18]

De Gaulle's decision to leave the North Atlantic Treaty Organization (NATO), the Soviet invasion of Czechoslovakia in 1968, the inability to advance strategic arms limitation talks with Moscow beyond preliminaries, and the resistance in Hanoi and Saigon to reaching a settlement before Johnson left office in January, 1969, are all additional examples of how conditions beyond Johnson's control largely shaped the outcome of other major foreign policy questions.

The 1965 decisions to escalate the war in Vietnam exhibited much the same determinism as that described in my previous examples. As Richard Neustadt and Ernest May pointed out in *Thinking in Time: The Uses of History for Decision Makers,*

> The more often we review the case the harder we find it to outline what LBJ could have said in 1965 to explain to the American people why he was dropping JFK's South Vietnamese allies or, alternatively, why he was beginning all-out war against Hanoi because of what impended in Saigon. Students, young and old, who try to outline the speech Johnson could have given over television, find the exercise distressing. They gravitate, as we do, toward a conclusion that LBJ's one real alternative was one scarcely hinted at even by [George] Ball, namely another dose of the 1963 medicine: engineering a change of regime in Saigon, but this time to bring in a clique that would call for neutralization and American withdrawal. . . . But when journalists picked up the scent, as they undoubtedly would, what then?[19]

The issue before us is not an either/or proposition. Did Lyndon Johnson have considerable leeway to chart an effective course in overseas affairs? Or was he essentially an unlucky president whose term of office coincided with external developments that lent themselves to little, if any, freedom of maneuver? It seems almost too easy to take the obvious middle ground here and reply yes to both propositions, depending on the particular country and the specific issue under consideration. But I see no substitute for case studies and the likelihood that we will find instances in each category. Before we can arrive at persuasive generalizations about LBJ's foreign policy leadership, however, we will need a lot of work on his direction of the many overseas challenges he faced during his term.

And even with these studies, there will never be uniformity of historical judgment on Johnson's performance. But thirty years after his presidency, it is time to begin doing the research and having this debate—time to free ourselves from conventional judgments about LBJ's personal limitations as a foreign policy leader and start discussing the specific options he did and didn't have. And where he made choices, we need to consider whether they were wise or shortsighted, beneficial or destructive to our national and the world's international well-being. Let the debate begin.

NOTES

1. Warren I. Cohen and Nancy Bernkopf Tucker, eds., Lyndon Johnson Confronts the World (New York: Cambridge University Press, 1994), chapter 10, p. 314 for the quote; also see H. W. Brands, The Wages of Globalism: Lyndon Johnson and the Limits of American Power (New York: Oxford University Press, 1995).
2. Eric Goldman, *The Tragedy of Lyndon Johnson* (New York: Dell, 1969), pp. 447–48, 625; Philip Geyelin, *Lyndon B. Johnson and the World* (New York: F. A. Praeger, 1966), p. 15.
3. Waldo Heinrichs, "Lyndon B. Johnson: Change and Continuity," *Johnson Confronts the World*, p. 26.
4. Brands, *Wages of Globalism*, p. vii.
5. See my interview with Francis Bator, Jan. 28, 1997, in *Flawed Giant: Lyndon Johnson and His Times, 1961–1973* (New York: Oxford University Press, 1998); Mac Bundy in *The Johnson Years: A Vietnam Roundtable*, edited by Ted Gittinger (Austin, Texas: LBJ Library, 1991), p. 138; Robert Dallek, *Lone Star Rising: Lyndon Johnson and His Times, 1908–1960* (New York: Oxford University Press, 1991), pp. 351–58. Richard E. Neustadt and Ernest R. May, *Thinking in Time: The Uses of History for Decision Makers* (New York: The Free Press, 1986), p. 79.
6. Clark Clifford, *Counsel to the President: A Memoir* (New York: Random House, 1991), pp. 527–28.
7. Meeting of the Pope and the President, Dec. 23, 1967, National Security File: Meeting Notes File, LBJ Library.

8. *Public Papers of the Presidents: Lyndon B. Johnson, 1968,* I, (Washington, D.C.: U.S. Government Printing Office, 1970), pp. 404, 409–13.

9. Lyndon B. Johnson, *The Vantage Point: Perspectives of the Presidency, 1963–1969* (New York: Holt, Rinehart & Winston, 1971), pp. 398–402; Clifford, *Counsel to the President,* pp. 496–97.

10. Undated, 1968 Clifford Memo, "S.V.N.," Clark Clifford Papers, LBJ Library; Walt W. Rostow to LBJ, "Summary of Dean Acheson's Proposal," Mar. 14, 1968; and "Draft Directive," Mar. 16, 1968, NSF: Memos to the President, LBJ Library; Clifford, *Counsel to the President,* pp. 507–509.

11. Memo, Mar. 14, 1968, Clifford Papers; Rostow to LBJ, Draft Directive, Mar. 16, 1968, NSF: Memos to the President, LBJ Library; Clifford, *Counsel to the President,* pp. 509–10.

12. See Clifford, *Counsel to the President,* pp. 511–19; McGeorge Bundy to LBJ, Mar. 27, 1968, White House Central File:EX/ND19/CO312, LBJ Library. Also see Rostow to LBJ, Feb. 1, 1968, describing General Matthew Ridgeway's growing skepticism about the war, Diary Backup, LBJ Library; and McGeorge Bundy's "Summary of Notes," Mar. 26, 1968; and "Summary," Mar. 26, 1968, NSF: Meeting Notes, LBJ Library.

13. Notes of meeting, Mar. 20, 1968; LBJ meeting with General Earle Wheeler, JCS, and General Creighton Abrams, Mar. 26, 1968, Tom Johnson Papers, LBJ Library; Luncheon meeting, Mar. 22, 1968, Diary Backup; Clifford, *Counsel to the President,* pp. 515–16.

14. *PPP:LBJ, 1968,* I, pp. 469–76. For a review of how the speech evolved into a peace address, see Rostow to LBJ, Mar. 19, 1970, NSF: Country: Vietnam.

15. An opening chapter on LBJ's vice presidency in the second volume of my biography is an ample demonstration of the point.

16. Brands, *Wages of Globalism,* p. 31; Joseph S. Tulchin, "The Promise of Progress: U.S. Relations with Latin America During the Administration of Lyndon B. Johnson," in *Johnson Confronts the World,* p. 227.

17. LBJ conversation with Charles Bailey, Aug. 7, 1967, Diary Backup, LBJ Library.

18. Brands, *Wages of Globalism,* chapter 7.

19. Neustadt and May, *Thinking in Time,* pp. 88–89.

2

Prague Spring and SALT

Arms Limitation Setbacks in 1968

JOHN PRADOS

Russia's representative at the funeral of John Fitzgerald Kennedy was Deputy Premier Anastas I. Mikoyan, a man with the reputation of being more moderate than the ideologues of the Communist Party of the Soviet Union. Succeeding to the presidency on the occasion of Kennedy's murder, Lyndon Baines Johnson met with Mikoyan during the somber days of the requiem. LBJ recounts telling Mikoyan, "he could be sure no day would go by in which I and my administration would not be working hard to ease world tensions and bring peace closer to us all."[1]

Over five years of a presidency often torn by dissension and strife, both foreign and domestic, Lyndon Johnson proved as good as his word. Though he would intervene against communism in Latin America and Southeast Asia and use fear of Russia's increasing involvement as justification for a policy in the Middle East, in bilateral Russian-American relations LBJ steered a non-confrontational course. The Johnson administration would increase trade and communication links with Russia, make use of a newly installed "hot line" directly connecting American and Soviet leaders, and reach accommodation with Russia on "arms control," that is, arrangements to limit or otherwise restrict weapons or military forces. The best-known arms control agreement consummated under President Johnson is the Nonproliferation Treaty, signed in July, 1968. There were also measures prohibiting weapons of mass destruction in outer space and substantial agreement on a similar regime for the seabed. Moreover, where Lyndon Johnson is often portrayed as ignorant of—perhaps even indifferent to—foreign policy, the record on Russian-American relations, especially arms control, shows a man actively engaged, grasping issues, exerting leadership in one of the thorniest policy areas facing his administration. Glenn T. Seaborg, a principal official throughout this period as chairman of the Atomic Energy Commission, had opportunity to observe LBJ in this field and argues that the president knew a lot more than is thought.[2] Clark Clifford, secretary of defense during the events at issue in this paper, and a connoisseur of presidents, writes, "I could see that arms control held the same importance to Lyndon Johnson in international affairs as civil rights did in the domestic arena."[3]

Least known among the arms control initiatives of the Johnson years is the effort to begin negotiations with Moscow on nuclear strategic forces. Yet across the spectrum of arms control the determination and commitment of this president are especially well demonstrated in the matter of nuclear forces. It should be added that Johnson's initiative failed, stymied by a foreign crisis, one triggered by Russian, not American, interventionism. But President Johnson's attempt to achieve something even after that tragic setback sheds a bright light on his endeavors in this area.

This paper describes Johnson administration preparations for Strategic Arms Limitation Talks (SALT); the Russian invasion of Czechoslovakia and its consequences for SALT; and the maneuvers through which LBJ sought to advance the negotiations. Although it fell to Richard Nixon, Lyndon's successor, to sign the first SALT agreement, Johnson merits much more of the credit than he has been accorded. This is that story.

Measures of SALT

When Lyndon Johnson took office there already existed an international forum for discussions on arms control. Located in Geneva, this was the Eighteen Nation Disarmament Committee (ENDC), operating under United Nations auspices and meeting, much like the UN General Assembly, with sessions every year. Early in the administration President Johnson asked his advisers to come up with proposals he could make at the ENDC, directly to the Soviets, or both. Before the 1964 elections LBJ made at least two such proposals, one for mutual destruction of bombers, the other for a verified "freeze" on strategic missile forces. Neither initiative gained much ground. Russian proposals in return were based on an ideal of universal and instantaneous reductions, called "general and complete disarmament," that never warmed hearts in the United States. Both sides also stumbled on the bugaboo of "verification," the actions required to ensure the provisions of any given arms control agreement were in fact being implemented.

Although Johnson's administration continued to attend the ENDC and engage in discussions at Geneva, during the middle years the government focused on unilateral measures, primarily concerning production of nuclear materials like plutonium. As LBJ had done on the bomber question in 1964, when the United States offered an international agreement on a measure it intended to carry out anyway (retire obsolete B-47 aircraft from inventory), the Russians were offered nuclear materials agreements. Nothing came of these initiatives, however. Between 1966 and 1968 the major arms control action concerned nonproliferation, with progress becoming rapid from the beginning of 1968, and a treaty completed and signed on July 1 of that year.

In the meantime technological developments were becoming increasingly central to the strategic nuclear balance and thus to arms control. Two major developments impended at this time: one was a relatively advanced (but only marginally effective) ballistic missile defense; the other, the advent of capability for independently targeting multiple warheads on a missile. With ballistic missile defense the Johnson administration withstood some political pressure to deploy an ABM (for "antiballistic missile") system against the Russians. Meeting at the Johnson Ranch before Christmas, 1966, Secretary of Defense Robert S. McNamara advised LBJ against any immediate ABM deployment decision. A couple of months later President Johnson made his first contacts with Moscow to offer ABM limits.

At Glassboro, New Jersey, in the summer of 1967, Johnson, Secretary of State Dean Rusk, McNamara, and other U.S. officials held a brief summit conference with Soviet Premier Alexei N. Kosygin. Separately and together, LBJ and McNamara made their pitch for an ABM agreement, but Kosygin rejected the proposal on the grounds that any defense against nuclear weapons was preferable to none. That fall McNamara gave a speech in San Francisco during which he announced the administration's decision to deploy a so-called "light" ABM network supposed to be oriented against Chinese rather than Russian attacks. Thus, in terms of eliminating a potential U.S. ABM system, the Soviets still stood to gain from an arms control agreement on missile defense. In addition, the recent memoir by Soviet Ambassador to Washington Anatoli Dobrynin informs us that Leonid I. Brezhnev, the other half of the Soviet duumvirate, who in fact had begun supplanting Kosygin in terms of political power, had a different attitude toward an ABM agreement. Brezhnev, writes Dobrynin, "was familiar with defense and industrial problems," and agreed with McNamara and Johnson's argument that missile defense would ultimately be futile, though he did not want to halt research in that area.[4] Kosygin told Dobrynin that missile defenses ought to be examined only in the context of offensive force reductions. Fundamentally, therefore, missile defense had not really been taken off the negotiating table.

Meanwhile, Lyndon Johnson himself retained an interest in offensive limits, not just defensive ones. The bureaucracy would be prodded for proposals, and the U.S. Arms Control and Disarmament Agency (ACDA), spearheaded by its deputy director, Adrian Fisher, was far along the road to a U.S. position even before Glassboro. The prospective position combined an ABM prohibition with an offensive force "freeze" of the sort suggested at Geneva a few years before. Though SALT historian John Newhouse views the 1964 freeze proposal as one of little consequence,[5] the Johnson administration's eventual negotiating position, as well as the SALT agreement actually concluded in Moscow in 1972, would not be very different. The major change related to verification—a switch from reliance upon physical inspection to remote sensing by reconnaissance satellites and other so-called "national technical means."

The discarding of any requirement for "on-site inspection" would not be a last-minute concession or eleventh-hour gambit. Rather, it reflected developments in intelligence technology and analysis. Under the Corona program, the Central Intelligence Agency and National Reconnaissance Office had developed sophisticated mechanisms for monitoring Soviet military activity, and since 1965 there had been secret experiments carried out by the United States to ascertain the degree of surety available from remote sensing.[6] From its earliest drafts, prepared under Adrian Fisher at ACDA in early 1967, the U.S. SALT freeze proposal incorporated verification by remote sensing. Moreover, the Johnson administration telegraphed this intention late that year when a senior Pentagon official gave a speech declaring the United States no longer felt it necessary to insist upon site inspection in arms control agreements.

In substance the U.S. SALT position would have frozen both offensive and defensive forces, including intercontinental ballistic missiles (ICBMs), submarine-launched ballistic missiles (SLBMs), medium-range ballistic missiles (MRBMs), and ABMs. In a concession to U.S. military interests, the SALT position excluded provisions that would have ruled out the most significant qualitative improvement then on the horizon, the multiple independently targeted warhead missile.

This last item is a key fact and warrants additional comment. Multiple warheads had existed in the SLBM force for years. With the advent of an active Soviet ABM system in 1964 the multiple warheads were touted as a "penetration aid," or device to help counter ABM defense. Weapons designers swiftly realized that multiple warheads that could be sent against different targets would greatly complicate the missile defense task, and eventually also understood that this capability conveyed a quantum jump to offensive force efficiency. The technology was called the multiple independently targeted reentry vehicle, or MIRV, and under that acronym became a headache to two generations of force planners and arms negotiators. By the late 1960s the United States had MIRVed missiles in advanced development for both its ICBM and SLBM forces.[7] The military wished to preserve the deployment option for these missiles, and arms controllers needed military support for a SALT position. As Robert Divine points out, under the ACDA freeze proposal of 1967, the military was simultaneously being asked to acquiesce in a nuclear regime in which Russia would have the only permitted ABM system (because it had already been deployed), and the military's preference for on-site inspection was being conceded.[8] Failure to constrain MIRV may have been the price.

The U.S. military in its own way was as much a sovereign entity as the Union of Soviet Socialist Republics. When the Committee of Principals began meeting on the position in the spring of 1967, the military made its predictable objections in spite of ACDA's preemptive concessions. The committee—a unit of top administration officials that included McNamara, Rusk, and Joint Chiefs of Staff Chairman General Earle Wheeler, in addition to other agency heads—wrestled over the SALT proposal. Central Intelligence Agency Director Richard M. Helms also expressed misgivings at the SALT provision that accepted verification by reconnaissance satellite in place of on-site inspection.

For approximately a year Washington made only glacial progress elaborating its SALT proposal. During this period Lyndon Baines Johnson exerted quiet leadership from the sidelines. As already noted, the president took a hand directly in the conversations with Kosygin at Glassboro. There is also the case of LBJ's celebrated "slip" in a speech at Nashville in the spring of 1967, when he admitted that satellite photographs told him exactly how many missiles the Russians really had. In the standard version, Johnson supposedly thought he was off the record when he said this. Of course, LBJ's sensitivity to what people quoted him saying is notorious, and his towering rages well documented; yet there is no record that Johnson ever complained about the leak of what had to be one of the biggest national security secrets in Washington. The possibility exists that LBJ's slip was deliberate, and that he intended to signal the military and CIA that he was satisfied with the satellite intelligence and they should be too.

In January, 1968, as Washington and Moscow began cooperating on the final stages of the negotiation that led to the Nonproliferation Treaty, LBJ again involved himself directly. President Johnson wrote Kosygin, advocating limits on offensive and defensive armaments as a way the superpowers could give example to all the nations being asked to face up to nonproliferation strictures. The Russian reply simply stated a willingness to look at issues in an indefinite future. At the end of a National Security Council meeting in late February, LBJ took aside Secretary of State Dean Rusk and encouraged him to redouble U.S. efforts. By April the State Department had news from the Soviets that Moscow would like to see a specific U.S. proposal.

By this time the SALT position of 1967 had evolved into a freeze incorporating ABM forces on both sides, that is, giving the United States advance credit for the Sentinel ABM program approved in late 1967 but yet to be deployed. The Joint Chiefs also continued to insist on the need for MIRV. The SALT position was finessed through the Department of Defense by a coalition of senior officials spearheaded by Morton Halperin, of the International Security Affairs Office, and Major General Royall B. Allison, representing the Joint Staff that served the Joint Chiefs of Staff. Instead of going straight to the top where service chiefs held entrenched positions, Halperin and his cohorts used the technique of getting the agreement of subordinate officers and only then approaching the senior ones. By summer the ACDA draft for a SALT position had been substantially agreed upon, even within the Pentagon.

Meantime, at the highest levels, on June 21 Kosygin wrote President Johnson that Moscow was willing to meet to exchange views "more concretely" on arms control measures. The president swiftly built on this response, enough so that on July 1, when the Nonproliferation Treaty was opened for signatures, the United States and Russia simultaneously announced agreement "to enter in the nearest future into talks on limitation and reduction of offensive strategic nuclear weapons delivery systems as well as systems of defense against ballistic missiles."[9] The next day Secretary Rusk met with Soviet Ambassador Anatoli Dobrynin and told the Russian diplomat that President Johnson would like another summit conference with Soviet leaders.

American SALT preparations now went into high gear. On July 8 the Committee of Principals for arms control, chaired by Rusk, gathered to consider an ACDA draft proposal embodying the current U.S. thinking on a SALT position. According to meeting notes, "Rusk said that President Johnson had worked hard on Kosygin . . . to get started on the missile talks. With the Kremlin's apparent assent, it was imperative now to bring the arms race under control."[10] This would mark the beginning of what Glenn Seaborg recalls as a "frenzied period of staff work."[11] Some issues were revisited. Clark Clifford, for example, who had replaced McNamara as secretary of defense, brought up anew the issue of verification and need for on-site inspection. Dean Rusk called upon Richard Helms to answer that concern, and the CIA chief replied that a study on the question would soon be available. Special National Intelligence Estimate 11-13-68 was duly completed about ten days later. Glenn Seaborg also raised the question of limits on qualitative force improvements and was assured that a treaty based on the U.S. position would permit them. Seaborg was thinking primarily of the warhead for the Sentinel ABM system, but the assurance applied equally to MIRV, as would soon become clear.

For a month there were intensive exchanges within the bureaucracy. The basic position paper was revised after consideration by the Committee of Principals, then again. By July 31 a third revision was available. The U.S. proposal provided for a freeze on ICBMs, MRBMs, SLBM submarines, a prohibition on deployment of any mobile ICBM systems, and, regarding ABMs: "the proposal would ban the deployment of more than a set and equal number of fixed, land-based antiballistic missile launchers and associated radars." As with ICBMs, mobile ABMs would be prohibited. Technological improvements were specifically permitted, and this was the language on ICBM launchers: "Building of additional silos, enlarging of existing silos, changing basic external configuration of silos and other launchers, and the relocation of launchers would be prohibited. No additional restriction would be imposed upon technological improvements of launchers of missiles already deployed including increasing the hardness of existing silos and deployment of MIRVs, or the retrofitting of existing launchers with new missiles."[12] This language, it should be noted, prefigured the agreed understanding in the 1972 SALT I agreement intended to prevent the Soviets from converting their smaller SS-11 ICBM launchers into emplacements for the large SS-9 (later SS-18 and SS-24) missiles.

The draft SALT position went before another session of the Committee of Principals on August 7. Dean Rusk opened this meeting "by reaffirming that the President wished to move ahead with the US-USSR talks on controlling the strategic arms race. He stated that it was the job of the Executive Committee not to find arguments why an agreement could not be attained but to determine how this could be done consistent with maintaining U.S. security."[13] It was, said Rusk, an "urgent" task. General Earle Wheeler's only objections this time concerned whether allies would be satisfied with U.S. provisions regarding the MRBMs that most directly threatened them; the danger of "clandestine" deployment of mobile ICBMs; and the need for limits on ABM radars. Dr. Ivan Selin, a senior systems analyst at the Pentagon, responded to Wheeler's concern over mobile ICBMs: they would have "little effect on the U.S. assured destruction capability since the U.S. forces must be prepared to withstand very much larger attacks from a MIRVed Soviet force that would be permitted under the agreement." The CIA estimates were that no more than two or three hundred mobile ICBMs could be deployed before there was high assurance of detection by U.S. reconnaissance satellites; by contrast, a MIRVed Soviet ICBM force would contain thousands of warheads.

Secretary Rusk, echoed by many of the other participants, advocated creation of a joint U.S.-Soviet "commission on strategic missiles," making the point in the context of verification. This prefigured the Standing Consultative Commission established by the SALT I Agreement, which still exists today.

Finally, there followed an important discussion of MIRVs. Adrian Fisher of ACDA remarked that the Soviets might propose banning MIRV, to which Ivan Selin added that the Pentagon's studies "had not addressed the question of whether it would be in the mutual interest of both sides to forego MIRVs." The fact of the matter was that the United States had two actual MIRVed missiles, the land-based Minuteman III, and the SLBM Poseidon, about to enter flight testing, with initial flights only about ten days away. "Secretary Rusk queried whether anyone felt the initiation of these tests should be postponed for fear that such action might foreclose options for future control. No one felt that such postponement would be desirable and, in fact, there were perhaps good reasons for not beginning the tests in the middle of the talks."[14] That is, U.S. officials preferred to have MIRV in testing *before* opening SALT negotiations.

Because analysts and historians of arms control generally agree that the fact that American MIRVs were in flight testing made it impossible to achieve any MIRV ban in negotiation with the Russians, this exchange on August 7, 1968, is pregnant with meaning and responsibility.

A fourth and final revision of the U.S. SALT bargaining position, prepared on August 13, contained no changes except to substitute a nine-year interval prior to review of treaty implementation for the previous proposal of a ten-year interval.

Approvals of the bargaining position quickly fell into place. Joint Chiefs Chairman General Earle Wheeler plus the chiefs of staff of the Army and Air Force concurred. The chief of naval operations and commandant of the Marine Corps held out for a few changes, especially ones that would enable the sides to shift more of their strategic forces to sea-based modes, but General Wheeler cut down their suggestions in his memorandum CM-3752-68 on August 9. Secretary Clifford's views went on record in a memorandum of his own on August 13. While making quite a number of stipulations, Clifford concluded: "on balance, and subject to the assumptions and conditions set forth . . . an agreement . . . would allow the actions necessary to preserve U.S. security."[15] President Lyndon Johnson gave formal approval to the SALT position, with a last minor change regarding ABMs, on August 27.

In the more rarefied atmosphere of Moscow's exchanges with Washington, events were also moving ahead toward a summit conference that would be the occasion to kick off the SALT negotiations. Ambassador Dobrynin writes that during July the Republican presidential candidate, Richard Nixon, asked to be received in Moscow by Soviet leaders. When Dean Rusk heard that Nixon's request had been accepted, he "observed rather gloomily that if Moscow was ready to receive Nixon, who he pointed out was 'not yet the president,' it might yet agree to meet the man who was still president of the United States."[16] Rusk asked to be called at any time, at the State Department or at home, whenever a reply came through to LBJ's proposal for a summit. Less than two weeks later Rusk prodded Dobrynin again for any message from Moscow. Finally, on July 25, Dobrynin handed Rusk a Soviet note agreeing to open SALT negotiations in a month or six weeks, but without anything about a summit. "Well, what about the main question?" Secretary Rusk asked. "Is there anything I can tell President Johnson?"[17]

Aside from Moscow's silence on the summit, Lyndon Johnson was visibly elated by the news of negotiations. Clark Clifford found the president very upbeat when he and Rusk met privately with LBJ on July 29. "I'll be in Moscow in exactly one month," Clifford quotes the president saying.[18]

Despite the optimism, however, Moscow's agreement to a summit was not immediately forthcoming. Days stretched into weeks, during which Washington put the final touches on its bargaining position as already described. It was on August 19, with Dean Rusk aboard the yacht *Honey Fitz,* that the Soviet invitation came through. Rusk scrambled to get the word to LBJ, who had gone to Detroit to address the Veterans of Foreign Wars. Just before deplaning from Air Force One, President Johnson learned that a message from Rusk was on the way. He waited to receive it. The word was that the Russians would receive President Johnson in Moscow on October 15 "or any other date close to that time." The next morning the White House staff prepared a press release and alerted journalists to stand by for an important announcement.

Suddenly other events intervened. The SALT summit announcement would never be made. Lyndon Johnson found himself embroiled in events of a much different kind.

Arms Control and Czechoslovakia

Upheaval occurred in Soviet Europe during 1967–68. Clearly major misunderstanding played a role. Soviet Foreign Minister Andrei A. Gromyko recounts the events, which took place in Czechoslovakia, this way:

> By 1968 the country occupied a stable position among the fraternal states, and the people had demonstrated their ability to heal the wounds inflicted by the war and Nazi occupation and to make progress both in their economic development and in strengthening the social order . . .
>
> Then suddenly the forces that were at one with the previous order, when power had been in the hands of politicians who cared nothing . . . decided to turn back the clock—and to do so with guns in their hands and without regard for casualties.[19]

In fact, Czechoslovakia groaned under the weight of communist economic planning and political organization, suffering production setbacks and other difficulties. The part of the nation known as Slovakia (today the Slovak Republic) in particular was not getting even the proportion of investment supposedly set aside for it in the economic plans. Not with guns, but at Czech Communist Party convocations, leader Antonin Novotny was voted out of many of his key offices, replaced by a then-Slovak party official, Alexander Dubček. Gromyko's reference to guns possibly concerns preliminary moves by Czech military forces toward a *coup d'état*, which Dubček tells us was called off by Novotny himself, who had also been the instigator. Soviet leader Leonid Brezhnev visited even before the end of 1967, and Dubček quotes him saying, "It's your business."[20]

Slovak leader Dubček, becoming leader of the entire republic as well as the Czechoslovak Communist Party, moved to the capital Prague. He began a series of reforms that became known as the "Prague Spring," a liberalization of communism, not the elimination of it, essentially similar to what Mikhail Gorbachev attempted in the Soviet Union of the 1980s. Unlike Hungary in 1956, when the liberalizing government had tried to sever ties with Russia by leaving its military alliance, the Warsaw Pact, Czechoslovakia made no effort to exit the socialist camp. Alexander Dubček's comments are illuminating:

> I had a keen sense of the historic importance of the moment and of the opportunities it offered, but I did not perceive the larger and more threatening obstacle on the distant horizon . . . the idea that I was twenty years too early did not occur to me in January 1968. . . . My problem was in not having a crystal ball to foresee the Russian invasion. At no point between January and August 20, in fact, did I believe that it would happen . . . Even looking back after twenty-five years, I do not see what I could or should have done otherwise.[21]

As the Czech liberalization proceeded over two hundred days, disquiet increased among neighboring Soviet allies, as well as in Russia itself. This was similar to the pattern in 1956, when unrest had occurred in Poland and East Germany as well as Hungary. In 1968, the East Germans and Hungarians were among those putting the most pressure on Moscow to do something about Czechoslovakia. Brezhnev and Kosygin grew increasingly concerned about the course of Dubček's Prague Spring.

These events in Soviet alliance politics were obviously taking place simultaneously with the diplomatic moves of the superpowers toward arms control talks. As Washington refined its negotiating position and LBJ cajoled Moscow to set a date for a meeting, in Moscow the need to act on Prague Spring more and more took the fore. The question arises whether Soviet moves toward

SALT, and minor concessions on commercial and other matters during the summer of 1968, were not intended to defuse international reaction to a Russian invasion of Czechoslovakia.

Unfortunately the lack of an actual record of Soviet foreign and military policy leaves us to reconstruct Moscow's decision solely from observable facts, and therefore our answer to the question of Soviet intentions in SALT is only informed speculation. Speculation or not, however, an answer here is important.

Between January 5, 1968, when Dubček became first secretary of the Czech Communist Party, and August 20, when the Warsaw Pact invasion took place, Dubček and other Czech leaders met with Soviet and other officials a number of times, including in Moscow in January and May, extended opportunities to speak with Kosygin, who vacationed at the Czech health resort at Karlovy Vary (Brno) from May 17 to 27, and at Cierna at the end of July. Russian pronouncements on the Prague Spring did not become openly hostile until after March, when Novotny resigned his last post as president of the republic. On May 24 Prague and Moscow announced that joint military maneuvers would be conducted in June. These were extended on July 2. The evidence indicates that during this early phase of the Czech crisis the terrain was dominated by Dubček's efforts to reassure Moscow. Thereafter the situation deteriorated.

On July 14 and 15 leaders of the Russian alliance met without Czech participation at Warsaw. Thereafter, on the 19th, the Soviet newspaper *Pravda* carried a story alleging that a cache of NATO (North Atlantic Treaty Organization) weapons, intended for sabotage and subversion, had been found in Czechoslovakia. On July 23 the Russians announced another military exercise, called "Nieman" after the river, supposed to test logistics along the Soviet border. Later Polish, East German, and Hungarian forces were publicly included in the exercise. In retrospect it is clear the Nieman exercise amounted to a cover for the preparations necessary to hurl an invasion into Czechoslovakia that would eventually comprise five hundred thousand troops with seven thousand tanks.

Alexander Dubček appreciated the danger of Prague's situation and held more meetings with Russian leaders at the end of July. This did not dissuade Moscow. Jiri Valenta, probably our best expert on Soviet decision making for the Czech intervention, concludes the final decision was made in Moscow between August 15 and 17.[22] Brezhnev sent one final letter to Dubček on August 19, and Warsaw Pact forces intervened against the Prague Spring the next day. In less than a week, and largely without organized opposition, Czechoslovakia would be completely occupied.

There are several disturbing coincidences in timing inherent in this chronology. Prime Minister Kosygin's letter to President Johnson stating a willingness to open SALT talks arrived on June 21, the day after the Warsaw Pact began its first set of military exercises. Those maneuvers were extended on July 2, the day after public announcement of SALT and the signing of the Nonproliferation Treaty. Kosygin's agreement for a date to open SALT negotiations, which was expressed in a note on July 25, followed by just two days Moscow's announcement of the Nieman exercise, its cover for a buildup to the Czech invasion. Finally, on August 19 we have Kosygin telling LBJ to come to Russia for a summit while Brezhnev writes Dubček, threatening Prague. The evidence is strong that these moves in different arenas were coordinated.

On August 20 Lyndon Johnson's aides were preparing their summit announcement for the U.S. press as Soviet and Warsaw Pact tanks crossed the Czech border. LBJ had scheduled one of his "Tuesday Lunch" national security meetings that day as well. As far back as July 12, Tuesday Lunch agendas indicate the group had discussed Soviet troops and Czechoslovakia, but the initial item this day was the summit, and toasts were drunk, with Prague Spring brought up later. Clark Clifford recounts, "Rusk believed that Moscow would not have agreed to a summit announcement if they were planning to do something in Czechoslovakia."[23] Director Helms of the CIA nevertheless reported the Soviets had just convened an emergency session of the Central Committee of the Communist Party of the Soviet Union. Walt Rostow takes credit for placing Czechoslovakia on the agenda for that day. Usually Rostow called around and asked what items were ripe for discussion, but this time he took the initiative himself.[24]

President Johnson's telephone rang at 7:06 P.M. It was Rostow, calling to say that Ambassador Dobrynin had an urgent message to deliver and would be around at eight.

"What's your guess?" LBJ asked. "Is it Czechoslovakia?" Rostow replied, "It could be."[25]

Anatoli Dobrynin writes that this exchange came about because he used President Johnson's personal phone number to request a meeting, which Moscow wanted to be between six and eight at night, rather than going through the usual State Department channels, which could make for delay. LBJ had given Dobrynin the number several years before, but the Soviet diplomat had never used it. Dobrynin has it that he spoke directly with Johnson, who first suggested noon for the meeting, details that are rather different from LBJ's own account.

Moscow's secret note to the president, which Dobrynin proceeded to read, maintained the fiction of foreign responsibility for events in Czechoslovakia, claiming "further aggravation of the situation which was created by conspiracy of the external and internal forces of aggression against the existing social order in Czechoslovakia and against the statehood established by the constitution of that country." This was asserted to be "a threat to the foundations of European peace and of security," which required "rendering necessary assistance to the Czechoslovak people." The Soviet note ended with the hope that "We proceed from the fact that the current events should not harm the Soviet-American relations to the development of which the Soviet Government as before attaches great importance."[26]

Dobrynin records of Lyndon Johnson, "Much to my surprise he did not react . . . at all, just thanked me for the information and said that he would probably discuss the statement with Rusk and others the next morning." He also claims LBJ went on to request Moscow's acknowledgment of his plan to announce the forthcoming summit the next morning, and ended the encounter with more recollections of the 1967 summit at Glassboro. Moscow sent along the acknowledgment within hours but, as Dobrynin adds, "events marched faster still."[27]

It seems farfetched that President Johnson remained oblivious to the Russian intervention against Prague Spring, unless he purposefully tried to calm Dobrynin. Johnson called for a meeting of his National Security Council, not for the next morning but for later the same night. LBJ spoke to the group quite clearly, according to Tom Johnson's meeting notes:

> It is one country invading another Communist country. It is aggression. There is danger in aggression everywhere.
>
> We need to give immediate thought to timing of meeting with Soviets. The agenda is more full now than before. We must discuss all problems before us. Is October agreeable or should we meet earlier.
>
> There are serious questions: (1) Can we talk now after this. (2) Does our presence look as though we condone this movement.[28]

The consensus of the meeting, including Lyndon Johnson in several remarks other than the questions he posed here at the outset, was that there could be no summit announcement and that Dobrynin should be told that very night. The former Soviet ambassador confirms that Dean Rusk summoned him to the State Department later that night. Dobrynin quotes Rusk about the summit: "We will keep in touch with you about this."[29]

Ambassador Dobrynin presents LBJ's desire for the summit as remarkable and slightly off-color, as if this were a matter of popularity or personal favor. Absent is the notion that Johnson wanted to move on arms control due to the urgency of the issue. Within a few weeks of the Soviet intervention, the U.S. government was again inching toward arranging a summit. Dobrynin records an exchange in mid-September in which Moscow not only agreed to a meeting but outlined a possible agenda. The indications are that Johnson concerned himself with the substance, the need, not his own popularity. The Russians, for their part, were no paragons of virtue in these events. As Dean Rusk put it, at a lunch-time meeting with Dobrynin on September 20, "The coincidence of the actions was like throwing a dead fish in the face of the President of the United States."[30]

Conclusion

So ended a serious attempt to open negotiations with Russia on limiting the most dangerous weapons in existence. Lyndon Johnson's failure to reach a summit with Brezhnev was a minor loss in terms of his accomplishments at president, though the collapse of arms control negotiations in 1968 would be much more grave, even tragic. This point can be analyzed from several perspectives.

In terms of the arms race as a whole, 1968 figured as a watershed year between the era of numerical expansion and the onset of the demon of technological improvement. Not that there had not been technical advances previously; in fact quite a few improvements had occurred. But the strategic environment of the earlier period had been markedly different. In 1969, and with increasing weight thereafter, a nascent and growing Russian lead in numbers of ICBM missiles created an imperative for Washington to counter that lead with technology. The multiple independently targeted warheads of the 1970s and strategic defense initiative of the 1980s proved highly destabilizing for the arms race and extremely costly for all the powers building nuclear weapons.

From the perspective of Washington, a key opportunity passed in 1968. Soviet missile forces that year were rapidly catching up to the United States in terms of numbers. The silos that would give Moscow numerical parity, and then a slight superiority, were already under construction or were just starting. Washington's arms control proposal was precisely to freeze nuclear forces at existing levels. Such a measure would have blunted the numerical trends that led to Washington's imperative for qualitative improvement.

Failing to open talks in 1968 also meant the job would be passed along to the next administration, that of Richard Nixon, with two additional consequences. Because the new administration understandably consumed time in putting its house in order on an arms control position, the delay permitted the first of the destabilizing qualitative developments, MIRV, to emerge from engineering development. Like the camel's nose entering the tent, Johnson's memorable phrase, the advent of unconstrained technical development quickly appeared a panacea to many and could only be capped much later with considerable difficulty. Moreover, because the eventual Nixon administration SALT proposal would in fact be a numerical freeze, nothing was gained on the arms control side from the delay due to Soviet intervention in Czechoslovakia.

An equally pernicious consequence of 1968 would be political. The numerical trends in missile forces eventually led to a Russian advantage of a good 50 percent (1,513 to 1,054 ICBMs). While many strategic analysts argue with good reason that there was no leverage to be gained from the disparity, and indeed that the qualitative status of the nuclear balance favored the United States, the mere perception of a disparity had political effects in the United States. As late as the presidential elections of 1980 and 1984, charges of Russian military superiority carried undue weight in American politics. Had President Johnson successfully led a push for a SALT agreement in 1968, the parity in forces that would then have been established would have helped curb some of the extreme rhetoric of later years.

Unfortunately, LBJ had very few cards to play when push came to shove in Prague. United States forces in NATO were not prepared for counter intervention. The NATO allies were, if anything, even less prepared, and they had little interest in military posturing over Prague Spring. Washington lacked treaty ties or substantial interests in Czechoslovakia to justify maneuvers beyond the diplomatic. Had Johnson had more warning of the Soviet intervention than he did, it would not have mattered. The Cold War in 1968 was simply not hot enough for the superpowers to come to blows over Czechoslovakia.

One final question is whether Lyndon Johnson ought to have gone ahead with SALT in spite of Czechoslovakia. He wanted to engage the Soviets in negotiations for the sake of capping the arms race, and, as the foregoing analysis suggests, the consequences of not moving to SALT were enormous. But LBJ, political to his fingertips, well knew that 1968 was a political year in the United States. His conversations with senators about ratification of the Nonproliferation Treaty, then impending, also served to warn Johnson against ignoring the political fallout of the Soviet intervention. The president could not afford to be seen as condoning the Russian invasion. Johnson squared the circle by canceling the immediate SALT summit and then attempting to revive the initiative in the waning days of his administration. By then Richard Nixon had won the presidential election and took arms control into his own hands. In sum, in 1968 the Cold War was simply not *cold* enough for LBJ to forge ahead with SALT despite Czechoslovakia.

From the Soviet standpoint Moscow's perspective on the conundrum of Prague Spring and SALT adds up to a weighty paradox. The decision to invade Czechoslovakia ultimately was Moscow's to make, and the results of that choice have reverberated down the years. Leonid Brezhnev thought it important enough that he consecrated the notion with his name—"Brezhnev Doctrine"—the idea that no Russian ally would be permitted to move out of Moscow's orbit. Threatening the Russians with cancellation of SALT, in retaliation for Soviet actions in Czechoslovakia, which was about the limit of U.S. diplomatic scope in the circumstances, simply did not affect any Soviet interest enough to turn Moscow aside.

With that said, it nevertheless remains true that Brezhnev's decision to invade Czechoslovakia went against Moscow's own best interests, and not merely for the Cold War types of reasons usually cited. In terms of the strategic nuclear balance Russia stood at the brink of parity. The Russians did not need any more than that, and Moscow definitely did not need a competition with the United States for qualitative improvements. To the degree that intervention against the Prague Spring prevented an early SALT agreement, Moscow lost over the long term. In fact, if the post–Cold War judgment is correct, that the military competition for high technology bankrupted the Soviet Union, Brezhnev's decision on Czechoslovakia can be seen as adding measurably to the extent and rate of the Soviet decline.

The most immediate and obvious losers in this whole episode were the Czech and Slovak peoples. The Dubček government's fall, and the Soviet occupation, destroyed all the reforms that had been put in place after Novotny's demise. The Prague Spring ended, to be followed by twenty years under the Soviet yoke. But when Dubček's successors succumbed in their turn, there would be no going back. It would be the end of communism in Czechoslovakia, indeed of the country itself, which splintered into the Czech Republic and the Slovak Republic, two national entities. Irony of ironies, had Moscow gone along with the Czech Spring and liberalized along the path Alexander Dubček had shown, Brezhnev might actually have accomplished what Mikhail Gorbachev failed at during the 1980s, a reform of Soviet communism. In that case, the Cold War thaw would have begun sooner, and with SALT in place at a state of parity, the technological arms race might have been headed off before developing its greatest impetus.

As it turned out there were many losers from the events of 1968, and no real winners in this analysis. The setback to Lyndon Johnson's plans for a triumphal summit cost arms control for years and spawned untold thousands of increasingly dangerous nuclear warheads. In fact, after two SALT agreements, two strategic arms reduction treaties, plus a treaty eliminating intermediate range nuclear missiles, today there continue to be more nuclear warheads atop land-based rockets than there were in 1967. LBJ himself suffered some grief in failing to get the summit, and there were political costs across America over many years. For Czechoslovakia there were two more decades of darkness. For

Moscow the ultimate cost would be the disintegration of the Union of Soviet Socialist Republics. And all these consequences stand entirely apart from the many other traumas, in the United States, Vietnam, and elsewhere, of that very fateful year. We can but hope there will never be another year like 1968.

NOTES

1. Lyndon B. Johnson, *The Vantage Point* (New York: Holt, Rinehart & Winston, 1971) p. 463.
2. Glenn T. Seaborg with Benjamin S. Loeb, *Stemming the Tide: Arms Control in the Johnson Years* (Lexington, Mass.: Lexington Books, 1987), pp. 13–14.
3. Clark Clifford with Richard Holbrooke, *Counsel to the President: A Memoir* (New York: Random House, 1991), p. 560.
4. Anatoli Dobrynin, *In Confidence: Moscow's Ambassador to America's Six Cold War Presidents, (1962–1986)* (New York: Times Books, 1995), p. 150.
5. John Newhouse, *Cold Dawn: The Story of SALT* (New York: Holt, Rinehart & Winston, 1973), p. 69.
6. In addition, the Central Intelligence Agency and National Reconnaissance Office under CORONA were in the process of introducing a new generation of reconnaissance satellites with even greater capacity. See Jeffrey T. Richelson, *America's Secret Eyes in Space* (New York: Harper & Row, 1990), passim. The CIA and NRO have recently declassified the CORONA program and its photography up to 1972. Relevant documents are collected in Kevin C. Ruffner, ed., *CIA Cold War Records: CORONA: America's First Satellite Program* (Washington, D.C.: CIA History Staff, 1995). For a study of intelligence reporting based on the remote sensing technology see John Prados, *The Soviet Estimate* (Princeton: Princeton University Press, 1986).
7. Ted Greenwood, *Making the MIRV* (Cambridge, Mass.: Ballinger, 1975).
8. Robert Divine, "Lyndon Johnson and Strategic Arms Limitation," in Divine, ed., *The Johnson Years, Vol. 3: LBJ at Home and Abroad* (Lawrence: University Press of Kansas, 1994), p. 259.
9. Johnson, *The Vantage Point,* quoted on p. 485.
10. Glenn Seaborg notes, July 8, 1968. In Seaborg, *Stemming the Tide,* p. 433.
11. Ibid., p. 432.
12. Arms Control and Disarmament Agency (ACDA), Paper 2956/Revision 3, "Strategic Missile Talks Proposal," July 31, 1968 (declassified Feb. 17, 1993). Lyndon B. Johnson Library (hereafter LBJ Library): Johnson Papers: National Security File (hereafter LBJP:NSF): Intelligence File, b. 11, folder "Arms Limitation Talks."
13. ACDA, Document 2990, Minutes, "Meeting of the Executive Committee of the Committee of Principals," August 7, 1968 (declassified Sept. 9, 1993). LBJ Library: Ibid.
14. Ibid., p. 6.
15. Memorandum, Clark Clifford–Lyndon Johnson, Aug. 13, 1968 (declassified June 27, 1990). LBJ Library: Ibid.
16. Dobrynin, *In Confidence,* p. 177.
17. Ibid., quoted on p. 178.

18. Clifford and Holbrooke, *Counsel to the President,* quoted on p. 559.

19. Andrei A. Gromyko, *Memoirs* (New York: Doubleday, 1989), p. 332.

20. Alexander Dubček, *Hope Dies Last: The Autobiography of Alexander Dubček* (New York: Kodansha International, 1993), quoted on p. 122.

21. Ibid., pp. 126, 128.

22. Jiri Valenta, *Soviet Intervention in Czechoslovakia, 1968: Anatomy of a Decision* (Baltimore: Johns Hopkins University Press, 1979), pp. 134–45, especially 140–41.

23. Clifford and Holbrooke, *Counsel to the President,* p. 561.

24. Interview with Walt R. Rostow, Austin, Tex., September 13, 1988. See also, John Prados, *Keepers of the Keys: A History of the National Security Council from Truman to Bush* (New York: William Morrow Publishers, 1991), p. 194.

25. Johnson, *The Vantage Point,* quoted on pp. 487–88.

26. Dobrynin, *In Confidence,* p. 180.

27. Soviet Note, Aug. 20, 1968. LBJ Library: LBJP: Tom Johnson's Notes of Meetings, box 2, folder "August 20, 1968—NSC." Also quoted in *The Vantage Point,* p. 488.

28. "Notes on Emergency Meeting of the NSC," Aug. 20, 1968 (declassified May 5, 1987) LBJ Library: Ibid.

29. Dobrynin, *In Confidence,* quoted p. 181.

30. Department of State, "Memorandum of Conversation," Sept. 20, 1968 (declassified June 17, 1994). LBJ Library: LBJP: NSF: Memos to the President, box 40, folder "Rostow v. 96."

3

Lyndon Johnson and Europe

Alliance Politics, Political Economy,
and "Growing Out of the Cold War"

THOMAS A. SCHWARTZ

In one of the most recent treatments of the foreign policy of the 1960s, historian H. W. Brands argues that "it was Lyndon Johnson's peculiar bad luck to preside over American foreign policy at the moment the scales of world power were tipping away from the United States." Most historical treatments of the Johnson era emphasize the debilitating effect of the war in Vietnam on America's international standing, seeing it as both a cause and a harbinger of America's overall political and economic decline.[1] As one recent book put it, "Lyndon Johnson's presidency, his plans for a Great Society, and his quest for national unity and universal adulation all sank and rotted in the rain forests and rice paddies of Southeast Asia."[2]

Despite some new studies that direct attention to other issues,[3] the overall verdict on Johnson foreign policy, including his policy toward Europe, remains a negative one. Lyndon Johnson himself usually shoulders the blame. As early as 1966, the journalist Philip Geyelin argued that Johnson "had no taste and scant preparation for the deep waters of foreign policy. . . ."[4] The contrast with his predecessor also affected perceptions of Johnson. Many contemporaries could not help but make an unfavorable comparison between the Northeastern, urbane, cosmopolitan John Kennedy, whose administration was absorbed with foreign policy crises, and his Southwestern, earthy, provincial successor, whose nickname in Georgetown salons was "Ole' Cornpone."[5] Even longtime friends of Johnson were not immune to this condescension. J. William Fulbright, the chairman of the Senate Foreign Relations Committee, who had known Johnson for years and even supported him for president in 1960, came to think of him as "an unlettered Texan desperately in need of enlightened guidance in matters of foreign policy." (No one was more aware of this than

Johnson, who once told Hugh Sidey, "I don't believe that I'll ever get credit for anything in foreign affairs, no matter how successful it is, because I didn't go to Harvard.")[6] Biographers echoed this, noting Johnson's mastery of domestic politics but arguing that with foreign policy, the president was "insecure, fearful, his touch unsure."[7] This view of Johnson, that he was a master of domestic politics but out of his element in foreign relations, was underlined recently in the Arthur Schlesinger, Jr., survey of historians, which ranks American presidents. Schlesinger commented on Lyndon Johnson's ranking by historians as an "above average" president, noting that it came about because [Johnson's] "domestic and foreign record [is] so discordant." This perception has also influenced most accounts of Johnson's policy toward Europe. Frank Costigliola concludes that Johnson and his advisers "remained imprisoned by the Cold War discourse that restricted even their most innovative policies," while David Kaiser has argued that the "years 1965–1969 [were] generally unproductive ones in East-West relations." Brands, although more generous to LBJ, concludes that Johnson suffered from a "dogged lack of imagination," which led him to "stick to the traditional verities of the Cold War."[8]

These judgments and assumptions about the Johnson presidency and its policy toward Europe are open to serious question. First of all, the Vietnam War, although having a powerful impact, did not fundamentally alter every other element of U.S. foreign policy. Dean Rusk was not exaggerating when he told German Foreign Minister Willy Brandt in February, 1967, that it was a "false impression that Viet-Nam pre-occupies us to the exclusion of everything else."[9] The war did not bring to a halt other Johnson foreign policy initiatives, nor did it paralyze the administration. Only in 1968, with the combination of the Tet offensive and Johnson's decision not to run for reelection, did the administration find it difficult to act decisively.

Secondly, the insistence on the "decline of American power" as the central model or paradigm for understanding any and all developments during this period is too simplistic and far too sweeping, both because it greatly exaggerates America's ability to control events in the 1950s and it underestimates America's continuing relative power in the 1970s and 1980s.[10] American decline was engineered purposefully by American leadership after World War II, with such programs as the Marshall Plan and assistance to Japan. The American position after World War II was artificially high, and the signs of a change in the U.S. economic position were already apparent at the end of the Eisenhower administration. Managing the adjustment in alliance relationships that this shift in the position of the United States would bring became one of the tasks of the Johnson administration. Johnson was as aware of this as anyone, and not only because of Vietnam. He understood that the recovery of

Europe had allowed "monetary strength" to be "spread more widely over the world than in the early postwar years, when the dollar dominated affairs," but unlike his successor, Johnson sought to make this adjustment through international negotiation, rather than unilateral American action.[11]

Thirdly, most historians have not framed their studies of Johnson's policy toward Europe with sufficient attention to the inherent dilemmas of U.S. leadership within a democratic alliance, a leadership role in which power must be used with caution and sensitivity toward the domestic politics of individual allies. The measure of accomplishment requires a more realistic understanding of both what is possible and desirable within such an arrangement, as well as an awareness of the intricate connection between political, security, and economic issues. This is particularly important in the case of European policy in the second half of the 1960s. This was a clear period of transition in Europe, with confrontation giving way to détente. The alliance was easier to hold together when the Europeans feared Moscow's intentions, and when they were too poor to worry about America's economic dominance. With the coming of de Gaulle, and progress toward the earlier alliance goals of European union and German reunification no longer possible, keeping Atlantic politics from turning cancerous was a new problem for the United States. The danger of an unraveling of the alliance as countries focused on internal questions, or as in the case of the United States, becoming committed in Southeast Asia, was a very real one. The true test of alliance leadership in this period came in its ability to solve problems and prevent disputes from escalating, not in extolling "grand designs" or proclaiming "the year of Europe."

Finally, a central factor in understanding Johnson's foreign policy comes from recognizing how inextricably linked it was to his domestic agenda. Geyelin recognized this at the time, noting that "Not since Roosevelt, or perhaps ever, have foreign politics been integrated so inextricably into the processes of domestic politics." In Johnson's mind, foreign policy was connected to what he sought to accomplish at home; it should reinforce those objectives and, in its own turn, be strengthened by them. Dean Rusk stressed this fact as well, arguing that tackling such issues as civil rights was a "fundamental prerequisite" to strengthening the American voice abroad. Johnson sought, as Joseph Califano has noted, "to mount a social revolution" in civil rights and the extension of the welfare state. He wanted a foreign policy that would help sustain and reinforce those changes. Even Johnson's critics recognized such a connection. As Fulbright's biographer notes, the senator from Arkansas came to support much the Great Society reform program from a conviction that "If his country were ever to pursue a policy of reason, restraint, and understanding abroad, it must do so at home as well."[12]

The argument presented here is revisionist: the Johnson administration's conduct of policy toward Europe, both Western and Eastern deserves consideration as among the most important achievements of his presidency. Despite the emphasis on domestic policy and the impact of the Vietnam War, the Johnson record on European questions is an impressive one. The administration held the Atlantic alliance together during what truly constituted its most severe internal crisis, the withdrawal of France from the unified military command of the North Atlantic Treaty Organization (NATO).[13] Defusing the challenge posed in the U.S. Senate from the Mansfield Resolution, Johnson initiated negotiations leading to the readjustment of the financial and military burdens of the alliance with the increasingly prosperous West Germany, at the same time assisting Great Britain through a succession of crises over the value of the pound sterling. Johnson's instincts and understanding of the importance of domestic politics, a characteristic frequently criticized by scholars of international affairs, largely served him well in dealing with European policy questions. They led him to recognize the problems inherent to the proposed Multilateral Nuclear Force, and move away from it and toward agreement on the nuclear nonproliferation treaty. Despite the escalating war in Southeast Asia, the administration was determined to "grow out of the Cold War" and followed a policy of "bridge-building" toward Eastern Europe and the Soviet Union.[14] It had a partial success in opening some avenues of trade and cultural exchange, as well as in lowering the rhetorical temperature of the Cold War. The administration sponsored initiatives, such as the creation of the International Institute for Applied Systems Analysis (IIASA), which were designed to create "non-political" links between Western and Eastern Europe, fostering changes within the Eastern bloc that helped undermine communist rule.[15] Johnson's October, 1966, speech, which encouraged a process of overcoming the division of Europe, was an important spur to movement in German politics and the German development of *Ostpolitik*.[16] The administration fully supported the Harmel Report, which provided the reconstructed NATO with a direction toward both deterrence and détente.

Neglected in most historical treatments, foreign economic policy is an area in which the Johnson administration had significant achievements. Despite intense domestic opposition, Johnson made a series of important decisions that allowed for the success of the Kennedy Round of tariff reductions, continuing the movement toward freer international trade and preventing a slide back toward protectionism. As one recent study concluded, "the Kennedy Round contributed to the substantial rise in the value of world exports in the early 1970s as the tariff cuts were phased in."[17] During a period in which the stability of the Bretton Woods system was increasingly questioned, Johnson sponsored negotiations that sought to create a new international money through international organization. These led directly to the breakthrough agreements at the Group of Ten's September, 1967, meeting and to the creation of SDRs, Special Drawing Rights on the International Monetary Fund. Although the role of SDRs has been limited, this important reform "planted a new permanent feature of international monetary organization that has the potential for further development over the long term."[18] Both the Kennedy Round and the international monetary negotiations required careful attention to the domestic politics of key allies, particularly West Germany and Great Britain, as well as a recognition of the connection between security issues and questions of political economy. De Gaulle's rejection of American leadership in NATO had a counterpart in the French attempt to derail the SDR negotiations and undermine the Bretton Woods system. In all of these questions—alliance politics, managing the international economy, creating a basis for détente—Lyndon Johnson's presidency emerges as significantly more creative and skillful than the picture presented in the standard historiography. At an important time of transition in the Atlantic relationship, with the Gaullist challenge, the need to readjust the burdens of the alliance and to ease tensions with the Russians, Johnson worked successfully to solve concrete problems with the allies "without overloading each other's politics, and thereby risk a splintering of the structure we had together built since 1945."[19]

Obviously no revisionism can neglect the failure of Johnson's Vietnam decisions. The war exacted a heavy price and limited the administration's achievements, both foreign and domestic. In European policy, it led Johnson to pressure the German government of Ludwig Erhard to keep to its schedule for offset payments, pressure which contributed to Erhard's demise. Although Johnson kept the British army in Germany, the administration was ultimately unsuccessful in retaining a British military commitment east of Suez and preventing the devaluation of the pound. The balance of payments deficits aggravated by the war contributed to the gold crisis of March, 1968, and accelerated the end of the Bretton Woods system. The bombing of North Vietnam also damaged America's image in Western Europe and burdened relations with the Soviet Union and Eastern Europe.

Nevertheless, it is now possible for a more balanced and positive assessment of the Johnson record. In this reassessment, historians need to do two things. First they need to reassess Johnson, both in his personal leadership qualities, and also, as Robert Dallek has argued, as a representative figure of the America of the 1960s. Johnson as a leader remains enigmatic, a difficult man to assess objectively. Historians have insisted on a static conception of Johnson in office, unwilling to recognize—largely because of Vietnam—any signs of learning or development, particularly in foreign policy. They have been too ready to accept some of the stereotypes of Johnson, reluctant to probe beneath the surface of an extraordinarily complex man. As his aide Joseph Califano put it: "The Lyndon Johnson I worked with was brave and brutal, compassionate and cruel, incredibly intelligent and infuriatingly insensitive, with a shrewd and uncanny instinct for the jugular of his allies and adversaries." Johnson's intimate connection to the America of his time has led Bruce Schulman to conclude that Lyndon Johnson is the "one modern President most Americans refuse to look in the eye, to consider in all his vulgarity, passion, weakness, and greatness."[20]

Secondly, historians need to take a new look at the interrelationship of foreign policy and domestic politics, especially in regard to America's relationship with Europe. Within the institutions and decision-making forums of the western alliance—both its security structure of NATO and its assortment of economic groupings, including the European Community, the International Monetary Fund, and the Group of Ten—foreign policy issues were increasingly "domesticated," with transnational political coalitions and networks playing decisive roles. The intellectual awareness that the behavior of the western countries deviated from the "realist" view of how nation states interact developed early in the postwar period. In 1957, the political scientist Karl Deutsch, schooled in Immanuel Kant's certainty that liberal democracies were inclined toward peaceful cooperation, used the term "pluralistic security communities" to refer to Atlantic alliance. Deutsch described a process whereby the nations within the alliance were developing a network of security relationships that made the resort to force between them unthinkable. This understanding of the importance of integration and interdependence permeated the intellectual atmosphere of the 1960s, leading analysts to look at the functioning of the alliance. Robert Keohane and Joseph Nye focused on the networks of "transnational relations, . . . contacts, coalitions, and interactions across state boundaries that are not controlled by the central foreign policy organs of government."[21] More recently Thomas Risse-Kappen has argued that the transatlantic alliance gradually came to constitute a community of liberal democracies, which deeply affected the collective identity of all its members, including the United States. Within such an alliance community, norms committed its members to timely consultation and consistently influenced the decision-making process. With military power or threats considered inappropriate among democratic allies, domestic pressures are frequently used to increase one's leverage in transatlantic interactions. Finally, within such a community, neither the Europeans nor the United States can be treated as unitary actors. Rather, transnational and transgovernmental coalitions among societal and bureaucratic actors frequently tipped the balance in tightly fought and difficult decisions. Louise Richardson's recent work dealing with Anglo-American relations during the Suez and Falklands crises also demonstrates the "centrality of transnational groups to policy outcomes."[22] In earlier research, I found this to be true in the course of trying to explain some of America's policies toward Germany, and finding that one could not explain these without reference to the transnational political coalitions that supported certain approaches and worked within the institutional framework of the alliance to achieve the adoption of such policies.[23]

Within the Western alliance community, with the concerns about answering to the electorate, the timing of elections, appeasing particular bureaucracies and economic interest groups, and arranging coalitions in support of proposals—the environment was becoming remarkably similar to the environment of American domestic politics. In such a political context, Lyndon Johnson excelled, bringing with him the skills that he had honed as Senate majority leader. Johnson recognized the need to build political coalitions, understood the constraints created by the domestic political situation of his allies, and forged the consensus necessary to implement solutions. Johnson believed these leaders were influenced "by the same grammar of power; whatever their countries' sizes or shapes, they shared a common concern with questions of rulership: which groups to rely on, which advisers to rely on, and how to conduct themselves amid the complex intrigues of politics."[24] Johnson thought, as Richard Barnet wrote, that the "the global political elite constituted a club like the Senate, not even as big." Whatever one might think of such a comparison, within the Western alliance Johnson's belief was not off the mark. Certainly he did not always have the type of detailed and intimate knowledge of his allies and adversaries that had contributed to his success in the Senate. He did often have to use his experts, but Johnson was, as Califano and others have pointed out, very good at exploiting the talents and skills of others in pursuit of his objectives.

One of those experts was Francis Bator, Johnson's deputy special assistant for National Security Affairs. Bator went to the White House in late April, 1964, to handle international economic policy matters for McGeorge Bundy, and in the summer of 1965 he received the portfolio for European policy. A native of Hungary, Bator's family had come to the United States before World War II. Trained at Massachusetts Institute of Technology, Bator joined the faculty there after receiving his Ph.D. He gained national prominence when the arguments of his book, *The Question of Government Spending*, were used by the Democrats to justify increased federal expenditures after their victory in 1960. Possessed of a sharp sense of European history as well as economics, Bator was particularly sensitive to the connections between security, political, and economic questions. He also possessed a number of "transnational" connections with his counterparts in allied governments, especially the British, which frequently smoothed the way toward agreement on contentious issues. Johnson, in fact, always sensitive to the particular perspective or bias of his advisers, dubbed him Britain's second ambassador in Washington. Indeed, upon his retirement from the Johnson administration, *The Economist,* whose coverage of the administration was generally friendly, called Bator "Europe's assistant," and noted that on a succession of matters relating to America's European policy, "a thread of lucidity, consistency, and balance has been traceable in the administration's handling and Mr. Bator has had a lot to do with it."[25] As holder of the portfolio for European policy from 1965–67, Bator was one of Johnson's "strong right arms" who helped the president make his judgments, frequently balancing political, economic, and security issues. Bator also reflected—and to an extent absorbed—Johnson's own acute sense of the importance of domestic politics, not only the politics of the United States, but the politics of each of the chief allies. Neglected in most historical accounts, Bator played a significant role in advising Johnson on European policy. His activity offers an insight into a different Lyndon Johnson, one capable of mastering the essentials of foreign policy as effectively as he had domestic affairs.

The Demise of the MLF and the Move Toward Détente

This essay will look briefly at three case studies to illuminate Johnson's approach to Europe. The first is the Multilateral Nuclear Force (MLF), which was the chief issue before NATO and the allies when Johnson became president.

Designed to head off German interest in national nuclear forces, and to give Germany a role in the decision to use nuclear weapons, the MLF proposal had changed considerably since it first emerged late in the Eisenhower administration. As part of his "Grand Design," Kennedy had supported the concept and allowed planning to proceed. Indeed, only two weeks before the assassination, Vice President Johnson publicly endorsed the idea, calling it "a first step toward a greater European voice in nuclear matters." By early 1964, the MLF proposal involved the creation of a "fleet of surface warships, armed with Polaris missiles, owned, controlled, and manned jointly by a number of NATO nations." After Kennedy's death, State Department supporters of the MLF, many of whom hoped to use the MLF to push their goal of a politically unified Europe, wanted Johnson to renew his earlier commitment and put pressure on the Europeans to act. At a meeting with the president on April 10, 1964, George Ball argued that the MLF would "give Germans a legitimate role in the defense of the Alliance, but on a leash." Thomas Finletter, the U.S. ambassador to NATO, reported that the Europeans had the impression Johnson wasn't interested in the project. He argued that the "U.S. had to stop being diffident about the MLF."[26] The only major reservations about the MLF came from William Foster, head of the Arms Control and Disarmament Agency, who worried that the MLF would damage the chance for a disarmament or non-proliferation treaty.[27]

Johnson took up the challenge that Finletter presented. The president was most interested in the argument that Germany would have to be treated as an equal with regard to nuclear weapons. In characteristic language, Johnson told his advisers, "the Germans have gone off the reservation twice in our lifetimes, and we've got to make sure that doesn't happen again, that they don't go berserk."[28] Rostow reinforced Johnson's fears when he told him, "if the multilateral solution is shot down now, as it was in 1932, the swing to the Right is all too likely to repeat itself."[29] But although Johnson thought the MLF could "satisfy the pride and self-respect of the Europeans," he "warned against trying to shove the project down the throats of potential participants."[30] Johnson did set a year-end deadline for signing a treaty, and in a speech to newspaper editors later that month announced, "We support the establishment of a multilateral nuclear force composed of those nations that wish to participate."[31]

Johnson's deadline brought the MLF to the center of American diplomacy toward Europe, with ambassadors urged to press their host countries for approval, and the USIA seeking to dispel the impression that the MLF was a bilateral U.S.-German arrangement.[32] (Thus it proved highly embarrassing to the administration when German Ambassador Wilhelm Grewe arrived in October, 1964, with a proposal from Chancellor Ludwig Erhard to proceed with MLF on a bilateral basis.)[33] But while the U.S. pressure elicited more support for the proposal, it also served to motivate the opposition. As the deadline approach, French attacks on the "two horned and apparently powerless body" of MLF increased, with the prediction of a "very serious situation" if the MLF were approved.[34] The Russians also stepped up their criticism, repeating their attack on giving the German "revanchists" nuclear weapons and contending that the MLF would doom a nuclear nonproliferation treaty. The U.S. ambassador in Moscow, Foy Kohler, believed they were "genuinely concerned that MLF will only hasten the day when the FRG [Federal Republic of Germany] becomes a nuclear power."[35]

After President Johnson's landslide victory, a conference was arranged with the new British Prime Minister Harold Wilson, whose Labor Party held only a two-seat margin in the House of Commons. Although he had moderated his opposition to an independent British nuclear deterrent, Wilson remained skeptical of the MLF. In the weeks before Wilson's visit, Bundy established a special committee, composed of himself, Ball, Rusk, and Robert McNamara, to work out a negotiating position. Bundy was particularly interested in evaluating the European prospects for MLF, and suspected that the picture being presented by MLF advocates—"who are determined to make the Europeans do what is good for them"—was seriously flawed.[36] As new information came in, Johnson's own doubts about the project grew. The president had just won an election against Barry Goldwater in which the nuclear question was the central issue, and though he had maintained his support for the MLF, he had also warned against "the fearful possibility of nuclear spread."[37] Now he was struck by the assessment that German support for the MLF was lukewarm and that one of the reasons Germany supported it was "it also believes that we want it very badly."[38] Henry Kissinger told Bundy that "it is simply wrong to allege that the future orientation of the Federal Republic depends on pushing through the MLF."[39] Even George Ball, an MLF supporter, reported that Erhard's Christian Democratic Union (CDU) was badly divided over the MLF, with its Gaullist wing bitterly attacking the idea.[40]

True to his understanding of all politics, domestic and foreign, Johnson now began to canvas the Senate, where he found little support for the MLF proposal. Conservatives disliked any sharing of the nuclear trigger, while liberals believed the MLF "would further imperil the prospects for arms control and divide the NATO alliance, all without adding to the security of the United States." The need to conduct a "great effort of political education" in order to secure passage of the MLF sobered Johnson to the dangers the MLF posed to his political power. With historical analogies in mind, LBJ decided he neither wanted to be a Woodrow Wilson, trying to push a League of Nations on a hostile Senate, nor a Franklin Roosevelt, squandering his electoral landslide in a Supreme Court–packing plan.[41]

Prime Minister Wilson arrived in the United States with a compromise proposal—an Atlantic Nuclear Force (ANF), which replaced the mixed-manned ships with various national components, thereby preserving British ownership of its V-Bomber and Polaris fleets. The prime minister might have been prepared to deal on the MLF, but Johnson decided that there was no good reason to press a fragile Labor government with an unpopular idea. Bundy convinced him that President Kennedy had the same doubts about the MLF.[42] "If Europe isn't for it, LBJ told a small group of advisers, "then the hell with it." Reminded of the argument that American prestige was already committed to the MLF, and that the United States had to save face, Johnson dismissed the concern with one of his favorite sayings: "While you're trying to save face, you'll lose your ass."[43] American pressure for the MLF came to an end, and although Johnson told the British and Germans that they were welcome to devise their own solution, the MLF lost its centrality in America's NATO policy.[44]

When the dust settled, Bundy praised LBJ, telling him that "this was without doubt the most productive and useful two days that we have had in foreign affairs since President Kennedy went to Berlin."[45] The demise of the MLF reinforced Johnson's own desire to pursue an easing of tensions with the Soviet Union and Eastern Europe. Fears about the effects of the MLF on nuclear proliferation and arms control negotiations were important to the opposition in the United States. From his first days in office, Johnson was determined to pursue the possibility of agreements with the Soviet Union, as well as encourage West Germany, the ally most skeptical about détente, to take its own initiatives. During his first meeting with Erhard in December, 1963, Johnson told him that the United States was "going down the road to peace, with or without others," and asked the chancellor to be more flexible toward the Soviet Union.[46] Johnson told Erhard that he believed that a policy of détente was the best approach to German reunification and progress with the Soviets. In February, 1964, Johnson used the surplus of fissionable material possessed by the United States to persuade the Soviets of the wisdom of a mutual cutback in the production of uranium for atomic weapons. In May, 1964, Johnson spoke of the need to "build bridges across the gulf which has divided us from Eastern Europe." He emphasized to his advisers that while they "work on the Atlantic nuclear problem, we keep Soviet interests in mind."[47]

Johnson's interest in détente had important consequences. First, for the issue of nuclear sharing within the alliance, it necessitated finding an alternative to the "hardware" solution of the MLF, ANF, or whatever acronym was used. Recognizing the likelihood that MLF would fail, Secretary of Defense Robert McNamara provided this "software solution" with his proposal for a Nuclear Planning Group (NPG) in May, 1965. Designed as a device to give the allies, especially the Germans, a greater insight and input into allied discussions of military strategy and nuclear weapons, the NPG itself proved extraordinarily successful at satisfying allied concerns. As Lawrence Kaplan has noted, Johnson accorded the NPG "a status it might not have had otherwise," recognizing its value in attempting to "tie in Germany with the U.S. and U.K." Ultimately the NPG would prove the key ingredient in what Bundy called "a real Johnson breakthrough" by opening the way "toward a non proliferation treaty and toward a new collective arrangement for command control and consultation in NATO."[48]

Secondly, Johnson's interest in détente meant an acceptance of the division of Germany for the foreseeable future, while helping Germany to recognize that reunification could only come about at the end of a long-term process of change. As part of that change, Germany needed to develop a "more active Eastern policy."[49] Bator added his own perspective, dismissing the idea held by some Germans that an official renunciation of the MLF would be a bargaining chip for reunification.[50] He argued that the "only tolerably safe path to unification is one which involves lessening fear of Germany in Eastern Europe and the USSR." Bator urged the president to steer Erhard and the Germans toward a recognition that they should make a virtue out of their non-nuclear status, using it to ease fears in Eastern Europe and hold open the long-run hope for reunification.[51]

Despite the escalating war in Vietnam, the administration pushed ahead toward détente. On October 7, 1966, Johnson told a conference of editorial writers that "we must improve the East-West environment in order to achieve the unification of Germany in the context of a larger, peaceful, and prosperous Europe."[52] The speech was an important signal and expressed "a doctrine congenial in Europe, different from de Gaulle's, without quarreling."[53] Johnson also affirmed that the United States respected "the integrity of a nation's boundary lines," and encouraged the removal of territorial and border disputes, a none-too-subtle reference to Germany's refusal to recognize the Oder-Neisse line and the loss of its eastern territories. The Bonn Embassy had sought a last-minute change that would have softened the reference, but the State Department insisted it remain, to provide "gentle support to those people in Germany who want slowly to back away from a self-defeating position."[54] In effect, the Johnson administration was lending its support to a transnational coalition in support of détente.[55] Among those who were encouraged by this was Willy Brandt, who became foreign minister in late 1966 and initiated his policy of *Ostpolitik*. The administration's new priorities were the Nonproliferation Treaty, which was signed in 1968, and a strategic arms control agreement with the Soviets, which Johnson discussed with Soviet Premier Kosygin in June, 1967, in Glassboro, New Jersey, and might have been achieved had the Soviets not invaded Czechoslovakia. By December, 1967, NATO adopted the Harmel Report on the future of the alliance and affirmed that "military security and a policy of détente are not contradictory but complementary."[56] The Johnson administration had created a firm basis upon which Nixon and Kissinger could build.

The French Challenge

French President Charles de Gaulle posed the most critical challenge to the Johnson administration and its alliance policy. Although he had supported the United States in the Berlin and Cuba crises, de Gaulle insisted on demonstrating his independence from the United States, witnessed in such moves as his veto of British entry into the Common Market, recognition of the People's Republic of China, and attacks on America's Vietnam policy. What appeared to be the final step came in March, 1966, when the general notified NATO that he was officially withdrawing French forces from the integrated military command. Johnson, whose relationship with de Gaulle never recovered from a misunderstanding they had at Kennedy's funeral, was stung by the attacks on his Vietnam policy but avoided personal criticism of the general. When the demand for withdrawal of American forces from France came, Johnson stifled the urge of his advisers to hit back sharply, fearing this would only confirm de Gaulle's claim of American domination. Johnson insisted that he saw "no benefit to ourselves or to our allies in debating the position of the French government."[57] George Ball noted that Johnson "incessantly restrained me from making critical comments," about de Gaulle. In one of his most famous remarks, the president told his aides, "When a man asks you to leave his house, you don't argue; you get your hat and go."[58]

Historians have generally not given Johnson credit for resisting the temptation to exploit the French action for his own short-term political gains.[59] Polls at the time demonstrated that an overwhelming majority of Americans disapproved of de Gaulle's action, and Johnson, in the midst of the Vietnam conflict, could have chosen to exploit this issue as a diversion. To arouse American anger, he need only have used Dean Rusk's question after de Gaulle told him that every American soldier must leave France: "Does that include the dead Americans in military cemeteries as well?"[60] (Canadian Prime Minister Lester Pearson told Johnson that he had also said this to de Gaulle.) Johnson chose not to arouse passions and stressed instead the last sentence of his response to de Gaulle's letter: "As our old friend and ally her place will await France whenever she decides to resume her leading role."[61]

Although Johnson favored a judicious and measured response to de Gaulle's withdrawal from NATO, many of his top advisers, including men like Dean Acheson and George Ball, wanted a much tougher approach. One opportunity to press their case came over the issue of French troops stationed in Germany. Consisting of air and army units comprising approximately 76,000 personnel, these forces posed less of a military question than a political one. The French government made it clear that although these forces would no longer come under NATO command, they would leave the forces in Germany if the German government wanted them. The German government faced a dilemma: if it insisted that French troops could remain only if they remained committed to NATO, it would precipitate a French withdrawal and cause a major setback in Franco-German relations, with important domestic political consequences. The Gaullists in the Christian Democratic Party, led by such figures as Franz Josef Strauss and having the support of former Chancellor Konrad Adenauer, would vigorously protest such a move, and would have significant public support. In a note of significant understatement, the American ambassador in Bonn, George McGhee, noted, "If the present confrontation results in a withdrawal of French forces . . . German public opinion will not react with exhilaration." Indeed McGhee suggested that such a clear failure in the attempt to "build Europe" would lead the Germans to a renewed focus on "the other elusive goal of German foreign policy-reunification," a game in which, McGhee commented, the "key cards are held by the other side."[62] On the other hand, if Germany agreed to seek a new arrangement with the French, that would seem to reward de Gaulle's nationalism, and it raised questions about a special status for France that would be particularly irritating to Washington. In effect, de Gaulle was forcing the Germans to choose between Paris and Washington, a choice no German political leader could afford.

On this issue most of Johnson's advisers wanted to take a firm stand. At a meeting on April 4, with Rusk, McNamara, Ball, and Acheson present, they decided that the United States "should fully support" the Germans if they took a hard line toward the French, "and do nothing to dissuade them." If the Germans decided to try to negotiate an agreement with de Gaulle, the "US should urge them to incorporate in these new arrangements effective safeguards assuring their use in accordance with NATO requirements and an adequate quid pro quo giving to other allies in Germany facilities in France such as transit and overflight rights."[63] These conditions were designed to be unacceptable to the French and call their bluff. They were the basis of the instructions given to John J. McCloy, the president's special envoy, as he prepared for talks with Chancellor Erhard a week later.

Johnson was at his ranch when the State Department finished drafting the instructions for McCloy. George Ball sent them to the president, with the note that this "will constitute Mr. McCloy's instructions." When Bator saw Ball's message, he objected to what he perceived as pressure on the Germans to take a hard line. He believed that such pressure would both complicate Erhard's position in German politics as well as go against Johnson's own clear preference for a muted response to de Gaulle's challenge. He feared that "if under U.S. pressure, German-French negotiations fail, and French Divisions withdraw, Germans will join other Europeans in blaming us for resulting grave damage to German-French relations." The desire to avoid choosing between Paris and Washington, Bator warned, is "still at the center of German politics." Bator immediately cabled LBJ at his ranch asking him to change McCloy's instructions. Bator urged a less conditional American approach, offering the Germans support for *whatever* they decided to do about the French troops.[64] Johnson, who was on vacation and "wanted to focus on his cows," did not look at Bator's message until later in the week, after McCloy had already met with Gerhard Schroeder, the German foreign minister, and delivered the tougher message. However, when Johnson read Bator's message, he immediately told Dean Rusk that he agreed with Bator, and that the secretary should change McCloy's instructions. Johnson wanted the Germans to know, as McCloy subsequently told Chancellor Erhard, that the "United States should support any position taken by the FRG that recognized the seriousness of the situation and provided an adequate response to the French. The FRG must itself decide the position it wishes to occupy in Europe. We are not thinking of forcing the FRG toward any policy or decision." The Germans ultimately decided that the political importance of the French troops outweighed any other considerations. France was allowed to keep its troops in Germany on its own terms, free, as Lawrence Kaplan noted, "from alliance obligations and free, for that matter to leave whether or not the Germans or Americans wished them to go."[65]

Johnson's "soft" treatment of de Gaulle aroused the fury of his advisers, notably Dean Acheson, who told Bator at a Washington dinner party, "You made the greatest imperial power the world has ever seen kiss de Gaulle's arse."[66] But the wisdom of Johnson's approach was that it recognized that for the United States to force the Germans to choose, as tempting an option as that might be, was unnecessary to preserve the alliance's vitality. Recognizing the extent of his differences with de Gaulle, Johnson kept them from damaging U.S. foreign policy, "not an insignificant achievement," as Lloyd Gardner concluded.[67] To a large extent, Johnson's reading of the European political situation and the French challenge was far more acute and incisive than some of the most experienced American diplomats and foreign policy "Wise Men."

Johnson and the Trilateral Negotiations

By 1966 the escalation of the war in Vietnam had increased the American balance of payments deficit dramatically and aggravated further the crisis over NATO's future that de Gaulle's withdrawal had precipitated.[68] In August the Mansfield Resolution, calling for the reduction of American forces in Europe, garnered forty-four votes in the Senate. Weakness in the British economy kept the pound sterling under severe pressure, culminating in a run on the pound in July, 1966. British austerity measures pledged savings of £100 million in overseas defense expenditures, and the British army on the Rhine looked like a prime candidate for cutbacks.[69] In early 1966, the German economy faced its first severe recession of the postwar period, and the Erhard government faced a large budget deficit. Under pressure to curb government spending, especially the expensive—and questionable—purchases of American military equipment, Germany was badly lagging in fulfilling its offset orders.[70] Erhard told Washington that he needed significant relief from the offset payments. Recognizing Erhard was in political trouble, and that the British were determined to cut as well, Bator suggested to Johnson the creation of some type of "mixed commission" of the United States, United Kingdom, and Germany, which might "protect our balance of payments" and hammer out a consensus "on an allied defense posture in Europe which will provide deterrence and the insurance of a reasonable conventional option."[71]

In late August, 1966, the United States suggested a form of "Trilateral Negotiations" between the United States, Britain, and Germany to resolve the offset problem. However, Erhard wanted to see Johnson before he agreed to the talks, hoping to strike his own bargain. With Erhard's political position in Germany now precarious, Bator told LBJ that "for us it is important—even more than Erhard's survival—that we not appear the culprit if he falls."[72] Press reports made it clear that Erhard "badly needs a success at the White House," but Johnson, backed strongly by McNamara and the Treasury Department, would not allow a "stretching out" of the offset payments.[73] Erhard implied that his successor might "not show the same loyalty and determination to cultivate close ties to the United States."[74] However, in the end Erhard put up little resistance.[75] When he returned to Germany and proposed a tax increase to meet the budget deficit, Erhard's government collapsed. The new government consisted of a "Grand Coalition" between the Christian Democrats and the Social Democratic Party (SPD). Kurt Kiesinger from the Gaullist faction of the CDU became chancellor, with SPD leader Willy Brandt taking over as foreign minister.

The collapse of Erhard's government might have proven a disaster for Johnson's European policy. Erhard had been the most loyal of allies, and Johnson felt a genuine warmth toward him. However, Erhard was increasingly ineffective as a political leader, and his weakness had shown at the polls in Länder elections.[76] In the weeks preceding the trip, his top aide had resigned and his defense minister only barely survived a vote of confidence. One recent analysis notes that "in Germany the prevailing opinion was that Erhard's fate was sealed anyway and the visit to Washington was just the last straw."[77] With his resignation and the coming of the Grand Coalition, Johnson now had a stronger, if more independent-minded, German government to deal with, one more capable of taking risks and far more interested in moving forward on détente.[78] Most importantly, however, Johnson and his advisers recovered rapidly, using the crisis to push for a solution that dealt with both the security and economic issues underlying NATO.

To handle the Trilateral negotiations, Johnson appointed John J. McCloy, the former American high commissioner in Germany.[79] McCloy strongly opposed significant troop reductions, and argued against the idea that the level of forces should depend on the offset payments. Opposing him was McNamara, who advocated a reduction of two divisions and personally favored an even more drastic cutback. In presenting the options to the president, Bator stressed that this "decision will cast a very long shadow on our relations with Germany and Europe, with consequences for domestic politics."[80] Johnson now took command. Through a series of meetings with the congressional leadership and his negotiators, Johnson laid down the path he wanted to follow. With the congressmen, Johnson "managed" a breakfast, taking a hard line "more arbitrary than I like, which made it difficult for them to disagree with the President of the United States." With McCloy, Johnson insisted that the former high commissioner pressure his German friends "that they have to be realistic." Noting that the Fredericksburg Germans with whom he grew up were "great people; but by God they are as stingy as Hell," Johnson told McCloy that "they have got to put in some money." They would have to help the British as well, as a BAOR withdrawal would encourage demands for a similar American action. Johnson feared that without a German offer, he would have to cut two divisions. When McCloy warned, "you are on the verge of the collapse of the Alliance," Johnson replied, "Jack, I know that; I'll try to hold this Alliance together longer than anybody else will, longer than the British will, and longer than the Germans. But they have got to put something in the family pot."[81]

The Germans did. They agreed to purchase and hold some $500 million in U.S. government medium-term securities, and even more importantly, agreed to make public their intention to refrain from buying gold. The so-called "Blessing Brief" was a significant German concession, one which would be extremely helpful in managing the balance of payments deficit. In effect, as Bator told the president, the United States had also scored a victory against the French, "negotiating the world onto a dollar standard," and to "recognition of the fact that, for the time being, the United States must necessarily play banker of the world and that the continuing threat to convert gold is simply unacceptable." Bator expected that America's concessions to the Germans in the Trilateral talks would contribute to gaining German support in the ongoing negotiations dealing with international money.[82] The United States withdrew one division and ninety-six aircraft, although for appearance's sake, these forces remained committed to NATO. The British proved more difficult, and the Americans had to increase their own spending in Britain to help the Germans reach a 90 percent offset of the exchange costs of the BAOR. McCloy wrote Johnson that "although from time to time the trading instincts of your Fredericksburg Germans cropped out in the F.R.G. representatives, I am not certain that the subtler but still acquisitive instincts of the British are any less formidable."[83]

The Trilateral Agreements of May, 1967, were in part a stopgap measure. They temporarily secured the alliance's financial basis—and protected the dollar—giving Johnson the weapon he needed to fend off congressional challenges. More importantly, they were one of the first examples of genuine burden sharing within the alliance. A German analyst recently noted the "greatest success of the trilateral talks" was that the offset question, rather than becoming an "explosive issue" within the alliance, "paved the way for the its consolidation."[84]

These three case studies suggest the need for a more intensive examination of the foreign policy of the Johnson years, both in pursuit of a balanced historical assessment and a better understanding of the dilemmas of that troubled decade. The war in Vietnam always overshadows this era, but there was more to Johnson's foreign policy than Vietnam. Lyndon Johnson guided the United States toward a policy that balanced the solidarity of the Western alliance with the need to begin "growing out of the Cold War."[85] His administration began a process of treating Western and Eastern Europe as a whole, recognizing that the division of the continent could be overcome only by a patient and sustained effort that sought a reduction of tensions and the building of bridges between East and West. These were important achievements and should be recognized among the administration's most significant and long-term successes. Charles de Gaulle once compared Lyndon Johnson with his martyred predecessor by saying, "This man Kennedy is America's mask. But this man Johnson, he is the country's real face."[86] De Gaulle did not mean to flatter Americans with this comparison, but for once, the general may have been unintentionally ironic.

NOTES

I want to thank Diane B. Kunz, Gustav Schmidt, Geir Lundestad, Odd Arne Westad, Jussi Hanhimaki, and Klaus Schwabe for their comments on earlier versions of this article. I also want to thank the Norwegian Nobel Institute in Oslo, Norway, for the opportunity to present a version of this paper in their research seminar on the United States and Western Europe.

1. H. W. Brands, *The Wages of Globalism: Lyndon Johnson and the Limits of American Power* (New York: Oxford, 1995), p. vii; Robert M. Collins, "The Economic Crisis of 1968 and the Waning of the 'American Century,'" *American Historical Review* 101:2 (Apr., 1996): 396–422.
2. Bruce J. Schulman, *Lyndon Johnson and American Liberalism* (New York: St. Martin's Press, 1995), p. 125.
3. Diane Kunz, ed., *The Crucial Decade* (New York: Columbia University Press, 1994); Warren I. Cohen and Nancy Bernkopf Tucker, *Lyndon Johnson Confronts the World* (New York: Cambridge University Press, 1994); and Robert Divine,

The Johnson Years: LBJ at Home and Abroad (Lawrence: University Press of Kansas, 1994).

4. Philip Geyelin, *Lyndon B. Johnson and the World* (New York: Praeger, 1966), p. 15.

5. Richard Barnet, *The Alliance* (New York: Simon and Schuster, 1983), p. 235.

6. Randall Woods, *Fulbright: A Biography* (New York: Cambridge University Press, 1995), p. 389; Theodore White, *The Making of the President, 1968* (New York: Atheneum, 1969), p. 101.

7. Doris Kearns, *Lyndon Johnson and the American Dream* (New York: André Deutsch, 1976), p. 256. She maintains that "Johnson's belief in the universal applicability of American values . . . was the source of his greatest weakness as president." Ibid., p. 194. See also John Kenneth Galbraith, *A Life in Our Times* (Boston: Houghton Mifflin, 1981), p. 457.

8. Arthur Schlesinger, Jr., "The Ultimate Approval Rating," *New York Times Magazine,* Dec. 15, 1996, p. 48; David Kaiser, "Men and Policies: 1961–1969," in Kunz, *The Crucial Decade,* p. 12; Frank Costigliola, "Lyndon B. Johnson, Germany, and the 'End of the Cold War,'" in Cohen and Tucker, *Lyndon Johnson Confronts the World,* p. 210, and Brands, *The Wages of Globalism,* pp. 28–29.

9. Despite his critical view of Johnson, Kaiser concludes that "even the foreign policy consequences of the Vietnam War already seem relatively minor." Kaiser, "Men and Policies," p. 37; *Foreign Relations of the United States, 1964–1968,* 13, p. 531. Indeed, Lloyd Gardner reminds us that the military strategy of slow and deliberate escalation, so often criticized today, was an example of "trying not to allow Vietnam to undermine policy in the rest of the world." Lloyd Gardner, *Paying Any Price: Lyndon Johnson and the Wars for Vietnam* (Chicago: Ivan R. Dee, 1995), p. 158.

10. To a certain extent, this concept reminds me of other historical clichés that are less than helpful in analyzing particular periods, such as the endlessly rising bourgeoisie of prerevolutionary France and the perpetually declining Ottoman Empire. They simply don't take you very far.

11. Quoted in Lyndon Johnson, *The Vantage Point* (New York: Holt, Rinehart & Winston, 1971), p. 321; Diane B. Kunz, *Butter and Guns* (New York: Free Press, 1997), p. 192, contains an insightful portrait of Nixon's determination to "do what was best for the domestic economy and his own political future and let the international economic system adapt to the United States."

12. Geyelin, *Lyndon B. Johnson and the World,* pp. 13, 147; Joseph A. Califano, Jr., *The Triumph and Tragedy of Lyndon Johnson* (New York: Simon & Schuster, 1991), p. 10. In considering this connection between Johnson's foreign and domestic policies, Lloyd Gardner has argued that there was an "ideological weld between the cold war vision of the world and American beliefs about the capacities of their society," and that "Johnson faced losing the Great Society without going forward in Vietnam." Gardner, *Pay Any Price,* p. 95; Woods, *Fulbright: A Biography,* p. 323.

13. Helga Haftendorn recently noted that "The NATO crisis of 1966–7 was viewed at the time as a situation in which the survival and future course of the Alliance were in jeopardy." Helga Haftendorn, *NATO and the Nuclear Revolution* (Oxford: Clarendon, 1996), p. 1.

14. Anatoly Dobrynin's memoirs make it clear that the Soviets appreciated Johnson's efforts despite their loyalty to their Vietnamese ally. Anatoly Dobrynin, *In Confi-*

dence: Moscow's Ambassador to America's Six Cold War Presidents (New York: Random House, 1995), pp. 188–89.

15. Mania concludes, "No other president had done as much since the end of the Second World War." Andrzej Mania, *Bridge Building: Polityka USA wobec Europy Wschodniej w latach 1961–1968* (Krakow: Uniwersytet Jagiellonski, 1996), p. 156. See also Bennet Kovrig, *Of Walls and Bridges* (New York: New York University Press, 1991), p. 109.

16. Despite the Nixon administration's historical reputation for pushing détente, "West German initiatives to the East had been repeatedly urged upon the Bonn government by the Johnson Administration." Seymour M. Hersh, *The Price of Power: Kissinger in the Nixon White House* (New York: Simon & Schuster, 1983), p. 416.

17. Steve Dryden, *Trade Warriors* (New York: Oxford, 1995), p. 112. Zeiler takes a less optimistic view, concluding that the Kennedy Round "kept the trade order, but failed to achieve America's aim of reversing the payments deficit through export expansion." Thomas W. Zeiler, *American Trade and Power in the 1960s* (New York: Columbia University Press, 1992), p. 239.

18. John S. Odell, *U.S. International Monetary Policy* (Princeton: Princeton University Press, 1982), p. 6. Harold James takes a more skeptical view of the SDR exercise, arguing that "the SDR appeared as the last and most controversial of the gadgets devised to deal with the weakness of the U.S. payments position, rather than the beginning of a new approach to managing the international order." Harold James, *International Monetary Cooperation since Bretton Woods* (Washington: Oxford University Press, 1996), p. 174.

19. This phrase is used by Francis Bator, in a note to Johnson on October 4, 1970. Bator was providing Johnson with his own assessment of the planned treatment of European issues in Johnson's memoirs. My thanks to Francis Bator for providing me a copy of his note.

20. Robert Dallek, *Lone Star Rising: Lyndon Johnson and His Times, 1908–1960* (New York: Oxford, 1991), p. 7; Califano, *The Triumph and Tragedy of Lyndon Johnson,* p. 10; Schulman, *Lyndon Johnson and American Liberalism,* p. 165.

21. Thomas A. Schwartz, "The United States and Germany After 1945: Alliances, Transnational Relations, and the Legacy of the Cold War," *Diplomatic History* 19:4 (Fall, 1995): 549–68; Robert O. Keohane and Joseph S. Nye, Jr., *Transnational Relations and World Politics* (Cambridge: Harvard University Press, 1972), p. xi.

22. Thomas Risse-Kappen, *Cooperation Among Democracies* (Princeton: Princeton University Press, 1995), pp. 4–5; Louise Richardson, *When Allies Differ* (New York: St. Martin's Press, 1996), p. 9. Paul Hammond also identified the transgovernmental relations involved in the MLF case. Paul Hammond, *LBJ and Presidential Management of Foreign Affairs* (Austin: University of Texas Press, 1992), pp. 157–59.

23. This was the case with measures to bring about greater European economic integration—namely the Schuman Plan for placing European coal and steel industries under a central authority—and the less successful European Defense Community, which sought to create a unified European army. See also François Duchêne, *Jean Monnet: The First Statesman of Interdependence* (New York: W. W. Norton, 1994).

24. Kearns, *Lyndon Johnson and the American Dream,* p. 195.

25. Barnet, *The Alliance,* p. 237; *The Economist,* Sept. 16, 1967, p. 989.

26. Johnson Speech, Nov. 8, 1963, in *Department of State Bulletin,* Dec. 2, 1963, p. 852; Gerard C. Smith, Speech, Apr. 22, 1964, in *American Foreign Policy: Current Documents 1964* (Washington, D.C.: Government Printing Office, 1967), p. 459; LBJ Library, NSF Subject File, Box 23, Memo, Discussion of MLF, Apr. 11, 1964.
27. *FRUS 1964–1968,* 13, p. 36, and LBJ Library, Henry Owen, Oral History, p. 11.
28. LBJ Library, Gerard Smith, Oral History, p. 7.
29. LBJ Library, NSF-SF, Box 23, Rostow to LBJ, Dec. 5, 1963.
30. *FRUS 1964–1968,* 13, p. 36. See also Geyelin, *Lyndon B. Johnson and the World,* p. 159.
31. Barnet, *The Alliance,* p. 240.
32. LBJ Library, NSF-SF, Box 23, USIA Circular, "MLF Information Activities," June 1, 1964.
33. *FRUS 1964–1968,* 13, pp. 78–83. Haftendorn notes that this may have been one of the events that caused McGeorge Bundy to take an even more critical look at the MLF. Haftendorn, *NATO and the Nuclear Revolution,* p. 132.
34. Jean Lacouture, *De Gaulle: The Ruler 1945–1970* (New York, 1991), p. 359, and *FRUS 1964–1968,* 13, p. 107.
35. LBJ Library, Gerard Smith, Oral History, p. 10; *FRUS 1964–1968,* 13, p. 65.
36. *FRUS 1964–1968,* 13, p. 105.
37. *Time,* Sept. 25, 1964, p. 17.
38. LBJ Library, NSF-SF, Box 23, Martin Hillenbrand to Klein, Nov. 25, 1964.
39. LBJ Library, NSF, Files of McGeorge Bundy, Box 15, Kissinger to Bundy, Nov. 27, 1964.
40. *FRUS 1964–1968,* 13, p. 113.
41. LBJ Library, NSF-SF, Box 23, Letter, Joseph Clark and eight other senators to Rusk, Sept. 7, 1964; *FRUS 1964–1968,* 13, pp. 136, 133.
42. Ibid., pp. 134–37.
43. Richard Neustadt, Memo of Conversation, "Wilson Visit and the MLF," Dec. 6, 1964. I want to thank Professor Ernest R. May for making this available to me.
44. To make sure that MLF supporters got the message, Johnson deliberately leaked his decision to James Reston of the *New York Times.* Geyelin, *Lyndon B. Johnson and the World,* pp. 171–77.
45. *FRUS 1964–1968,* 13, p. 158.
46. *Time,* Jan. 10, 1964, p. 23. The account of the Erhard-Johnson talks in the German documents makes it clear that Erhard was sensitive about any perception of difference in the American-German approach to détente. *Akten zur Auswärtigen Politik der Bundesrepublik Deutschland 1963* Vol. III, (Munich: Oldenbourg, 1994), p. 490.
47. George McGhee, *At the Creation of a New Germany* (New Haven: Yale, 1989), p. 148; *FRUS 1964–1968,* 11, pp. 22, 264. See also Glenn T. Seaborg, *Stemming the Tide: Arms Control in the Johnson Years* (Lexington, Mass.: D.C. Heath, 1987), pp. 39–49; *FRUS 1964–1968,* 17, p. 12.
48. Lawrence S. Kaplan, "The United States and NATO in the Johnson Years," in Divine, *Johnson Years, Vol. 3,* p. 133; Deborah Shapley, *Promise and Power: The Life and Times of Robert McNamara* (Boston: Little Brown, 1993), p. 404; *FRUS 1964–1968,* 11, p. 264.
49. LBJ Library, George McGhee, Oral History, p. 14.
50. LBJ Library, NSF-CF, Box 186, "A Reexamination of Premises on the German Problem," Dec. 9, 1965.

51. LBJ Library, Bator Papers, Chronological File, Box 3, Memorandum for the President, "A Nuclear Role for Germany: What Do the Germans Want?" Apr. 4, 1966.
52. LBJ Library, NSF Speech File, Box 5, Speech to Editorial Writers, Oct. 7, 1966. Zbigniew Brzezinski, later to be Jimmy Carter's National Security adviser, took full credit as author of the speech in his oral history at the LBJ Library. He modestly believed that it "fundamentally reversed the priorities of the United States in Western Europe." In truth, the idea of a major speech on European policy was one of the contributions of the Acheson group, and had a number of contributors. The first drafts were written by Bator. *FRUS 1964–1968*, 13, p. 385, and Interview with Francis Bator, Cambridge, Mass., Dec. 16, 1995.
53. LBJ Library, NSF Speech File, Box 5, Rostow to LBJ, Oct. 6, 1966.
54. LBJ Library, NSF Speech File, Box 5, Bator to LBJ, Oct. 13, 1966.
55. I am not arguing that the United States deserves the credit for *Ostpolitik*, only that at this time it was ahead of the Germans on the issue and capable of lending considerable political support to those in Germany who wanted to move in that direction. For the signs of interest in Germany for such a policy, see Roger Morgan, *The United States and West Germany, 1945–1973* (London: Oxford University Press, 1974), pp. 155–58.
56. Barnet, *The Alliance,* p. 289.
57. Philip H. Gordon, *A Certain Idea of France* (Princeton: Princeton University Press, 1993), pp. 3–22, has one of the most succinct and clear expositions of de Gaulle's ideas; LBJ Library, David Bruce, Oral History, p. 7; Johnson later said of de Gaulle, "I always had trouble with people like him, who let high rhetoric and big issues take the place of accomplishments." Kearns, *Lyndon Johnson and the American Dream,* p. 195. There is a parallel here to Johnson's unwillingness to arouse American passions about Vietnam, for fear that it would compel him to escalate the war; *FRUS 1964–1968,* 13, p. 376.
58. George Ball, *The Past Has Another Pattern* (New York: Norton, 1982), p. 336; Lyndon Johnson, *The Vantage Point,* p. 305.
59. Brands is a noteworthy exception to this tendency. Brands, *Wages of Globalism,* p. 102.
60. Thomas J. Schoenbaum, *Waging Peace and War: Dean Rusk in the Truman, Kennedy, and Johnson Years* (New York: Simon and Schuster, 1988), p. 421.
61. *FRUS 1964–1968,* 13, pp. 452, 349. Frank Costigliola argues that this sentence contains a "gender-coded" formulation that indicates the continuing American desire to dominate both France and the alliance. Frank Costigliola, *France and the United States: The Cold Alliance Since World War II* (New York: Twayne, 1992), pp. 145–46.
62. *FRUS 1964–1968,* 13, pp. 357, 376.
63. Ibid., p. 354.
64. LBJ Library, NSF, Agency File, NATO, Vol. 3, George Ball, Memorandum for the President, "Guidance for John J. McCloy," Apr. 10, 1966; LBJ Library, Bator Papers, Chronological File, Box 3, Telegram, Bator to LBJ, Apr. 11, 1966.
65. *FRUS 1964–1968,* 13, p. 367; Lawrence S. Kaplan, *NATO and the United States* (Boston: Twayne, 1988), p. 121.
66. Interview with Francis Bator, Cambridge, Mass., Dec. 16, 1995. Acheson had other reasons for his anger, including Johnson's use of the press to paint him, Ball, and McCloy, as "anti-de Gaulle extremists." This led to an extraordinarily

heated confrontation between Acheson and the president at a White House meeting on May 19, 1966. For Acheson's account, and their subsequent rapprochement, see his letter to Anthony Eden, June 29, 1966, in *Among Friends: Personal Letters of Dean Acheson,* eds. Davis S. McLellan and David C. Acheson (New York: Dodd, Mead & Co., 1980), p. 279.

67. Lloyd Gardner, "Lyndon Johnson and De Gaulle," in *De Gaulle and the United States,* eds. Robert O. Paxton and Nicholas Wahl (Berg: Oxford, 1994), p. 278.

68. By the end of 1966 roughly three-quarters of the military deficit in the balance of payments was attributable to the Vietnam conflict, and it continued to worsen until the end of Johnson's presidency. David Wightman, "Money and Security," *Rivista di storia economica* 5 (Jan., 1988): 57.

69. Diane Kunz, "Cold War Dollar Diplomacy: the Other Side of Containment," in Kunz, *Crucial Decade,* p. 100.

70. Some of these purchases, like the F-104 Starfighter planes, had already had an alarming run of sixty-six accidents. Gregory F. Treverton, *The Dollar Drain and American Forces in Germany* (Athens: Ohio University Press, 1978), p. 65; Wightman, "Money and Security," p. 46. By September 1, 1966, Germany had placed less than half the orders due by the end of 1966, and made less than 25 percent of the payments due by the end of the agreement in June, 1967.

71. *FRUS 1964–1968,* 13, p. 455.

72. LBJ Library, NSF, NSC History, Trilateral Negotiations and NATO, 1966–67, (TNN), Box 50, Bator to LBJ, Sept. 25, 1966,

73. *Time,* Sept. 30, 1966, p. 29; To meet an estimated yearly gap of $500 million between what the Germans would pay and what the costs were, McNamara advocated reducing American spending in Europe by $200 million, and considering the withdrawal of a significant number of American combat personnel, which he acknowledged would have a "traumatic" effect on NATO. LBJ Library, NSF, NSC History, TNN, Box 50, McNamara to LBJ, Sept. 19, 1966.

74. *FRUS 1964–1968,* 13, p. 473.

75. McGhee, *At the Creation of a New Germany,* pp. 192–93.

76. Dennis L. Bark and David R. Gress, *A History of West Germany, Vol. 2: Democracy and its Discontents 1963–1988* (Oxford: Basil Blackwell, 1989), p. 57. Although Bark and Gress repeat the argument that American obstinacy caused Erhard's downfall, the evidence they present suggests otherwise.

77. Hubert Zimmermann, "Dollars, Pounds, and Transatlantic Security: Conventional Troops and Monetary Policy in Germany's Relations to the United States and the United Kingdom, 1955–1967," doctoral dissertation, European University, Florence, 1997, p. 241.

78. Rusk was particularly impressed with Brandt's appearance at NATO, noting that he demonstrated that the new German government "will not be bound by the rigid theology of the Adenauer period . . ." *FRUS 1964–1968,* 13, p. 517.

79. Kai Bird, *The Chairman* (New York: Simon and Schuster, 1992), esp. pp. 590–93.

80. *FRUS 1964–1968,* 13, p. 535.

81. LBJ Library, NSF, NSC History, TNN, Box 50, LBJ to McCloy, Mar. 1, 1967, and Memorandum for the Record, "President's Conversation with John J. McCloy," Mar. 2, 1967.

82. LBJ Library, NSF, NSC History, TNN, Box 50, McCloy to LBJ, May 17, 1967; LBJ Library, Bator Papers, Chronological File, Box 4, Memorandum for the President, Mar. 8, Feb. 23, and Apr. 21, 1967.

83. LBJ Library, NSF, NSC History, TNN, Box 50, McCloy to LBJ, Mar. 22, 1967.
84. Haftendorn, *NATO and the Nuclear Revolution,* p. 397. Kaplan ends his study by noting that John Leddy's 1968 conclusion that "NATO is in a better state of health than the pessimists predicted a few years ago," may have understated Johnson's achievement. Kaplan, "The United States and NATO," in Divine, *Johnson Years, Vol. 3,* p. 143.
85. Interview with Francis Bator, Cambridge, Mass., Dec. 16, 1995.
86. Merle Miller, *Lyndon* (New York: Putnam, 1980), p. 344.

4

The Struggle for the Americas

The Johnson Administration and Cuba

WILLIAM O. WALKER III

The United States and Cuba were engaged in a struggle for the Americas when Lyndon Baines Johnson became president in November, 1963. For nearly four years Fidel Castro had tried to create an ideological counterweight to U.S. power. The contest would soon be over. The Mann Doctrine of March, 1964, signaled the extent to which the United States would go to prevent the spread of Castro's influence and communism in the Western Hemisphere. Henceforth, building a hemispheric fortress against communism on a foundation of order and stability would take precedence over the reform programs promised in the early days of the Alliance for Progress.

U.S.-Cuban relations in the Johnson years divide into three phases. From November, 1963, to April, 1965, the United States acted to isolate Cuba within the hemisphere even while it explored and ultimately dismissed indications that Castro was interested in a modus vivendi. From May, 1965, until October, 1966, relative calm prevailed. Castro tried but failed to find a way to outflank the United States by rhetorically upping the ante in their conflict. The final two years of the Johnson presidency witnessed a surge of revolutionary activism on Castro's part, notably in Bolivia. His inability to develop a solid base of support among Communist Parties in the hemisphere guaranteed his political isolation and furthered Cuban economic dependence upon the Soviet Union.

Ideology, Identity, and Foreign Policy

Agreeing about the outcome of the fierce battle between the United States and Cuba for ideological supremacy is relatively easy. Explaining that outcome, however, can land the analyst in a conceptual thicket. Is it accurate, for instance, to explain the Cuban-U.S. imbroglio primarily as a function of the Cold War and the growth of communism in Cuba?[1] What role should the long history of "singular intimacy" between the two countries play in an analysis of U.S.-

Cuban relations?[2] How much weight should be assigned to persistent patterns of Cuban dependence and U.S. hegemony in their relationship?[3] Should analysts interpret U.S. dominance in strategic or economic terms?[4] Each of these ways of understanding the contours of U.S.-Cuban relations has its merits and drawbacks.[5]

It may nevertheless be possible to escape the conceptual underbrush. If we explain interstate relations as a process entailing forms of conflict, accommodation, competition, and cooperation between political systems at the decision-making level, then foreign policy emerges as a manifestation of a particular world view, or ideology. Scholars more often assume than explain what they mean by ideology. Michael H. Hunt, one major exception to this practice, defines ideology as "an interrelated set of convictions or assumptions" that engenders ways of comprehending and dealing with reality.[6] Ideology thus sets the boundaries for the ways in which authorities seek to project and protect their core values.

Exploration of the historical origins and development of the ideology that undergirds U.S. foreign policy belongs elsewhere. Let it suffice here to observe that from its birth the United States sought to make a place for itself in the world by positing an ideology with missionary characteristics, which presupposed its universal appeal. Public officials and private citizens were deeply committed to the preservation of a political culture that had its roots in devotion to the ideal of representative government and the operations of a marketplace economy. An enduring concern for the United States ever since the War of 1812 has been how to guarantee the viability of this cultural system in an often alien world.[7]

Without a robust foreign policy to give it voice, the ideology of the United States would possess no explanatory relationship to the actions of officials. Yet, as political scientist David Campbell cogently argues in *Writing Security,* foreign policy has become a "political practice central to the constitution, production, and maintenance of American political identity."[8] That is, the process of making and implementing a foreign policy over two centuries has legitimated the sense of exceptionalism and, thus, the expansionism and universalism that form the essence of the world view of U.S. policy elites.

Cuba and U.S. Foreign Relations

How crucial has Cuba been to understanding the presence of the United States in the world arena? Historian Louis A. Pérez, Jr., contends that from the early nineteenth century the "destinies of both countries seemed not merely intertwined but indissoluble." If that is the case, it may not be possible to understand the history of U.S. foreign relations without some reference to Cuba.

Thomas Jefferson imagined a place for Cuba within his "empire of liberty." John Quincy Adams assumed that Cuba, "incapable of self-support, can gravitate only towards the North American Union, which . . . cannot cast her off from its bosom." The tale of Narcisco López, the mid-nineteenth-century adventurer who sought to wrest Cuba from the domain of Spain, is partly a poignant story about a presumptive love of republican institutions that had long lain dormant in the hearts of many Cubans.[9]

The importance of Cuba to a self-image of beneficence in the United States has been even greater in the twentieth century. In 1904 President Theodore Roosevelt, through Secretary of State Elihu Root, reflected on his adminis-tration's Cuba policy: "We freed Cuba from tyranny; we then stayed in the is-land until we had established civil order and laid the foundations for self-government and prosperity; . . . I hail what had been done in Cuba not merely for its own sake, but as showing the purpose and desire of this nation toward all the nations south of us."[10] The potential for disorder paradoxically offered the United States a chance to demonstrate the universal appeal of its basic values. Prolonged disorder, however, would not only threaten vital in-terests abroad but also imperil the construction of a political culture at home.

Consequently, the strengthening of authority abroad might of necessity have to precede completion of the transition to a truly representative form of gov-ernment. Sumner Welles, whom President Franklin D. Roosevelt sent to Cuba in 1933 to preside over the abrogation of the Platt Amendment, clearly under-stood the vital importance of order to U.S. identity. Of his relationship with Fulgencio Batista, Welles acknowledged that Batista was the sole authority of any consequence on the island. Prefiguring the Mann Doctrine by three de-cades, he determined that the association with Batista would have to be main-tained "in the event of further disturbances which may endanger lives and properties of Americans or foreigners in the Republic."[11]

The Cold War and fears among authorities of the spread of communism led not only to a stronger assertion of the universal qualities of U.S. ideology but also to a recurring inability, if not unwillingness, to diagnose the severity of a particular threat. The point is not whether fears of communism were real or self-induced, but rather whether the messianic qualities of U.S. political culture made those fears of foreign danger essential to its continued existence. Campbell forcefully argues that "in the cold war, when numerous overseas obligations were constructed, . . . the identity of the United States became even more deeply [linked to] the external reach of the state."[12]

President Dwight D. Eisenhower's administration thus had little choice but to respond to the unprecedented ideological challenge to U.S. interests in the hemisphere posed by Castroism and Cuba. Special National Intelligence Estimate 85-3-60 of December 8, 1960, described that threat: "The Castro regime enjoys a considerable measure of sympathy among the general public in Latin America because it appears to stand for social progress and for emancipation from US economic dominance. Its revolutionary character is not regarded as a defect by those who are out of power." From a State Department official in Havana came this assessment of Castro's regime: it "represents the negation of many spiritual and cultural values associated with the Christian democratic civilization of the Western world."[13]

The struggle for the Americas between the United States and Cuba in the 1960s was therefore considerably more than a contest with its roots and meaning in the Cold War. Theoretically, the struggle could be a peaceful one. Even if Woodrow Wilson never actually said that the United States would teach the people of South America to elect good men, he surely acted in that spirit. In remarkably similar fashion, Eisenhower believed that "we must encourage the governments [of Latin America] to be more active in teaching their people about the problem" of communism.[14] Putting the burden of the effort on leaders outside of the United States acknowledged their role in contributing to the persistence of Washington's global vision and, hence, to the composition of U.S. political culture, or identity, in the Cold War.

Kennedy and Cuba

Eisenhower's immediate successor, President John F. Kennedy, also believed that Latin America was indispensable to the success of his country's ideological mission. "I regard Latin America as the most critical area in the world today," Kennedy told a news conference in February, 1963. Within weeks of his inauguration two years earlier, the National Security Council (NSC) had asked: "Have we determined what we are going to do about Cuba?" To be more precise NSC members should have asked what they were going to do about revolutionary Cuba. Since January 1, 1959, Cuba had become a dangerous, pariah state. Characterization of Cuba as alien, or "other," depended upon equating Cuba with its most prominent leaders, the two Castro brothers, Fidel and Raúl, and Ernesto "Che" Guevara. By December, 1958, the Department of State was already linking Raúl and Che with Soviet communism.[15]

Associating Fidel with communism took a bit longer. At the end of 1958, Chief of Naval Operations Admiral Arleigh A. Burke had to admit that "Castro is not a Communist." Nearly two years later the U.S. embassy in Havana was reporting that "the Castro regime is now believed to be so firmly committed to the communist camp that it could not extract itself even in the unlikely event that it might wish to do so."[16] Philip W. Bonsal, the last U.S. ambassador in Cuba who had been recalled from Havana in October, 1960, was not so sure.

The strength of Cuba's revolution, he believed, derived from the personal charisma of its leader. The regime "rests upon a Cuban base of coercion and acceptance."[17] The Soviet Union also had its own doubts about the extent of Castro's devotion to communism.[18]

Even so, advisers to Kennedy rejected Bonsal's counsel of moderation toward Castro's revolution.[19] Moreover, few of them found any reason to engage in what they deemed a superfluous debate about whether Fidel Castro really was a Communist. Walt W. Rostow called him "a classic revolutionary romantic." Arthur M. Schlesinger, Jr., depicted Castro as "the passionate leader of the Cuban Revolution." Adolf A. Berle, chair of Kennedy's Task Force on Latin America, called him "personally brave," but also "irresponsible." Early in 1961, Berle observed: "Full-scale Latin American 'cold war' is underway."[20]

If the language employed by Rostow, Schlesinger, and Berle was dismissive in tone, it nevertheless portrayed Castroism as a threat to U.S. leadership in the Americas—and hence to U.S. identity. In Cuba itself, contends historian Lester D. Langley, Castro "challenged liberal American beliefs about the social and economic reforms that Cuba merited."[21] They worried just as much, though, about Castro's ability to do the presumed work of the Soviet Union in the Americas by striving to subvert established governments.[22]

Notwithstanding the overwhelming disparity of power favoring the United States, whether measured in strategic or economic terms, there was a remarkable similarity in the ideological ardor brought to their struggle by the two protagonists. If officials in Washington believed that U.S. identity was at stake in the late 1950s and early 1960s, Castro similarly shared that concern, but his fears were about the fate of revolutionary Cuba. Like the United States, Cuba situated its self-identity in a strong sense of mission. To be sure, survival of the regime was Castro's foremost goal; the act of exporting revolution, however, became indistinguishable from the protection of Cuba's core values. Castro understandably denied that other Latin American nations could import revolution like some purchasable commodity. He nonetheless believed, presumably without regard for geographic boundaries, that "the duty of every revolutionary is to make revolution."[23]

Perhaps because his was the more difficult task of creating state identity virtually anew, Castro's view of Kennedy showed little consistency. At the United Nations in September, 1960, he spoke of the presidential candidate in terms laced with contempt. Many years later in a more reflective mood, he lauded Kennedy's courage and observed that Kennedy might have been the "president best able to rectify American policy toward Cuba."[24]

The sentiments of an aging Castro do not gainsay the fact that the policy of the Kennedy administration was intended to counter the Cuban revolution by ways other than a direct invasion of the island by U.S. military forces. In their entirety, the Alliance for Progress and other plans for economic development, the establishment of counterinsurgency and military training programs, the support of exile groups based in Florida, relations with the Organization of American States (OAS), and many bungled assassination attempts were intended to contain the scourge of Cuban-style revolution and, if need be, eliminate its leader.[25] The first goal had largely been achieved by Kennedy's death in November, 1963, but Castro's own appeal and Cuba's territorial security, though not the cause of revolution elsewhere in the region, were enhanced after the failure of the Bay of Pigs and the missile crisis of October, 1962.[26]

Castro later described the events at Playa Girón, or Bay of Pigs, as "the prelude to the October crisis" and "a severe political blow" to Kennedy's prestige in the hemisphere.[27] The missile crisis may have led Washington to consider some form of military pressure against Cuba, but its peaceful resolution left Castro unscathed. It surely resulted in a redoubled effort within the White House to remove Castro by assassination. The irony of his own survival and the murder of his enemy Kennedy was not lost on the Cuban leader who has stated, "In a strange way, we believe, Kennedy had to die so that the Cuban Revolution could live."[28]

Isolating the Cuban Revolution

"The Johnson Administration is not giving up the fight for Cuba," declared the NSC in December, 1963.[29] However true that commitment may have been in the abstract, in reality Johnson and his advisers could do nothing to rid Cuba of the Castro regime without risking another confrontation with the Soviet Union. Accordingly, LBJ's administration began to reconsider the wisdom of existing policy.

In his final weeks Kennedy had followed a two-track approach toward Cuba. The Central Intelligence Agency (CIA) apparently still possessed carte blanche to assassinate Castro if it could. Meanwhile, the White House was trying to determine whether some kind of modus vivendi could be worked out with the Cuban leader. It is not possible to conclude whether Kennedy was serious about easing tensions, just as it is not possible to prove that the president would have pulled U.S. forces out of Vietnam had he lived. Not even Arthur Schlesinger makes a case for so momentous a change in Cuban policy in November, 1963. Richard N. Goodwin, however, contends that Kennedy had abandoned "the fierce rhetoric of the dedicated Cold Warrior" after the missile crisis and was determined to revamp the U.S. approach to Cuba.[30]

What is certain is that the Johnson administration, during its first few months in office, sought to distance itself from the most extreme policies of its predecessor. Early in April, 1964, it apparently decided to quit the assassination business where Castro was concerned. Some CIA officials believed they still had the authority to plot against Castro's life; Johnson had, however, clearly ordered an end to CIA-sponsored sabotage inside Cuba. This is not to argue that the administration ceased defining the nation's identity with reference to successes and failures vis-à-vis Cuba. Rather, by rethinking its mission, it hoped to avail itself of a greater range of policy options. Assassination was never so much a policy as an overreaction to the ideological challenge posed by Castro's Cuba. The goal of murdering foreign leaders was destined not to win many friends throughout the Americas, and the Johnson White House knew it.[31]

Spawning the reconsideration of policy toward Cuba was the "Plank-Chase Report on U.S.-Cuban Relations," a White House and Department of State undertaking that analyzed how the Eisenhower administration had dealt with Cuba from 1959 to 1961. This document suggests that Washington lost a chance during that time to influence the course of Cuba's revolution because "when effective cooperation with Cuba was called for, the U.S. was generally not co-operative enough; and when effective opposition to Cuba was called for, this country did not sufficiently oppose."[32] The brief window of opportunity closed by May, 1960, if not before. The Plank-Chase report assumed that Cuba might have responded to U.S. pressure in a positive way. Hence, the "lost chance in China" thesis about whether U.S. authorities missed a chance to establish cordial relations with Mao Zedong in the late 1940s seems to have had a Cuban variant in 1964.

The lost chance idea implicitly reasserted the universalism of U.S. core values. It did not at all indicate that Johnson was prepared to stray too far from the Cuban policy set forth by his two predecessors. (Secretary of State Dean Rusk denied there existed "dramatic differences between Kennedy and Johnson" over Latin American policy.)[33] The preferred relationship between the two countries, as Eisenhower's and Kennedy's policies attested, was one conducted without Castro in power. Absent his removal from office, or his death, the optimal course of action was to reach an accommodation with Castro on terms set by the United States. That result would necessarily have entailed surrender rather than negotiation on Castro's part.

Accordingly, it is worth asking why Johnson and his major advisers placed any faith at all in the chimera of a lost chance by continuing Kennedy's overtures to Castro's regime in the fall of 1963 and winter of 1963–64. The answer reveals much about Johnson's approach to foreign policy. U.S. officials rightly suspected that the missile crisis had strained Soviet-Cuban relations. It was also apparent that the Cuban economy, under pressure from the United States, was not performing as well as Castro had expected. Moreover, the news about

Kennedy's death had badly shaken Fidel. "Es una mala noticia," he reportedly said.[34] (Castro, it should be noted, feared that Johnson's ascent to the presidency could be even worse news for the Cuban revolution.)

In assessing the shortcomings—as they saw them—of U.S. policy during Castro's early months in power, administration officials believed that the Cuban leader not only would act on what they defined as his and his nation's interests apart from ideological considerations, but also would respond favorably over time to U.S. entreaties. How, though, could they seriously consider such a scenario? Johnson, historian Waldo Heinrichs notes, thought that as a Texan he possessed a special affinity for Latin America even though his actual knowledge of the region was slight. The president accordingly advocated "an American mission to the Third World" where he "could establish cultural beachheads."[35] Some analysts have pointed out that the prospect of perpetual U.S. presence in Cuban affairs, which augured poorly for the future of the revolution, actually helped to move Castro toward the Soviet Union in the first place.[36] Johnson's inner circle could not, of course, entertain a proposition so damning to their underlying assumptions about Castro and Cuba.

The same liberal political precepts that impelled Johnson to build the Great Society at home also influenced his conduct of foreign affairs. Doris Kearns [Goodwin] observes how "Johnson assumed that in war, as in the Senate, everyone knew the rules of the game, what kind of agreement would be reasonable, and that eventually an agreement would be reached."[37] The president's magnanimity in dropping the plan to assassinate Castro symbolized the political style he had cultivated during his many years in Washington. He could not imagine that the implicit deal he made with Castro, Fidel's life in exchange for curbing subversion, would not result in the desired benefits.

Just as he publicly offered in a speech at Johns Hopkins University in April, 1965, to aid the development of North Vietnam (while also promising to prosecute the war if need be), at which time he proposed a program like the Tennessee Valley Authority for the Mekong River, Johnson privately extended the carrot and stick to Cuba in early 1964. For Johnson, nothing less than the integrity of the liberal beliefs he had come to personify was at stake. That Latin America was serving as a testing ground for the core values, and thus the self-image of the United States, evoked a pattern present in hemispheric relations throughout the twentieth century.[38]

The carrot consisted of more than an end to the attempts on Castro's life; it offered the prospect of further dialogue with Cuba. Castro evidently was intrigued and did not abandon hope for some kind of accommodation until U.S. forces landed on the shores of the Dominican Republic in April, 1965.[39] The sticks were understandably far greater in number than the carrot: increased economic and diplomatic isolation; continued support for exile groups in Florida; enhancement of the forces of order throughout the hemisphere; and unequivocal condemnation of real and perceived attempts to export revolution.

The idea to open exploratory lines of communication with Cuba originated in January, 1963, with National Security Adviser McGeorge Bundy.[40] For Castro, dialogue with Washington accorded him a measure of de facto legitimacy, and might serve as a useful bargaining tool in relations with Moscow and Beijing. Optimally, negotiations would enable him to find a niche on the world scene somewhere between the United States and the Soviet Union.

Beginning in September, 1963, William Attwood, an adviser on African affairs to U.S. Ambassador Adlai Stevenson at the United Nations, met intermittently with Cuban representative Carlos Lechuga about the Bundy initiative, which President Kennedy had encouraged. Attwood, as he later wrote, favored "neutralizing Cuba on our terms." Lisa Howard of the American Broadcasting Company served as a go-between for Attwood and the government of Cuba. Meanwhile, Jean Daniel, a leftist French journalist, met with Castro in Havana to discuss a possible U.S.-Cuban démarche. The tragic events of November 22 in Dallas appeared to cut the effort short. Attwood was named ambassador to Kenya in January, 1964.[41]

Meanwhile, Bundy did not abandon the idea of an opening to Castro, although in NSC meetings he cast it as one in a package of many available measures. The political explosiveness of an overture to revolutionary Cuba in an election year and strong doubts about the wisdom of the operation within the Department of State and the CIA compelled Bundy and his deputy, Gordon Chase, to slow the pace of the initiative to a crawl. Available evidence suggests that indirect contacts with Castro, through Howard, who was reporting from Cuba on a frequent basis, continued into the summer of 1964. By then, Howard was carrying messages to Cuba's leader that she had received from the White House through Stevenson at the United Nations.[42] Johnson therefore may not have foreclosed the possibility of carefully structured discussions with Castro. At length, the overture to Castro was so tentative that it got swept away in the flow of events and the related policy-making process. Johnson himself displayed great indecisiveness about what course of action he preferred.

Bundy and Chase failed, though, to generate sufficient support to pursue in-depth discussions with Castro. At the same time, the White House had several reasons for keeping alive the initiative. First, in mid-February Castro had told Howard, who conveyed the message to the administration, that he "earnestly desire[d]" Johnson's election in November. Castro expressed his appreciation for the beginning Kennedy had made. He recognized, too, that any further approach would be unlikely until after the November elections. Perhaps to convey his seriousness, Castro said he understood Johnson's need "during the campaign to make bellicose statements about Cuba." If informed about ostensibly hostile words or actions, he promised not to take retaliatory measures.[43] Howard found Castro's interest in further discussions genuine; Bundy and Chase apparently did as well.

From another quarter, pressure mounted for an overhaul of Cuban policy. On March 25, Senator J. William Fulbright (D-Ark.), chairman of the Senate Foreign Relations Committee, called for a major change in administration thinking. Later in the year, he elaborated on his remarks in the introductory essay of his book, *Old Myths and New Realities*. "Castro is a nuisance but not a grave threat to the United States," he wrote. Fulbright did not actually recommend direct negotiations with the Cuban government. He did, however, indicate his belief that the administration's "fixation" with Cuba was counterproductive and imperiled other U.S. objectives in the region.[44]

Fulbright's criticism reverberated in the White House. He had publicly raised the issue of Cuban policy while officials were vacillating between conciliation and confrontation. In a larger sense he had implicitly questioned the very conceptual underpinnings of Johnson's foreign policy toward much of the Third World. He would give further voice to these doubts, and gain the enmity of the president, in his adverse reaction to the invasion of the Dominican Republic in 1965 and through his break with Johnson over the war in Vietnam.[45]

Scholars have faulted the administration for viewing Latin America through a Cuba-colored lens.[46] As Fulbright intimated, it could hardly have been otherwise. Just one week before the senator made his remarks, Assistant Secretary of State for Latin American Affairs Thomas C. Mann issued the statement regarding administration policy toward Latin America that bears his name, the so-called Mann Doctrine. Henceforth, military and economic assistance in the region would depend not on the character of a given regime but on the extent to which it could maintain order and contain subversive activities.[47] Because of this ostensibly conservative turn in policy, in April when Johnson renounced the option of assassinating Castro, it was unclear what that decision meant in concrete terms. In November, 1963, as Jean Daniel was meeting with Castro on Kennedy's behalf, the CIA dispatched an operative, a Cuban ex-revolutionary known as "AM/LASH," with instructions to kill Castro. Deputy Director for Plans Richard Helms did not believe that the president's change of heart should negate AM/LASH's mission; the relationship between the CIA and AM/LASH would last until the Cuban government discovered it in February, 1966.[48]

Meanwhile, covert plans to engage in sabotage against Cuba continued apace as the majority of officials, Johnson included, were predisposed to see Castro's hand in every development that challenged administration goals. Castro was "fanning the fires of violence in Venezuela, Colombia, Panama, Brazil, Bolivia, Guatemala, Nicaragua, Ecuador and Peru," warned the Department of State in a message to U.S. diplomats throughout the hemisphere.[49] This sweeping allegation did not, however, mean that Cuba was engaged in a systematic campaign to distribute arms to insurgents throughout Latin America.[50]

The discovery of a sizeable cache of weapons in Venezuela in late 1963 (which may have been planted by CIA operatives) and evidence of meddling thereafter nevertheless offered anti-Castro hardliners in Washington an opportunity to take advantage of Castro's supposed determination to export violent revolution. The Organization of American States soon formed a committee to look into the matter, with the approval of the White House. The OAS acted in July, 1964, to increase Cuba's diplomatic isolation from the other American republics, as we shall see.[51] In discussing the arms issue at an NSC meeting on March 5, Mann and Johnson explored the idea of getting advance approval from the OAS for military action against Cuba should the need arise. Several others, including Bundy, demurred and reminded them of Kennedy's pledge—made after the missile crisis—not to invade Cuba.[52]

Their dissent scarcely mattered because Johnson, Mann, and others chary of compromise with Castro viewed the Venezuelan affair as a providential weapon in their ideological battle for the Americas. Journalist Philip Geyelin wrote of Thomas Mann, he was "a hard-liner . . . and Lyndon Johnson's kind of man." The two, he continued, "were more interested in where the power lay than where, in the best of all possible worlds, it ought to lie." This conscious pragmatism helped to allay the president's fear that failure in foreign policy would undermine the vitality of the nation as embodied in his Great Society programs.[53]

Concern about the likelihood of communist subversion also arose when riots erupted in Panama on January 7, 1964, over the flying of the U.S. flag. Johnson saw Castro's handiwork behind the anti-American activity. So, too, did Mann, who, as one of Johnson's special envoys, warned President Roberto Chiari that "Castro [sic] agents in Panama were as great a danger to Panama as they are to the US government." The Standing Group on Cuba within the NSC also believed that Castro was partly responsible for the crisis in Panama. An OAS investigation would later reach a different conclusion.[54] Tensions between the United States and Panama had begun to ease by early April, yet Johnson stubbornly maintained his belief that Castro "had not abandoned his plans for testing the United States and its new President." As the president wrote about the 1965 Dominican crisis, "The Communist leader in Havana was always alert to any exploitable weakness among his neighbors."[55]

Mann's policy-making star rose during the Panama crisis. The Mann Doctrine, with its emphasis on economic progress through order and stability, was taking shape on several fronts. The substance of the doctrine was not new. In 1952, as director of the Office of Middle American Affairs in the State Department, Mann prepared an assessment of the state of U.S.–Latin American relations and concluded, in Walter LaFeber's words, that the Americas "were forming a natural economic unit on which U.S. prosperity and security largely rested." The region thus had to be protected from the irresponsibility of extreme nationalism, to paraphrase Mann.[56]

Twelve years later in endeavoring to thwart the ideological challenge emanating from Cuba, Mann believed that the Alliance for Progress was not structured to serve as the primary line of defense. Local military and police forces needed training programs and modern equipment for effective antisubversion and counterinsurgency activities. The Agency for International Development (AID) held oversight authority for these efforts through the public safety programs of its Office of Public Safety. National Security Action Memorandum 177 of June, 1964, reiterated the importance of public safety assistance as an instrument of U.S. policy. Consistent with Mann's thinking in the early 1950s, U.S. foreign aid should be used to help "control civil disturbances and dissident elements . . . so that economic and social development can proceed."[57]

The symbiotic relationship between U.S. aid and regional stability became axiomatic in Johnson's administration. A well-structured aid program was a prerequisite for the construction abroad of economic development and political democracy. That is, it served as a conduit for the projection of U.S. core values. Conversely, the absence of an assistance program as an arm of foreign policy encouraged challenges to U.S. leadership such as those posed by Cuba. In a midyear review of progress made since he took office, Mann clearly made a link between aid and "growing political stability in Latin America" where "new and direct investment on the part of Americans [sic] in Latin America was $26 million during the first quarter of this year, compared with *minus* figures of $8 million last year and $37 million in 1962."[58]

Foreign assistance, whether through investment or trade, served to reward friends, whereas deprivation of aid promised to punish enemies of the United States. The underlying assumption, as political scientist Robert Packenham writes, that "under no circumstances are radicalism and revolution appropriate for economic aid and political development," was not really shared by Washington's closest allies. In an appearance before the North Atlantic Council on March 23, Undersecretary of State George W. Ball called for adherence to a program of economic denial, which to date was "not fully accepted by all of our NATO partners." Indeed, since early 1962, the United States had been endeavoring with limited success to persuade European allies to curtail trade with Cuba. Ball feared that the extension of credits to Cuba by NATO members, following the precedent set by Great Britain, would "frustrate a serious policy affecting the defense of free world interests in a vital area of the world."[59] Economic denial did not become a policy that Washington's NATO allies warmly or substantially embraced, although Johnson's inner circle never deviated from the objective of making Cuba pay for its challenge to the United States.

Ball's speech was ironically and unintentionally revealing in that his depiction of Cuba's desire to attain certain foreign policy objectives in order to bolster state identity could have applied, with scant modification, to U.S. foreign policy as well. Castro "looks upon the Southern Half of the American Continent as the proper field for the fulfillment of his ambitions. He seeks a revolutionary millennium in which the example of Cuba will have swept the Continent. . . . This vision . . . is necessary to the man and his followers, whose revolutionary enthusiasm must be constantly fed on the prospect of further advance beyond the confines of the island." In strikingly similar fashion, two proponents of liberal developmentalism, social scientists Max F. Millikan and Walt W. Rostow of the Massachusetts Institute of Technology, had in 1957 concluded a small book about aid and foreign policy with a chapter entitled, "The American Mission," which extolled the universal appeal of the U.S. economic model. Seen from this perspective, the ideological divide between the United States and Cuba was so great as to be as impassible as the Florida Straits in a hurricane.[60]

Fidel Castro, of course, more than matched Ball's rhetoric in his speeches to the Cuban people. On the fifth anniversary of the revolution in January, Castro declared that the revolution was "not just any victory, . . . not the victory against Batista and his clique. . . . It is the victory against the imperialist Yankees. These have been five years of resistance against Yankee imperialism!" Then, after the April coup against João Goulart in Brazil, Castro excoriated the United States. He called Mann "a known reactionary, an archenemy of our revolution." The coup itself was "hatched," the revolutionary asserted, "by the Yankee Pentagon and State Department."[61]

These doses of vitriol emanating from Havana and Washington make it all the more remarkable that the overtures concerning negotiations lasted as long as they did. To be sure, the speech on the fifth anniversary of the revolution contained passages with conciliatory language in which Castro backed away from a policy of exporting revolution. The same can be said about the April speech but to a substantially lesser degree. Hence, it is fair to surmise that Castro actually believed he had struck an implicit bargain in February with Johnson and was using Lisa Howard as his intermediary.

Accepting that analysis places Castro's statements to the *New York Times* during an interview in July in a positive light. The "erratic Cuban leader," as the *Times* subsequently referred to him, told that paper's Richard Eder that he would stop supporting revolution elsewhere if Washington put an end to its subversive activities. In addition to covert backing for forays against Cuba by exiles headquartered in Florida, Castro was referring to overflights of the island's air space. At present, neither side "ha[d] confidence in the good faith of the other." He also said that it would be easier for him than for U.S. leaders to reach a mutual understanding, whether before or after the coming elections.[62]

The immediate reaction in the White House doubted good faith by Castro because his "whole record is one of broken promises and duplicity." It was therefore unthinkable "that he will stop his subversion."[63] Subversion encompassed a range of activities from extending moral support to left-wing movements to funneling arms to revolutionaries—as had presumably occurred in the case of the Venezuelan arms cache.

Like beauty, subversion largely depended upon the eye of the beholder. A CIA report on arms trafficking in the Caribbean in 1963, which included the discovery on the Venezuelan beach, concluded that the "information was far too incomplete . . . to identify the sources of arms and, in particular, the extent of Cuban involvement." The NSC's Chase wondered whether "we are cranking up to go after something that really isn't there." Of much "greater significance," suggested the report, was Cuban involvement in the training of potential rebels and Havana's rhetorical campaign to foment revolution.[64] The response in the State Department echoed the Mann line: "Castro's policy toward Latin America is essentially hostile, with emphasis on efforts to overthrow established governments." As for improving relations with Washington, he "does not seem prepared to give up much."[65]

The crucial issue in relation to subversion, contended the State Department's Bureau of Intelligence and Research, was how to prevent the Soviet Union, through Castro, from "breaking US hegemony in the Western Hemisphere." The Cuban revolution had made more difficult the task of repelling the threat of communism in the U.S. sphere of influence. Unfortunately, State Department officials lamented, innocent Cubans would have to suffer for Castro's hostility, because "Cuba cannot grow and prosper while he is fighting with Cuba's traditional friend, the United States."[66]

The close relationship between U.S. identity and Johnson's Cuba policy was demonstrated soon after Castro's interview with the *New York Times*. Wayne S. Smith, who served in the Office of Cuban Affairs, has written that Secretary of State Dean Rusk and others of like mind interpreted Castro's peace feelers as a sign of weakness and threw the "olive branch back in his face." The State Department had spent months lining up votes among OAS members to punish Cuba for intervention in Venezuelan affairs. It was hardly coincidental that the OAS voted fifteen to four to break diplomatic and trade relations with Cuba as Castro was speaking in conciliatory tones on July 26, the anniversary date of the 1953 attack on the Moncada Barracks. Just after the OAS vote, the State Department depicted Castro as adopting a tougher line against the United States in the speech, whereas the *Washington Post* reported that he had called for improved relations.[67] In a mood of self-congratulation, the State Department termed the OAS meeting "a substantial victory for the US and Venezuela." Rusk exalts in his memoirs about a defeat for "Marxism-Leninism" in the Western Hemisphere.[68]

U.S. relations with Cuba receded into the background as events in the Gulf of Tonkin off the coast of North Vietnam and the election campaign captured the attention of the White House. Cuba was not absent from the presidential campaign, however. Johnson declared on September 7 that the OAS resolution in July and the Tonkin reprisal raids in August "proved that we would stand firm in the defense of freedom."[69] Like his predecessors, Johnson was determined to maintain his nation's global mission in the Cold War. That Cuba, a "traditional friend," had rejected Washington's beneficence through programs like the Alliance for Progress was all the more reason to remain vigilant.

Those states like Cuba, who would seek to spread communism in the Third World, were meeting their match. Such was the blunt message the administration sought to convey. The argument had considerable merit in the short term. The lack of a diplomatic presence in much of Latin America would reduce Cuba's capacity to wield as much financial and ideological influence as before, and it would present the appearance of hemispheric unity. In order to preserve his status as a leader who was independent of U.S. actions, Castro had to respond.

A meeting of Latin American Communist Parties in Havana in November ended with declarations of greater Cuban support for armed struggle in Guatemala, Honduras, Colombia, Paraguay, Haiti, and Venezuela. Yet Soviet Premier Nikita Khrushchev's ouster from power and the entry of the People's Republic of China into the nuclear club in October may have delayed the inception of such a campaign. Castro had come to regard the Soviets as uncertain allies, and what the coming of the nuclear age to China meant for the unpredictable Sino-Cuban relationship could not readily be divined.[70]

Castro, though giving off mixed signals as usual, still may have desired better relations with Washington. Interviewed just before the U.S. elections, he told C. L. Sulzberger of the *New York Times,* "A big Johnson triumph would signify an opportunity to make realistic policies." Castro's words did not fall on receptive ears. To the extent they ever existed, chances for an accommodation seems to have been lost by that time. Even as the *Times* interviews appeared, the Johnson administration was applauding the promise of stability in Bolivia offered by the seizure of power by a military government. The Mann Doctrine had no room for tinkering with Cuban policy. Also, the CIA had recently hired Cuban exiles as mercenary pilots to defend U.S. interests in the Congo.[71] Havana must have looked upon these regional and global developments with great apprehension.

As if in response, Castro sent Che Guevara to address the United Nations in December. Cuba had initially planned to keep a low profile at the session. An NSC report at the time indicated that the threat of subversion was low but warned that "the situation could change explosively overnight."[72] Johnson's advisers saw Guevara as "the architect and principal advocate of . . . subversion and violence throughout the Hemisphere." They anticipated Guevara's speech on December 11 with much trepidation, however, fearing charges that Washington was violating Cuban sovereignty through its U-2 spy flights over the island.[73]

To their surprise, Che denounced U.S. imperialism in mild terms, glossing over the U-2 flights and emphasizing Washington's backing for repressive regimes. Taking Guevara's temperate presentation as a cue, Bundy and Chase hastily asked Lisa Howard to arrange a meeting on December 16 between Guevara and Senator Eugene McCarthy (D-Minn.). The talks focused on Cuba's economic isolation and the possibility of U.S. recognition of the regime. In a postmortem held in the office of Undersecretary of State George Ball, no consensus emerged about what to do next. Ball fretted about giving a propaganda advantage to Cuba should the existence of the meetings become known; Thomas Mann, also in attendance, kept his own counsel.[74] His preference for a policy of economic denial and diplomatic isolation remained unchanged. The intermittent search for a modus vivendi with revolutionary Cuba, begun early in 1963, had ground to a halt.

An Interlude of Relative Calm

Not until U.S. forces landed in the Dominican Republic in April would it be possible to comprehend how total was the break. In early 1965, Cuba was in some ways more isolated than it had been since 1960 when it first made overtures for trade to the Soviet Union. Fidel Castro, who had exhibited marked flexibility toward the United States, would thereafter take a harder line in condemning what he considered to be U.S. imperialism. In so doing, he would bestow an air of legitimacy on the Mann-Johnson-Rusk approach that spurned negotiation. By late 1966 Castro would be desperate for some advantage over his powerful neighbor. As the Johnson administration became more committed to defending controversial interests in Southeast Asia, policy makers welcomed the evident success of their Cuban policy. If the United States was facing grave challenges on the world stage, close to home in the Americas there still remained allies on whom Washington could rely to confront the Communist enemy. The very existence of that enemy, officials believed, testified to the ultimate wisdom of the president's foreign policy. Seen in that light, as Johnson had often intimated, it was the solemn job of the United States to stand tall as the guardian of freedom.

Che Guevara traveled to Africa upon leaving the United Nations. Why he made the trip was easy to understand. Intelligence reports indicated that the Cuban revolution had lost its cachet in Latin America. To be sure there were exceptions: Colombia, Guatemala, and Venezuela were considered prime targets for subversion. The *Ejercito Liberación Nacional,* or National Liberation Army, in Colombia, for example, had fashioned a Cuban-style appeal to the urban masses. Bolivia, however, once seen as a prime target for revolution, had reportedly vanquished terrorist threats.[75]

Guevara's message to Africans was therefore an effort to rejuvenate Cuba's revolutionary stature among the world's poor and oppressed peoples. So concluded Thomas L. Hughes, the State Department's director of intelligence and research. Che visited Algeria, Mali, Congo, Guinea, Ghana, Dahomey, Tanzania, and the United Arab Republic. Hughes deemed the trip "a modest success." Most striking to U.S. analysts about Guevara's message was his clear warning "privately and publicly of the dangers that can arise from extensive Soviet or Chicom [*sic*] involvement in their countries."[76]

Then on April 28 came Johnson's decision to dispatch troops to the Dominican Republic to quash a revolt against the pro-U.S. military government. Were Communists in charge of the rebellion? Secretary Rusk doubted it. President Johnson feared otherwise, sensing the influence of Cuba over the rebels. "We knew," he later wrote about Castro, that "he had his eye on the Dominican Republic."[77] The CIA reached the same conclusion even though it found "no evidence that the Castro regime is directly involved in the current insurrection." The CIA did find "45 extremists" who had presumably received training "in Cuba and/or elsewhere in the Communist bloc." In another report on the revolt, the agency referred to the rebels as "Castroites."[78] The CIA, predisposed like Johnson to see the specter of Cuban influence in the revolt, found what it was looking for.

U.S. intervention in the Dominican Republic alarmed Castro, who, like Guevara, had generally lost faith in the two Communist superpowers. As U.S. troops poured into Santo Domingo, Castro had to wonder whether Cuba was about to be sacrificed on the altar of U.S.-Soviet friendship. Early in March, the Cuban leader had made a gesture through the British indicating that he was still interested in normalizing relations with Washington. He received no recorded response.[79]

Castro's speeches to the Cuban people in May brought out the animosity he felt toward the United States. His objective became the rupture of the OAS; Castro found it inconceivable that fellow Latin Americans would abide the imperial attitude exhibited by the United States in the Dominican Republic. His outrage earned Cuba no show of support from OAS members, however. If anything, it suggested that Castro had abandoned the caution he had evinced in his policies toward the rest of the hemisphere since the fall of 1963.[80]

Castro's heated rhetoric played into the hands of those in Washington who were desirous of portraying him as an intractable ideologue. To be sure, his surge of revolutionary fervor did seem to bring him out of the malaise that had set in following the OAS vote the previous July. The State Department analyzed Castro's actions as producing "a resurgence of Cuban confidence" in the ultimate victory of revolution in Latin America. Castro also said that the "phantom of revolution" terrified the United States, but that assertion—however valid it may have been—passed without comment.[81]

That phantom, such as it was, became quite important to the conduct of Johnson's foreign policy. In the 1964 presidential campaign, he told an audience in Detroit that "*everywhere* we have worked to extend the domain of liberty."[82] The decisive issue, as his administration was pondering the road that would enmesh it in Vietnam, became how best to safeguard the ostensible domain of liberty in the Americas. A debate arose in the spring and summer of 1965 over the nature of military and, to an extent, economic assistance and what it could accomplish. While Castro was giving virtually no indication of a campaign to export revolution, U.S. officials endeavored to fortify hemispheric defenses against the anticipated coming assault.

That task would not be easily accomplished. Ball informed Johnson that not all high-level U.S. officials had agreed with his course of action in the Dominican Republic. The Department of State's Policy Planning Council acknowledged that "we have not made our case to these countries [in the hemisphere] that the Dominican revolt was at a certain stage Communist dominated." The creation of an Inter-American Defense Force, which some in Johnson's administration vigorously advocated, therefore seemed unlikely; the force could be seen as a harbinger of further U.S. intervention. At the present time, the Policy Planning Council argued in June, a regional force "limits the freedom of US unilateral action."[83]

The key, then, was to provide assistance to maintain U.S. freedom of action while prolonging Latin American dependence on the United States. How much aid was considered enough? Within the Department of Defense, some sentiment existed for cutting the Military Assistance Program for Latin America, a savings of $55 million. The State Department objected, arguing that "influence on the military in the internal political context . . . would very probably decline." It also feared that without U.S. aid, Latin American security would suffer. The joint chiefs of staff concurred with the State Department's view, stressing the vital role of the Latin American military in security matters "until the efforts at police improvement are assured." Secretary of Defense Robert S. McNamara also found persuasive the views expressed in the State Department, telling McGeorge Bundy that reducing aid might "alienate the military forces on whom the Alliance for Progress must depend to maintain stability in the area."[84]

Security in the Americas in the mid-1960s had an economic component as well as a military one. Walt Rostow was calling for "a new look at Latin American policy," which would necessarily mean improving the conditions for regional trade. Likewise, Thomas Mann, then about to be replaced as assistant secretary of state by Jack H. Vaughn, believed that the administration should support David Rockefeller's Business Group for Latin America as it expanded to become the Council for Latin America. The council operated throughout Latin America, and its 224 member corporations "benefit[ed] directly from AID-financed orders for the sale of goods."[85] The fate of North American businesses in Latin America depended in large measure at that time upon the preservation of order and stability, which further validated the administration's hard line toward Cuba.

CIA-orchestrated covert operations had declined somewhat in frequency but remained a part of the campaign to keep Castro off balance. It was Guevara's disappearance from Cuba, though, soon after his return to Havana from Africa in March that threatened to throw Washington off its guard. Guevara and Castro reportedly differed strongly over Cuba's role in the Communist world, with Fidel pragmatically accepting an orientation toward Moscow and Che leaning toward Beijing. The CIA analyzed the disagreements between the two comrades as a consequence of Castro's opposition to Che's economic and foreign policies, which Castro deemed too centralized and overly dogmatic. Agency analysts also speculated that Guevara was intending to foment revolution in foreign lands, though perhaps not at Castro's behest. It is not clear whether U.S. officials knew that Guevara was going to return to Africa, specifically to the Congo, to take up the cause of the Kinshasa rebels.[86]

The indications of self-denial on Castro's part contained in the CIA memo had no effect on Johnson's policy, because, as the State Department explained, "Cuba's foreign policy continues to center on the encouragement of revolution in Latin America [and] denigration of the US." Revealingly, the State Department's Bureau of Intelligence and Research admitted that Castro's interest in negotiations in 1964 failed "because of the lack of US interest in his proposals." U.S. policy makers clearly believed that they had successfully contained the spread of Cuban influence. Reports indicating extensive discord at the Tri-Continental Conference, convened in Havana in early January, 1966, for the purpose of showcasing Third World solidarity, appeared to confirm that perception. The ideological rift with China, for example, was widening, which meant future volatility for Cuba's already unstable economy.[87]

Other than capitulation to the dictates of Washington, Castro's options were few—as had been the case after the July, 1964, OAS vote to isolate Cuba. In his closing speech at the Tri-Continental Conference, he offered a preview of what was to come: an intensified ideological contest with the United States. "The imperialists are everywhere in the world," Castro declared. "And for Cuban revolutionaries the battleground against imperialism encompasses the whole world."[88] The uncertain status of Cuba's relationship with Moscow and Beijing had prevented Castro from carrying out a similar struggle after the Communist Party meeting in Havana in November, 1964. That impediment had no influence on Castro's planning in the early months of 1966. The CIA did not believe he would try to export armed struggle on a grand scale. Rather, the agency assumed that he would seek to identify targets of opportunity in countries like Haiti, Guatemala, and Colombia with "exceedingly shaky political structures."[89] Trouble with the Cuban economy because of a poor sugar harvest demanded Castro's immediate attention, concluded U.S. authorities.[90]

Seeking to take advantage of Castro's difficulties, the United States began a campaign in the OAS to embarrass the Cuban leader and highlight the failings of his revolution. In early February, the OAS Council passed a resolution condemning the Tri-Continental Congress for espousing intervention and aggression in violation of the right to self-determination, a right Castro had adamantly defended as he sought coexistence with Washington. The dispute moved to the United Nations, where all Latin American governments other than Mexico protested the Havana meeting in a letter to Secretary General U Thant. Castro then had no recourse except to denounce again the United States and the "cowardly and shameless complicity" of the other American republics in the endeavor.[91]

For the first time since the administration of President Eisenhower broke relations with Castro, the National Security Council in early 1966 was not constantly wondering what it "was going to do about Cuba." The Johnson administration had a firmly established policy that it moved to bolster throughout the year. This is not to argue that the White House and the NSC were at all complacent about Cuba. Indeed, high-level officials worried that Johnson's job would immeasurably increase in difficulty if the president had to deal with Cuba as well as Vietnam.[92] Lessening the rhetorical jousting did not indicate, as some policy makers feared, that Cuban policy had been put on the back burner.

The State Department, as usual, scrutinized Castro's public appearances, judging his annual 26th of July speech "consistent with his heightened revolutionary stridency of the past seven months."[93] In practical terms, the U.S. response consisted of a reexamination of existing aid programs for Latin America. The NSC defended the "modest" $80 million annual outlay in security assistance, seeing it as a small insurance payment for a dividend comprised of "economic, social and political development," which entailed a "major investment" of $1 billion yearly.[94] From the State Department Rusk concurred. He and Lincoln Gordon, named as assistant secretary for inter-American affairs in February, believed that the military assistance could help stem Castroite mischief until Alliance for Progress programs eliminated the potential for civil unrest.[95]

Rusk, Gordon, and Rostow saw security assistance as a means to the larger objectives of democratization and prosperity. Aid bought time, officials averred, for the democratic process to take root; it also promised to safeguard outlets for investment in social change and economic development. Troubles regularly plagued the economic arm of administration policy, however. Congress began to question the value of the alliance and wanted to scale back the extent of resources committed to it. Also, the Treasury Department sought to link export credits to the purchase of North American products.[96] A CIA assessment termed the lack of export markets "the most severe economic constraint on growth in Latin America." The report should additionally be understood as an implicit critique of the Alliance for Progress.[97]

Into the breach stepped Walt Rostow, who in April, 1966, took McGeorge Bundy's place as national security adviser. In the president's inner circle, the so-called Tuesday Cabinet, Rostow conveyed a "misleading aura of authority," in the words of Henry F. Graff. Yet it was Rostow, Kearns Goodwin notes, "who screened what the President heard and saw."[98] If Kearns overstates Rostow's influence, it is still true that Johnson welcomed his counsel. It was axiomatic for Rostow that the nation "had to have about [it] a situation where it is possible to continue to develop a society at home" intent upon preserving traditional core values. Seen from that perspective, "subversion and guerrilla warfare in the developing nations" by definition posed serious threats to U.S. national security.[99]

Rostow, acting as social scientist and policy maker, devised a response to the threats, which might fairly be termed Rostow's "Frontier Thesis." Like the historian Frederick Jackson Turner in the 1890s, Rostow identified the frontier as a safety valve with the capacity to revitalize the nation's identity—its unique political and economic institutions. Whereas Turner had pondered the meaning of the closing of the frontier, Rostow viewed the frontiers of Latin America as lands of new opportunity where the United States, through judicious programs of economic aid, would lead others to unprecedented prosperity. In conveying his ideas to Johnson, he asserted that "the opening of the South American frontiers has an important role to play in the region's future." It is indicative of the missionary imperative in U.S. foreign policy in the 1960s that Johnson requested, in the form of a National Security Action Memorandum, regular reports on so nebulous a concept as open frontiers in Latin America.[100]

Rostow's thesis about development and security, reminiscent of his work with Max Millikan in the 1950s, ran aground on the shoals of nationalism, which was itself intensified by concerns over market share for commonly produced South American goods. As slow starting as the alliance itself, the proposal to open remote frontiers had made scant headway by the time Johnson left office. In sum, it hardly contributed to the spirit of a common mission that U.S. officials hoped to instill among their counterparts below the Rio Grande. A CIA evaluation of the future potential for revolution indirectly suggested why Rostow's idea failed to catch on: the lure of the city for peasants and the accompanying urban problems would lessen the likelihood of capital investment, and thus development in frontier areas.[101]

Also bringing into question the concept of mutual security through economic development, or, alternatively, through economic stagnation for Cuba, was the revival in late 1966 of European, Canadian, and Japanese trade with Cuba. Trade between Cuba and U.S. allies had decreased since 1964, but that situation would undergo a modest change from late 1966 through 1968. Washington exhorted its friends, most notably the British, to reconsider their decisions to make credit available to Cuba—largely to no avail. On several occasions when diplomacy failed to curb trade with Cuba, the CIA likely sabotaged some goods before they were shipped. Overall, the United States succeeded in keeping to a minimum allied commerce in strategic commodities.[102]

Revolutionary Challenge and U.S. Response

But for Fidel Castro's own ideological needs in his disputes with China and the Soviet Union, an atmosphere approaching stasis would have characterized the last two years of Cuban policy for the Johnson administration. That quiescence was not to be. By November, the CIA was reporting the presence of Cuban-trained subversives in Venezuela. Agency analysts feared that "the Cuban timetable for revolution in Latin America calls for successful socialist revolution in one or two countries as model cases by 1970." The elusive Guevara, whose activities remained a mystery, was presumably leading the drive to foment revolution.[103] (In fact, Che had established operations in Bolivia in autumn, 1966.)

Reports about Cuban-inspired or Cuban-directed rebellion in South America had a renewed air of urgency about them. "Abundant evidence" indicated that the Fidelistas of the *Fuerzas Armadas de Liberación Nacional* (FALN) were preparing to engage in an armed insurgency against the government of Raúl Leoni. Conditions did not, however, appear to be quite so desperate in Caracas. The pro-Castro *Ejército de Liberación Nacional* (ELN) was employing ever more violent tactics against the Colombian state, possibly in concert with other rebel groups. The situation would rapidly worsen, the CIA predicted, if "Castro is willing and able to sustain the guerrillas."[104] In reality, neither Venezuela nor Colombia were seriously threatened at that time, although on September 24, 1967, the OAS again condemned Cuba for exporting aggression and inciting revolution.[105]

Guerrilla activity in Bolivia presented a graver problem for authorities in Washington. In June the CIA concluded that "Cuba has played a key role" in the recent buildup of radical leftist opposition to the government of General René Barrientos Otuño. Che Guevara himself was reportedly in charge of guerrilla activity. The government, hostile to the traditional Bolivian left, denied the presence of guerrilla fronts until clashes between guerrilla bands and military forces compelled Barrientos to do otherwise.[106]

In a report to Johnson about Cuban support for the guerrilla movements in Latin America, Rostow added a handwritten notation to the effect that "each organized guerilla [*sic*] can tie up 10–20 government soldiers. We do better in Viet-nam only because of air power, mobility, firepower, etc." Rostow's choice of words surely resonated with Johnson. Despite their limited numbers and relative lack of sophisticated weaponry, guerrillas employed tactics with the potential to create a domino effect in unstable Latin American nations. Rostow's note implicitly asked whether Guevara's bold promise to create "dos, tres, muchos Viet-Nam" throughout the Americas would actually come to pass.

Johnson the internationalist, already on the defensive for his Indochina policy, believed that all he stood for was under seige. Twenty years earlier, he had staunchly defended the creation of the Marshall Plan because the alternative was unthinkable. "One day," he prophesied, "we will wake up in a world in which the Western Hemisphere is a lonely island and all the rest of mankind behind the iron curtain." As Rostow's note clearly intimated, a Cuban-guerrilla victory presented the prospect of the worst possible defeat for U.S.-led globalism short of a nuclear war.[107]

By early July, the NSC was advocating more aid for rural police; in the meantime Green Berets were on their way to Bolivia to go after Guevara.[108] Why was Guevara in South America? Had he lost Castro's favor? Or did he go to Bolivia on Castro's orders? If so, what was Castro's motivation in sending the Argentine revolutionary to the jungles there? Documentary evidence from the Cuban side remains beyond the reach of scholars, but the context of the times suggests that Che was not acting on his own. Castro was feeling hemmed in by the U.S. economic offensive; he strongly believed that Communist Parties in Latin America, over which he exerted scant influence, were far more bourgeois than revolutionary; and he wanted to cast himself as an independent actor as relations with Moscow continued to sour.[109] As such, he gambled on Guevara in Bolivia in a failed effort to rejuvenate his own revolutionary credentials.

It is probably erroneous, therefore, to interpret Guevara's presence in Bolivia as the work of a rogue revolutionary. He went, it would appear, with Fidel's blessing, thinking that "objective conditions" existed to make ideological inroads among Bolivia's peasants through guerrilla warfare.[110] The error in judgment by Che, who could not communicate directly with the Quechua-speaking Indian miners he was committed to free from imperialism, cost him his life on October 9.[111]

Guevara's death also brought to an end the brief revival of the struggle for the Americas between Cuba and the United States. Cuban-style revolution could not easily be replicated elsewhere. Consequently, Castro had no reliable means of recruiting the masses of impoverished Latin Americans into a battle against U.S. imperialism. Although Castro did not give up his rhetorical commitment to armed struggle, within months of Che's death his seemed to be the faith of an agnostic. Soviet Premier Aleksei Kosygin had briefly visited Cuba after meeting with Johnson at Glassboro, New Jersey, in June. He told Fidel that it was time to end the campaign for armed struggle in Latin America and also criticized the decision to send Guevara to Bolivia.[112] The events of October would reduce Cuba to a Platt-like relationship with the Soviet Union.

On the ninth anniversary of the revolution, Castro spoke to the Cuban people not about Che and armed struggle during 1968, the "year of the heroic guerrilla," but about agricultural matters. Maurice Halperin, a friendly critic of the revolution, has noted that "there was less for the population to celebrate than at any previous anniversary." Sugar was being rationed; morale was low.[113] U.S. intelligence reports about the speech and its aftermath were triumphalist in tone. The return of rhetorical "venom and fury" directed against the United States at the Havana Cultural Congress on January 12 caused no alarm in Washington. The CIA discounted the short-term prospects for armed insurgency, remarking: "The old ways and systems [in Latin America] have shown quite a lot of staying power." Ever aware of its role in the furtherance of the U.S. mission abroad, agency analysts did warn that "over a longer period, however—certainly within the next decade—we see conditions developing *throughout the area* which will be much more conducive to revolution."[114]

In the final year of the Johnson presidency, Fidel Castro, the once fearsome revolutionary, became mostly a nuisance factor to U.S. policy makers who meanwhile continued their vain struggle against another revolution thousands of miles away. Castro and radical opponents of the war in Vietnam made common ideological cause. He provided some financial resources to help fund their activities, yet this endeavor entailed no risk at all. And a number of reports about Cuban interest in fomenting insurgency in Haiti or the Dominican Republic had no empirical evidence to back them up. Just after the election of Richard M. Nixon to the presidency, U.S. intelligence analysts found nothing to worry about in Cuba's training of potential guerrillas from around the Caribbean.[115] With no other option, Castro was in the process of easing himself back into the ideological embrace of the Soviet Union.

Ideology, Identity, and Foreign Policy Revisited

Fidel Castro's failure in his ten-year struggle with the United States resulted from more than the critical disparity in military resources. It derived partly from the shortcomings in the self-image he had fashioned for himself. On the one hand, Castro was unquestionably a revolutionary. On the other hand, his skewed vision of continental nationalism, which placed him in the tradition of Simón Bolívar, was an illusion built on willful self-delusion in several respects. Most Communist Parties in Latin America followed the Soviet line of peaceful coexistence with their capitalist enemies. Also, nationalists across the region found themselves remarkably at odds with Castro's more universalist revolutionary ideals.[116] Ultimately, revolution in the Cuban style was not an exportable commodity.

The war in Vietnam may also have encouraged Castro in his and Guevara's promotion of armed struggle in Latin America. This consideration recalls Campbell's sound insight that states create their identity through their foreign policy objectives. For Castro's Cuba, envisioning the United States as a direct or indirect threat to its existence led it to try to defend itself by exporting revolution. Cuban leaders evidently did believe that, upon terminating the war in Vietnam, the White House would then turn its military attention to Cuba.[117] Fear of the United States was fundamental for the manufacture of Cuba's self-image and, hence, to its very existence as a revolutionary state.

In turn, for policy makers in the Johnson administration—as for their predecessors under Eisenhower and Kennedy—Castro's ongoing commitment to revolution underscored the wisdom of U.S. policy toward Latin America since

1959. Washington's willingness to tolerate Castro's presence in the hemisphere—one plausible interpretation of Kennedy's non-invasion pledge—also reinforced the messianic course of U.S. policy. The symbiotic linkage between self, the beneficent state, and the inimical other, in this case Cuba, remained intact.

As Latin American leaders internalized U.S. objectives, the White House found itself having to decide how to allocate limited resources. President Barrientos of Bolivia requested additional military aid to counter subversion. The fight "was not solely for Bolivia's behalf," he told U.S. officials, "but [Bolivia] was doing it for the whole Western Hemisphere."[118] Would credits from the Military Assistance Program be enough to keep Bolivia under Washington's wing? A similar dilemma arose relating to foreign economic policy. At a meeting of the presidents of the hemisphere, held under the auspices of the OAS in April, 1967, Latin American leaders made clear to Johnson their hope for commodity price stability and for larger market share through trade preferences.[119]

This appeal greatly frustrated U.S. officials because it implied that the Alliance for Progress and associated programs had been less than a success. U.S. government analyses deemed the extent of recent economic progress "poor" in the region. Rates of growth remained low; capital outflow to service debts and remit profits was rising. Worst of all, the alliance had failed to stem the worrisome economic tide.[120] The administration knew it could not count on Congress for large capital outlays, given the short- and long-term fiscal costs of the Vietnam War.

Nor did the White House find in evidence at the 1967 summit the economic self-reliance that Rostow believed essential for a secure future of economic progress and regional integration. In the absence of commitments to open and developed frontiers, he lamented in a memo to Johnson, Latin America cannot "achieve the cohesion and strength necessary to play its proper role on the world scene."[121] Ironically, the persistence of nationalism had the capacity to impair the realization of U.S. foreign policy goals just as it thwarted the revolutionary plans of Castro's Cuba.

Segments of the North American business community believed that governance by military regimes might break the impasse created by excessive nationalism. In November, 1967, business interests with investments in Peruvian copper were telling the army that they would support a military coup.[122] That kind of involvement by North Americans in Latin American affairs was not greatly out of line with the logic of the Mann Doctrine. (What the businessmen got the following October—a leftist military regime—was not what they had been seeking.) It makes the point, though, about the association between an activist foreign policy and national identity, even as it questions what it meant to be a "winner" in the struggle for the Americas in the 1960s.

As indicated at the outset, the United States assuredly won the battle with Cuba for dominance in the Western Hemisphere. A clear Cuban victory was unimaginable without the retirement of the United States from regional affairs. To conceive of winners or losers misses an essential point: U.S.-Cuban relations in the Johnson years, and since Castro seized power in 1959, reflected a struggle between two political cultures.

Neither combatant emerged unscathed from the confrontation. Castro was endeavoring to create a revolutionary culture where one had not existed before. This process would take years if it were to reach much beyond the elite, ruling level. Internal contradictions and U.S. efforts to isolate Cuba prevented the emergence of a new Cuban political culture. In contrast, the U.S. ruling elite embodied a political culture that accepted international obligations as its chief defining characteristic. Lyndon Johnson epitomized that perspective and believed in the responsibilities that came with it. The Vietnam War destroyed the faith in liberal internationalism embraced by the informed body politic in the United States. "Neo-Wilsonian ideology," Frank Ninkovich writes, "always full of inconsistencies, [had] reached the most critical stage of its intellectual journey."[123]

The self-image of the United States and its global identity were arguably at stake as Johnson turned over the reins of power to Nixon in January, 1969. The core values of the United States faced rejection around the globe; in some quarters they were already judged irrelevant. Logically, Castro was not wrong to fear an invasion from North America. The history of U.S. foreign policy indicates the centrality of Cuba to its neighbor's sense of self, that is, to U.S. identity. In that sense, it is perhaps not possible to separate the threat Cuba may have actually posed to U.S. security from the need of the U.S. government to portray Fidel Castro's Cuba in such a way.

NOTES

A generous grant-in-aid from the Lyndon Baines Johnson Foundation made research for this essay possible.

Abbreviations:
CIA: Central Intelligence Agency
CO: Country File
DIA: Defense Intelligence Agency
DS: Department of State
FBIS: Foreign Broadcast Information Service
GC: Gordon Chase

INR: [Bureau of] Intelligence and Research
NIE: National Intelligence Estimate(s)
NSAM: National Security Action Memorandum
NSC: National Security Council
NSF: National Security File
OAS: Organization of American States
RS: Regional Security

1. For emphasis upon Castro as a Communist see Earl E. T. Smith, *The Fourth Floor: An Account of the Castro Communist Revolution* (New York: Random House, 1962); Richard M. Bissell, Jr., with Jonathan E. Lewis and Frances T. Pudlo, *Reflections of a Cold Warrior: From Yalta to the Bay of Pigs* (New Haven, Conn.: Yale University Press, 1996), p. 152. Few scholars contend that Castro was a Communist before sometime in 1959, 1960, or even 1961. Robert Freeman Smith skirts the issue by writing that "the Cuban leader began in April 1959 to reveal his true intentions." See Smith, *The Caribbean World and the United States: Mixing Rum and Coca Cola* (New York: Twayne Publishers, 1994), p. 42.

2. On the influence of historical tensions between Cuba and the United States on relations at the time of the revolution, see Richard E. Welch, Jr., *Response to Revolution: The United States and the Cuban Revolution, 1959–1961* (Chapel Hill: University of North Carolina Press, 1985); Jules R. Benjamin, *The United States and the Origins of the Cuban Revolution: An Empire of Liberty in an Age of National Liberation* (Princeton: Princeton University Press, 1990); Louis A. Pérez, Jr., *Cuba and the United States: Ties of Singular Intimacy* (Athens: University of Georgia Press, 1990). The words, "singular intimacy," are those of President William McKinley spoken in 1899.

3. Early work by Robert Freeman Smith charted a dependent relationship between the United States and Cuba. See Smith, *The United States and Cuba: Business and Diplomacy, 1917–1960* (New Haven, Conn.: College and University Press, 1960). For an analysis of the ties between U.S. foreign policy and Cuban dependence see William Appleman Williams, *The United States, Cuba, and Castro: An Essay on the Dynamics of Revolution and the Dissolution of Empire* (New York: Monthly Review Press, 1962). A measured, yet critical look at U.S. policy that considers the span of U.S.-Cuban relations is Lester D. Langley, *The Cuban Policy of the United States: A Brief History* (New York: John Wiley and Sons, 1968).

4. The case for interpreting the antecedents of the U.S.-Cuban crisis in strategic terms is found in two books by Dana G. Munro, *Intervention and Dollar Diplomacy in the Caribbean 1900–1921* (Princeton: Princeton University Press, 1964); idem, *The United States and the Caribbean 1921–1933* (Princeton: Princeton University Press, 1974). For emphasis upon the economic origins of the crisis see Benjamin, *The United States and the Origins of the Cuban Revolution;* Morris H. Morley, *Imperial State and Revolution: The United States and Cuba, 1952–1986* (New York: Cambridge University Press, 1987). Thomas G. Paterson offers a more comprehensive assessment, focusing on "a major phenomenon of twentieth-century world history: the steady erosion of the authority of imperial powers." See Paterson, "Fixation with Cuba: The Bay of Pigs, Missile Crisis, and the Covert War Against Castro," in Thomas G. Paterson, ed., *Kennedy's Quest for Victory: American Foreign Policy, 1961–1963* (New York: Oxford University Press, 1989), pp. 123–

55, 343–52, 126. See also idem, *Contesting Castro: The United States and the Triumph of the Cuban Revolution* (New York: Oxford University Press, 1994).

5. I have muddied the explanatory waters myself in an essay that cast the Latin American policies of the Kennedy and Johnson administrations in a Cold War context without paying heed to a sufficiently broad historical framework. William O. Walker III, "Mixing the Sweet with the Sour: Kennedy, Johnson, and Latin America," in Diane B. Kunz, ed., *The Diplomacy of the Crucial Decade: American Foreign Relations during the 1960s* (New York: Columbia University Press, 1994), pp. 42–79.

6. Michael H. Hunt, *Ideology and U.S. Foreign Policy* (New Haven, Conn.: Yale University Press, 1987), pp. xi, 11–17.

7. Anders Stephanson, *Manifest Destiny: American Expansion and the Empire of Right* (New York: Hill and Wang, 1995). Helping to shape my thinking about the nature of elite political culture in the United States are Drew R. McCoy, *The Elusive Republic: Political Economy in Jeffersonian America* (Chapel Hill: University of North Carolina Press, 1980); Charles Sellers, *The Marketplace Revolution: Jacksonian America, 1815–1846* (New York: Oxford University Press, 1991). For an analysis of the importance of conflict for the shaping of ideology see Steven Watts, *The Republic Reborn: War and the Making of Liberal America, 1790–1820* (Baltimore: Johns Hopkins University Press, 1987).

8. David Campbell, *Writing Security: United States Foreign Policy and the Politics of Identity* (Minneapolis: University of Minnesota Press, 1992), p. 8.

9. Pérez, *Cuba and the United States,* p. 38. See, for example, John A. Logan, Jr., *No Transfer: An American Security Principle* (New Haven, Conn.: Yale University Press, 1961), p. 101, on which Logan writes: "Cuba would be . . . the most consistent object of application of the No-Transfer principle in American diplomacy." John Quincy Adams to Hugh Nelson, Apr. 28, 1823, in Worthington C. Ford, ed., *The Writings of John Quincy Adams,* 7 vols. (New York: Macmillan, 1913–17), vol. 7, p. 373; Tom Chaffin, *Fatal Glory: Narciso López and the First Clandestine U.S. War against Cuba* (Charlottesville: University of Virginia Press, 1996), p. 8.

10. Theodore Roosevelt to Elihu Root, May 20, 1904, in Elting E. Morison, ed., *The Letters of Theodore Roosevelt,* 8 vols. (Cambridge: Harvard University Press, 1951–54), vol. 4, p. 801.

11. Welles quoted in Louis A. Pérez, Jr., *Cuba Under the Platt Amendment, 1902–1934* (Pittsburgh: University of Pittsburgh Press, 1986), p. 331.

12. Campbell, *Writing Security,* p. 172.

13. United States, Department of State, *Foreign Relations of the United States, 1958–1960,* vol. 6: *Cuba* (Washington, D.C.: Government Printing Office, 1991), pp. 1171, 1142 (hereafter *FRUS*).

14. Ibid., p. 1130.

15. *Public Papers of the Presidents of the United States: John F. Kennedy, Containing the Public Messages, Speeches, and Statements of the President, January 1 to November 22, 1963* (Washington, D.C.: Government Printing Office, 1964), p. 154.; National Security File, Meetings and Memoranda Series, National Security Action Memorandum 10, Feb. 6, 1961, Box 328, John F. Kennedy Presidential Library, Boston, Mass.; *FRUS, 1958–60,* vol. 6, pp. 310, 324, 581.

16. *FRUS, 1958–60,* vol. 6, pp. 326, 1125.

17. Philip W. Bonsal, *Cuba, Castro, and the United States* (Pittsburgh: University of Pittsburgh Press, 1971), p. 191.

18. Fedor Burlatsky, *Khrushchev and the First Russian Spring: The Era of Khrushchev through the Eyes of His Adviser,* trans. Daphne Skillen (New York: Charles Scribner's Sons, 1988), p. 169. And see Vladislav Zubok and Constantine Pleshakov, *Inside the Kremlin's Cold War: From Stalin to Khrushchev* (Cambridge: Harvard University Press, 1996), pp. 206–207; the authors write: "Had Stalin been in the Kremlin, the Soviets would never have assisted the radical Cuban regime."

19. Arthur M. Schlesinger, Jr., *A Thousand Days: John F. Kennedy in the White House* (Boston: Houghton Mifflin, 1965), pp. 221–22; Adolf A. Berle, *Navigating the Rapids 1918–1971: From the Papers of Adolf A. Berle,* Beatrice Bishop Berle and Travis Beal Jacobs, eds. (New York: Harcourt Brace Jovanovich, 1973), p. 704; W. W. Rostow, *The Diffusion of Power, 1957–1972: An Essay in Recent History* (New York: Macmillan, 1972), pp. 100–102.

20. Rostow, *Diffusion of Power,* p. 100; Schlesinger, *Thousand Days,* p. 187; Berle, *Navigating the Rapids,* pp. 685, 695, 725.

21. Lester D. Langley, *America and the Americas: The United States in the Western Hemisphere* (Athens: University of Georgia Press, 1989), p. 191.

22. NSF, RS Series, Latin America, Memorandum for McGeorge Bundy, Feb. 1, 1961; Memorandum for Bundy, Feb. 3, 1961, Box 215, JFK Library. That Cuba might fan the flames of revolutionary unrest throughout much of the Americas was a theme that pervaded administration thinking in the early 1960s; *FRUS, 1961–63,* vol. 12: *American Republics* (Washington, D.C.: Government Printing Office, 1996).

23. Jorge I. Domínguez, *To Make a World Safe for Revolution: Cuba's Foreign Policy* (Cambridge: Harvard University Press, 1989), pp. 3, 6, 113; Fidel Castro, "Second Declaration of Havana [February, 1962]," in James Nelson Goodsell, ed., *Fidel Castro's Personal Revolution in Cuba: 1959–1973* (New York: Alfred A. Knopf, 1975), pp. 263–68, 267.

24. Maurice Halperin, *The Rise and Decline of Fidel Castro* (Berkeley and Los Angeles: University of California Press, 1972), p. 81. Castro's remarks are contained in James G. Blight, Bruce J. Allyn, and David A. Welch, *Cuba on the Brink: Castro, the Missile Crisis, and the Soviet Collapse* (New York: Pantheon, 1993), p. 193.

25. See Walker, "Mixing the Sweet with the Sour," pp. 46–57. As is well known, the United States tried to assassinate Castro; see *Alleged Assassination Plots Involving Foreign Leaders: An Interim Report of the United States Senate Select Committee to Study Governmental Operations with Respect to Intelligence Activities* (New York: W. W. Norton, 1976), pp. 71–180; William Colby, *Honorable Men: My Life in the CIA* (New York: Simon and Schuster, 1978), pp. 189–90, 213–14, 410. Perhaps the most credible account of the underside of the assassination campaign is Warren Hinckle and William Turner, *Deadly Secrets: The CIA-Mafia War Against Castro and the assassination of J.F.K.* (New York: Thunder's Mouth Press, 1992).

26. On ties between the Bay of Pigs and Castro's prestige see CIA, NIE 80/90-61, "Latin American Reactions to Developments in and with Respect to Cuba," July 18, 1961, NSF, NIEs, Box 8–9, LBJ Library. Richard N. Goodwin of the State Department, a former special counsel to Kennedy, denies that the October crisis aided Castro in any way; Goodwin, *Remembering America: A Voice from the Sixties* (Boston: Little, Brown, 1988), p. 218.

27. Castro, as quoted in Blight, Allyn, and Welch, *Cuba on the Brink,* pp. 194–96. Carlos Franqui, who fought against Batista with Castro and served as director of the newspaper *Revolución,* and who broke with Castro in 1968, called Girón "an

extraordinary triumph" for Cuba; Franqui, *Family Portrait with Fidel,* trans. Alfred MacAdam (New York: Random House, 1984), p. 126.

28. On the possibility of military action, see James G. Hershberg, "Before the 'Missiles of October': Did Kennedy Plan a Military Strike against Cuba?" *Diplomatic History* 14 (Spring, 1990): 163–98; Colby, *Honorable Men,* pp. 189–90; Castro, as quoted in Blight, Allyn, and Welch, *Cuba on the Brink,* p. 191.

29. Memorandum by Gordon Chase of a Meeting with the President, Dec. 19, 1963, NSF, CO: Cuba Meetings, Dec., 1963–Mar., 65, Dec. 27, 1963, Box 24–25, LBJ Library.

30. Schlesinger, *A Thousand Days,* pp. 999–1000; idem, *Robert Kennedy and His Times* (Boston: Houghton Mifflin, 1978), pp. 556–57; Goodwin, *Remembering America,* p. 219.

31. *Alleged Assassination Plots,* pp. 176–78; On the importance of finding a sense of proportion in response to ideological challenges such as those presented by Cuba, see John Lewis Gaddis, *The United States and the End of the Cold War: Implications, Reconsiderations, Provocations* (New York: Oxford University Press, 1992), pp. 13, 16.

32. NSF, GC Files, "Plank-Chase Report on U.S.-Cuban Relations," Feb. 3, 1964, Box 4, LBJ Library.

33. Dean Rusk, as told to Richard Rusk, *As I Saw It,* ed. Daniel S. Papp (New York: W. W. Norton, 1990), p. 370.

34. Blight, Allyn, and Welch, *Cuba on the Brink,* pp. 189–90, 225; Memorandum by Gordon Chase, "U.S. Policy Towards Cuba," Dec. 2, 1963, NSF, CO: Cuba, U.S. Policy, Vol, II, Box 26, 27, 28, 29, LBJ Library; Halperin, *Fidel Castro,* p. 297.

35. Waldo Heinrichs, "Lyndon B. Johnson: Change and Continuity," in Warren I. Cohen and Nancy Bernkopf Tucker, eds., *Lyndon Johnson Confronts the World: American Foreign Policy, 1963–1968* (New York: Cambridge University Press, 1994), p. 27.

36. Compare Pérez, *Cuba and the United States,* pp. 238–49, and Domínguez, *To Make a World Safe for Revolution,* pp. 16–26. President Kennedy made a similar point in November, 1963, about how U.S. ties to Batista had helped to set the stage for Castro's movement; see Schlesinger, *Robert Kennedy,* p. 555.

37. Doris Kearns, *Lyndon Johnson and the American Dream* (New York: Harper & Row, 1976), p. 265.

38. Lloyd C. Gardner, *Pay Any Price: Lyndon Johnson and the Wars for Vietnam* (Chicago: Ivan R. Dee, 1995), develops this theme in the case of Vietnam; Jules R. Benjamin, "The Framework of U.S. Relations with Latin America in the Twentieth Century: An Interpretive Essay," *Diplomatic History* 11 (Spring, 1987): 91–112.

39. Halperin, *Fidel Castro,* p. 297.

40. *Alleged Assassination Plots,* p. 173.

41. William Attwood, *The Twilight Struggle: Tales of the Cold War* (New York: Harper & Row, 1987), pp. 259, 257–64; Schlesinger, *Robert Kennedy,* pp. 551–56.

42. Chase Memorandum, Dec. 27, 1963, NSF, CO: Cuba Meetings, Dec., 1963–Mar., 1965, Box 24–25, LBJ Library; Assistant Secretary of State Edwin M. Martin to Bundy, Nov. 8, 1963, NSF, CO: Cuba, Contacts with Leaders, May, 1963–Apr., 1965, Box 21, LBJ Library; Adlai E. Stevenson to Lyndon Johnson, June 26, 1964, ibid.; Chase memo to Bundy, July 7, 1964, ibid.

43. Fidel Castro to Johnson, Feb. 12, 1964, verbally conveyed by Lisa Howard, ibid.

44. *New York Times,* Mar. 26, 1964; Senator J. W. Fulbright, *Old Myths and New Realities and Other Commentaries* (New York: Random House, 1964), pp. 24–35.

45. For a thorough accounting of the "old myths and new realities" address and its aftermath see Randall Bennett Woods, *Fulbright: A Biography* (New York: Cambridge University Press, 1995), pp. 334–39.

46. See Lester D. Langley, "Latin America in the Cold War and After," in John M. Carroll and George C. Herring, eds., *Modern American Diplomacy,* rev. and enlarged ed. (Wilmington, Del.: Scholarly Resources, 1996), pp. 232–33; H. W. Brands, *The Wages of Globalism: Lyndon Johnson and the Limits of American Power* (New York: Oxford University Press, 1995), pp. 30–61.

47. *New York Times,* Mar. 19, 1964. For information on Mann's background and his influence on U.S. policy toward Latin America in the late 1950s and 1960s see Walter LaFeber, "Thomas C. Mann and the Devolution of Latin American Policy: From the Good Neighbor to Military Intervention," in Thomas J. McCormick and Walter LaFeber, eds., *Behind the Throne: Servants of Power to Imperial Presidents: 1898–1968* (Madison: University of Wisconsin Press, 1993), pp. 166–203. Military forces in Latin America saw the Mann Doctrine as giving them carte blanche for authoritarian control of political dissent.

48. *Alleged Assassination Plots,* pp. 176–80; Schlesinger, *Robert Kennedy,* pp. 543–49. Cuban expert Jorge Domínguez contends that Johnson's rejection of the assassination option indicates the creation of a limited security regime with Cuba. Domínguez, *To Make a World Safe for Revolution,* pp. 44–49; the problem with this interpretation, as Domínguez admits, is that the administration may not have conveyed its intent to the Cuban government.

49. NSF, CO: Cuba, Chase File, Vol. A, Nov., 1963–May, 1964, Dec. 17, 1963, Box 18, LBJ Library.

50. Thomas L. Hughes, Bureau of Intelligence and Research, Department of State, to Rusk, Nov. 29, 1963, NSF, CO: Cuba, INR, Nov., 1963–June, 1965, Box 24–25, LBJ Library.

51. M. Margaret Ball, *The OAS in Transition* (Durham: Duke University Press, 1969), pp. 468–69; Sheldon B. Liss, *Diplomacy & Dependency: Venezuela, the United States, and the Americas* (Salisbury, N.C.: Documentary Publications, 1978), pp. 225–30. The possibility that the CIA may have been responsible for the arms found on a Venezuelan beach is raised in Stephen G. Rabe, "The Caribbean Triangle: Betancourt, Castro, and Trujillo and U.S. Foreign Policy, 1958–1963," *Diplomatic History* 20 (Winter, 1996): 76. On this issue see Joseph Burkholder Smith, *Portrait of a Cold Warrior* (New York: Putnam, 1976), pp. 381–84; Philip Agee, *Inside the Company: CIA Diary* (Middlesex: Penguin Books, 1975), p. 322.

52. NSC Meeting No. 523, Mar. 5, 1964, NSF, NSC Meetings File, NSC Meetings, Vol. 1, Tab 4, Box 1, LBJ Library.

53. Philip Geyelin, *Lyndon B. Johnson and the World* (New York: Frederick B. Praeger, 1966), pp. 44, 97, 99.

54. Thomas C. Mann to Rusk, Jan. 11, 1964, NSF, NSC History: Panama Crisis, 1964, Box 1, LBJ Library; "Review of Current Program of Covert Action against Cuba," Jan. 27, 1994, NSF, CO: Cuba Intelligence, Covert, Jan., 1964–June, 1965, Box 24–25, LBJ Library; Walter LaFeber, *The Panama Canal: The Crisis in Historical Perspective,* updated ed. (New York: Oxford University Press, 1989), pp. 103–16.

55. Lyndon Baines Johnson, *The Vantage Point: Perspectives of the Presidency, 1963–1968* (New York: Holt, Rinehart and Winston, 1971), pp. 184, 188.

56. Mann was serving as Johnson's chief adviser on Latin American policy, assistant

secretary of state for inter-American affairs, and head of the Alliance for Progress; LaFeber, "Thomas C. Mann," pp. 173–74.

57. Assessments like the one made about the prospects for stability in Guatemala were typical; see U.S. Ambassador John O. Bell, Guatemala, to the State Department, Mar. 9, 1964, NSF, CO: Guatemala Cables, Vol. I, Box 54, LBJ Library; Memorandum for Special Group (CI) [Counterinsurgency], Apr. 5, 1965, NSF, GC files: untitled, Box 6, LBJ Library.

58. Memorandum by Thomas C. Mann, June 17, 1964, NSF, CO: Latin America, Vol. II, June, 1964–Aug., 1964, Box 2, LBJ Library (emphasis in original). On the meaning of aid for the foreign policy of liberalism in the 1960s, see Robert Packenham, *Liberal America and the Third World: Political Development Ideas in Foreign Aid and Social Science* (Princeton: Princeton University Press, 1973), pp. 115–16, 121, 132, 144.

59. Packenham, *Liberal America*, p. 144. Text of Address by George W. Ball, Mar. 23, 1964, NSF, CO: Cuba, Chase File, Vol. A, Nov. 1963–May, 1964, Box 18, LBJ Library; and Morley, *Imperial State and Revolution*, pp. 191–214.

60. Ball address, Mar. 23, 1964, NSF, CO: Cuba, Chase File, Vol. A, Nov., 1963–May, 1964, Box 18, LBJ Library; Max F. Millikan and W. W. Rostow, *A Proposal: Key to an Effective Foreign Policy* (New York: Harper & Brothers, 1957), p. 151. Years later in writing about what aid programs could accomplish, Rostow observed that the answers to Latin America's problems lay well beyond the reach of "North American magic and money." Rostow, *Diffusion of Power,* p. 216. Historian Diane B. Kunz notes, however, that "the United States did not want Latin American countries to find their own answers." Diane B. Kunz, *Butter and Guns: America's Cold War Economic Diplomacy* (New York: Free Press, 1997), p. 147.

61. Foreign Broadcast Information Service, Jan. 3 and Apr. 20, 1964, in NSF, CO: Cuba, Castro's Speeches, Vol. I, Oct., 1963–Sept., 1964, Box 20, LBJ Library.

62. On overflights see NSC Action 2486, May 2, 1964, NSF, NSC Meetings File: NSC Meetings, Vol. II, Tab 2, Box 1, LBJ Library; *New York Times,* July 6 and July 8, 1964.

63. Memorandum by Robert M. Sayre to Bundy, July 7, 1964, NSF, Name File: Sayre Memos, Box 8, LBJ Library.

64. CIA Report, "Arms Traffic in the Caribbean Area, 1963," May 18, 1964, NSF, CO: Cuba Subversion, Pt. 1, Vol. I, Box 31–32, LBJ Library; Chase to Bundy, Dec. 10, 1963, NSF, CO: Cuba, OAS Resolution, Vol. II [I], Box 24–25, LBJ Library.

65. Hughes to Rusk, Apr. 17, 1964, NSF, CO: Cuba, INR, Vol. I, Nov., 1963–June, 1965, Box 24–25, LBJ Library.

66. Ibid.; Sayre memo to Bundy, July 7, 1964, NSF, Name File: Sayre Memos, Box 8, LBJ Library.

67. Wayne S. Smith, *The Closest of Enemies: A Personal and Diplomatic Account of U.S.-Cuban Relations since 1957* (New York: W. W. Norton, 1987), pp. 87–89; Hughes to Rusk, July 28, 1964, NSF, CO: Cuba, Castro's Speeches, Vol. I, Oct., 1963–Sept., 1964, Box 20, LBJ Library; *Washington Post,* July 28, 1964.

68. Hughes to Rusk, Sept. 14, 1964, NSF, CO: Cuba, OAS Resolution, Vol II [II], Box 24–25, LBJ Library; Rusk, *As I Saw It,* pp. 374–75.

69. *Public Papers of the President of the United States: Lyndon Baines Johnson, Containing the Public Messages, Speeches, and Statements of the President, 1963–64,* Book II: *July 1–December 1, 1964* (Washington, D.C.: Government Printing Office, 1965), p. 1050.

70. DS Report, Mar. 1, 1965, NSF, CO: Cuba Subversion, Pt. 1, Vol. I, Box 31–32, LBJ Library; DS, INR Memorandum, Apr. 1, 1965, ibid.; Theodore Draper, *Castroism: Theory and Practice* (New York: Frederick A. Praeger, 1965), pp. 210–13.

71. *New York Times,* Nov. 4, 1964; Berle, *Navigating the Rapids,* p. 799; NSF, CO: Latin America, CIA Memorandum, May 18, 1965, Box 2, LBJ Library; Piero Gleijeses, "'Flee! The White Giants Are Coming!' The United States, the Mercenaries, and the Congo, 1964–65," *Diplomatic History* 18 (Spring, 1994): 207–37.

72. Chase memo to Bundy, Dec. 1, 1964, NSF, CO: Cuba memos, Box 20, LBJ Library.

73. William G. Bowdler to Bundy, Dec. 10, 1964, NSF, CO: Cuba, Personalities, Oct., 1964–Feb., 1965, Box 20, LBJ Library.

74. FBIS, Dec. 15, 1964, with Address by Che Guevara, Dec. 11, 1964, ibid.; Memorandum by Ball, Dec. 17, 1964, NSF, CO: Cuba, Contacts with Leaders, May, 1963–Apr., 1965, Box 21, LBJ Library.

75. DS Report, Mar. 1, 1965, NSF, CO: Cuba, Subversion, Pt. 1, Vol. I, Box 31–32, LBJ Library; Memorandum by George C. Denney, Jr., Apr. 8, 1965, ibid.

76. Hughes to Rusk, Apr. 19, 1965, NSF, CO: Cuba Personalities, Oct., 1964–Feb., 1965, Box 20, LBJ Library.

77. Rusk, *As I Saw It,* pp. 373–74; Johnson, *The Vantage Point,* p. 188. The Dominican revolt, concludes its foremost historian, "ow[ed] nothing to Castro and in no way follow[ed] the Cuban model." See Piero Gleijeses, *The Dominican Crisis: The 1965 Constitutionalist Revolt and American Intervention,* trans. Lawrence Lipson (Baltimore: Johns Hopkins, 1978), p. 301; see also Peter Felten, "The Politics of Intervention: The Dominican Republic and the United States during the 1960s," unpublished ms., pp. 49–52.

78. CIA Intelligence Memorandum, Apr. 29, 1965, NSF, GC Files: Communism in the Dominican Republic, Box 3, LBJ Library; CIA Memorandum, "The Communist Role in the Dominican Revolt," May 7, 1965, ibid.

79. Memorandum by Chester L. Cooper, Mar. 4, 1965, NSF, CO: Cuba, Chase File, Vol. C, Jan., 1965–June, 1965, Box 18, LBJ Library.

80. I. J. M. Sutherland, British Embassy, Washington, to Wayne Smith, May 14, 1965, ibid.; copy of dispatch, British Embassy, Havana, to the Foreign Office, May 20, 1965, ibid.

81. Hughes to Rusk, May 20, 1965, NSF, CO: Cuba, INR, Vol. 1, Nov., 1963–June, 1965, Box 24–25, LBJ Library.

82. *Public Papers: LBJ, 1963–64,* Book II, 1050 (emphasis added).

83. Memorandum of a telephone call between Johnson and Ball, June 22, 1965, Ball Papers: Dominican Republic [I], Box 3, LBJ Library; Policy Planning Council Memorandum, June 10, 1965, NSF, Chase Files: Latin American, Inter-American Military Force, Box 4, LBJ Library.

84. Assistant Secretary of State for Inter-American Affairs Jack H. Vaughn to Assistant Secretary of Defense John T. McNaughton, Mar. 29, 1965, NSF, CO: Latin America, Vol. III, Jan., 1965–June, 1965, Box 2, LBJ Library; Joint Chiefs of State memorandum (undated), ibid.; Secretary of Defense Robert S. McNamara to Bundy, June 11, 1965, ibid.

85. Sayre to Bundy, Mar. 8, 1965, NSF, Name File: Sayre Memos, Mar. 8, 1965, Box 8, LBJ Library; Mann to Johnson, Mar. 15, 1965, NSF, CO: Latin America, Vol. III, Jan., 1965–June, 1965, Box 2, LBJ Library. And see Jerome Levinson and Juan de

Onís, *The Alliance That Lost Its Way: A Critical Report on the Alliance for Progress* (Chicago: Quadrangle Books, 1970), pp. 159–60.

86. Cyrus Vance to Bundy, July 20, 1965, NSF, CO: Cuba, Bowdler File, Vol. I, Apr., 1964–Jan., 1966, Box 18, LBJ Library; Maurice Halperin, *The Taming of Fidel Castro* (Berkeley and Los Angeles: University of California Press, 1981), pp. 125–28; CIA Intelligence Memorandum, "The Fall of Che Guevara and the Changing Face of the Cuban Revolution," Oct. 18, 1965, NSF, CO: Cuba, Bowdler File, Vol. I, Apr., 1964–Jan., 1966, Box 18, LBJ Library; Victor Marchetti and John D. Marks, *The CIA and the Cult of Intelligence,* 3d ed. (New York: Dell Publishing, 1989), pp. 111–12; Louis A. Pérez, Jr., *Cuba: Between Reform and Revolution,* 2d ed. (New York: Oxford University Press, 1995), p. 377.

87. Hughes to Rusk, Aug. 10, 1965 and Jan. 19, 1966, NSF, CO: Cuba, Bowdler File, Vol. I, Apr., 1964–Jan., 1966, Box 18, LBJ Library.

88. *Documentos políticos: Política internacional de la revolución cubana,* vol. 1 (Havana: Editora Política, 1966), p. 83.

89. CIA Intelligence Memorandum, "Latin America's Communist Developments," Mar. 15, 1966, NSF, CO: Latin America, Vol. IV-a, Sept., 1966–Dec., 1966, Box 3, LBJ Library.

90. Halperin, *Taming,* p. 281, n. 7; CIA Memorandum, May 28, 1966, NSF, CO: Cuba, Bowdler File, Vol. II, Feb., 1966–July, 1967, Box 19, LBJ Library.

91. DS circular letter, Feb. 2, 1966, NSF, Name File: Bowdler Memos, Box 1, LBJ Library; Bowdler to Bundy, Feb. 18, 1966, ibid.; Telegram (copy) from Castro to U Thant, Feb. 10, 1966, ibid. The CIA later took satisfaction from Castro's "unusual sensitivity to international and domestic irritants since the beginning of the year." CIA to Rostow, June 14, 1966, NSF, CO: Cuba, Bowdler File, Vol. II, Feb., 1966–July, 1967, Box 19, LBJ Library.

92. Bowdler to Bill Moyers and Rostow, Aug. 3, 1966, NSF, CO: Cuba, Bowdler File, Vol. II, Feb., 1966–July, 1967, Box 19, LBJ Library.

93. Hughes to Rusk, July 27, 1966, ibid.

94. Bowdler to Rostow, June 24, 1966, ibid.

95. Rusk to McNamara, Nov. 15, 1966, ibid,; Lincoln Gordon to Rusk, Nov. 16, 1966, ibid.

96. Joseph S. Tulchin, "The Promise of Progress: U.S. Relations with Latin America During the Administration of Lyndon B. Johnson," in Cohen and Tucker, eds. *Lyndon Johnson Confronts the World,* pp. 232, 237–38. About the tying of aid see Gordon to Rostow, May 3, 1967, NSF, CO: Latin America, Vol. V, Apr., 1967–Nov., 1967, Box 3, LBJ Library.

97. CIA National Intelligence Estimate 80/90-67, "Economic Trends and Prospects in Latin America," July 20, 1967, NSF, NIEs: 80/90, Latin America, Box 8–9, LBJ Library.

98. Henry F. Graff, *The Tuesday Cabinet: Deliberation and Decision on Peace and War under Lyndon B. Johnson* (Englewood Cliffs: Prentice Hall, 1970), p. 21; Kearns, *Lyndon Johnson,* p. 320.

99. Rusk, *As I Saw It,* pp. 518–19; Brands, *Wages of Globalism,* pp. 12–13. Report by Walt Rostow, "Some Reflections on National Security Policy, February 1965," NSF, DS, Documents from Unprocessed Files, Policy Planning, Vol. 4, Box 1, LBJ Library.

100. Rostow to Johnson, May 27, 1966, NSF, NSAM: NSAM 349, Box 8, LBJ Library; NSAM 349, "Development of the Frontiers of South America," May 31, 1966, ibid.

101. CIA, NIE, "The Potential for Revolution in Latin America," NIE 80/90-68, Mar. 28, 1968, NSF, NIEs: 80/90 Latin America, Box 8–9, LBJ Library.

102. Rusk to the U.S. Embassy London, Nov. 16, 1966, NSF, CO: Cuba, Bowdler File, Vol. II, Feb., 1966–July, 1967, Box 19, LBJ Library; Bowdler memo to Rostow, Sept. 26, 1966, ibid.; Morley, *Imperial State and Revolution,* pp. 218–39; Jonathan Kwitny, *Endless Enemies: The Making of an Unfriendly World* (New York: Congdon & Weed, 1984), pp. 243–46.

103. CIA memo, Oct. 26, 1966, NSF, Name File: Bowdler Memos, Box 1, LBJ Library; CIA intelligence cable, Sept. 23, 1966, NSF, CO: Cuba, Bowdler File, Vol. II, Feb., 1966–July, 1967, Box 19, LBJ Library.

104. Castro spoke about Venezuela and insurgency in his annual speech on March 13; see FBIS, Mar. 14, 1967, in *Castro Speech Data Base,* UT-LANIC (http://lanic.utexas.edu [Cuba]); CIA memo, "Evidence of Cuban Violations of Venezuelan Sovereignty," undated [Mar., 1967], NSF, IF: Guerrilla Problem in Latin America, Box 2–3, LBJ Library; CIA memo, "Status of Insurgency in Colombia," Apr. 7, 1967, ibid; Liss, *Diplomacy and Dependency,* pp. 224–25.

105. Ball, *OAS in Transition,* pp. 480–82.

106. CIA memo, "Cuban Sponsorship of Bolivian Guerrillas," June 14, 1967, NSF, IF: Guerrilla Problem in Latin America, Box 2–3, LBJ Library; Herbert S. Klein, *Bolivia: The Evolution of a Multi-Ethnic Society,* 2d ed. (New York: Oxford University Press, 1992), pp. 245–50.

107. Rostow to Johnson, June 24, 1967, NSF, IF: Guerrilla Problem in Latin America, Box 2–3, LBJ Library; "Mensaje del Che a la Tricontinental, 16 de Abril de 1967," *Documentos de Política Internacional de la Revolución Cubana,* 3 vols. (Habana: Ediciones Políticos, 1971), vol. 3, p. 166; Johnson, as quoted in Frank Ninkovich, *Modernity and Power: A History of the Domino Theory in the Twentieth Century* (Chicago: University of Chicago Press, 1994), p. 277.

108. Bowdler to Rostow, July 5, 1967, NSF, IF: Guerrilla Problem in Latin America, Box 2–3, LBJ Library; Rostow to Johnson, June 23, 1967, NSF, CO: Bolivia Memos, IV, Box 8, LBJ Library.

109. Frank Mankiewicz and Kirby Jones, *With Fidel: A Portrait of Castro and Cuba* (Chicago: Playboy Press, 1975), pp. 129–31; Domínguez, *To Make a World Safe for Revolution,* pp. 124–25; Lee Lockwood, *Castro's Cuba, Cuba's Fidel,* rev. ed. (Boulder: Westview Press, 1990), p. 356. On the Soviet side, "irritation with Cuba has reached a new high," concluded the State Department. Hughes to Rusk, June 27, 1967, NSF, CO: Cuba, Bowdler File, Vol. II, Feb., 1966–July, 1967, Box 19, LBJ Library.

110. Fidel Castro, "Speech Made on Occasion of the Commemoration of the XIV Anniversary of the Attack on the Moncada Garrison in Santiago de Cuba, July 26, 1967," in *Fidel Castro: Major Speeches* (London: Stage 1, 1968), p. 87; Fidel Castro, "Speech Made at the Closing of the First Conference of the Latin American Organization of Solidarity (OLAS) at the 'Chaplin' Theater on August 10, 1967," ibid., p. 118; "Mensaje del Che," pp. 160–62.

111. The story of Che Guevara's death and U.S. involvement is retold in Felix Rodriguez and John Weisman, *Shadow Warrior: The CIA Hero of a Hundred Unknown Battles* (New York: Simon and Schuster, 1989), pp. 9–19, 127–72; Henry Butterfield Ryan, *The Fall of Che Guevara: A Story of Soldiers, Spies, and Diplomats* (New York: Oxford University Press, 1998).

112. Lockwood, *Castro's Cuba,* pp. 354, 358; CIA Intelligence Report, "Cuban Subversive Policy and the Bolivian Guerrilla Episode," May, 1968, NSF, CO: Cuba, Bowdler File, Vol. IV, 1965–1968, Box 19, LBJ Library; Halperin, *Taming,* p. 247; CIA intelligence cable, Oct. 17, 1967, NSF, CO: Cuba, Bowdler File, III, Aug., 1967–Mar., 1968, Box 19, LBJ Library. The lack of Soviet support for Guevara's exploits gives some credence to the thesis that Castro sent him to Bolivia in order to limit Guevara's influence over Cuban policy making—at the least.

113. Halperin, *Taming,* pp. 318–24 (quote: 319). In the preface to the paperback edition of his first volume on Castro, Halperin stated: "Essentially, the Cuban Revolution is over." Halperin, *Fidel Castro,* p. vi.

114. Hughes to Rusk, Jan. 3, 1968, NSF, CO: Cuba, Bowdler File, Aug., 1967–Mar., 1968, Box 19, LBJ Library; Hughes to Rusk, Jan. 15, 1968 (with quoted words), ibid.; CIA, "The Potential for Revolution in Latin America" (n. 101 supra).

115. Hughes to Rusk, Oct. 7, 1968, NSF, CO: Cuba, Bowdler File, Vol. IV, 1965–1968, Box 19, LBJ Library (emphasis added); DIA memo, Nov. 9, 1968, ibid.; Samuel W. Lewis memo to Rostow, Nov. 20, 1968, ibid.

116. This image of Castro as a modern Bolívar is discussed in Blight, Allyn, and Welch, *Cuba on the Brink,* pp. 13–14, 309–10; it has as one inspiration the writing of Castro's friend Gabriel García Márquez in *The General in His Labyrinth;* these points form the basis of the CIA report, "Cuban Subversive Policy" (n. 112 supra).

117. CIA report, "Cuban Subversive Policy" (n. 112 supra); CIA intelligence cable, Sept. 30, 1967, NSF, CO: Cuba, Bowdler File, Vol. III, Aug., 1967–Mar., 1968, Box 19, LBJ Library.

118. Raul H. Castro, U.S. embassy, to Rusk, Oct. 19, 1968, NSF, CO: Bolivia memos, Vol. IV, Box 8, LBJ Library.

119. "Latin American Reaction to Summit," Apr. 18, 1967, NSF, CO: Latin America, Vol. V, Apr., 1967–Nov., 1967, Box 3, LBJ Library.

120. CIA, "Economic Trends and Prospects."

121. Rostow to Johnson, Jan. 27, 1967, NSF, NSC History, OAS Summit Meeting, Apr., 1967, Tabs 16–25, Box 12, LBJ Library.

122. CIA intelligence cable, Nov. 9, 1967, NSF, CO: Peru Cables, Vol. III, Box 73, LBJ Library.

123. Julie Marie Bunck, *Fidel Castro and the Quest for a Revolutionary Culture in Cuba* (University Park: Pennsylvania State University Press, 1994); Ninkovich, *Modernity and Power,* p. 277.

5

Yankee, Go Home and Take Me with You

Lyndon Johnson and the Dominican Republic

PETER FELTEN

In April, 1966, as U.S. troops neared the end of their first year in the Dominican Republic, someone scrawled on a public wall in Santo Domingo a quirky
twist on a familiar theme: "go home yankee y llevame contigo [and take me
with you.]"[1] This simple statement captured the ambiguity at the heart of United
States–Dominican relations during the Johnson years. Dominicans rejected U.S.
involvement in their nation's affairs, yet they generally expected Yankees to
dominate their country. At the same time, Washington assumed it controlled
important matters in Santo Domingo, but Dominicans repeatedly manipulated
U.S. behavior to suit their own aims. The dynamics of U.S.-Dominican relations should not be viewed statically as a superpower exercising authority over
its helpless neighbor. Rather, Washington held the preponderance of power,
but Dominicans often used their leverage to direct the course of relations.

During the 1965–66 United States military intervention in the Dominican
Republic, President Lyndon Johnson established the general parameters of U.S.
policy. Johnson opposed a "second Cuba," and he favored the creation of a
stable, pro-Washington and at least mildly democratic government in Santo
Domingo. Within the president's broad guidelines, Dominicans frequently
manipulated United States behavior. Dominicans shaped Washington's actions
because administration officials, including the president, underestimated Dominican capabilities and failed to understand Dominican goals.[2] Johnson's
pragmatic attitude toward the acceptable means to achieve his general aims also
allowed him to accept and even encourage outside influence.

The intervention ultimately met its primary objective. The president's success in Dominican policy resulted in part from his persistent pursuit of his
overall policy outlines and in part from his permitting others to shape the details of events in Santo Domingo. His failures emerged mainly from his awk-
ward efforts to win public support for his policies. Both Johnson's flaws and

his strengths reveal not only his character but also his priorities. President Johnson never considered Santo Domingo to be a vital concern for its own reasons; instead, he saw the Dominican Republic, and Latin America in general, as a distraction from the Great Society and Vietnam.

Johnson's domestic dreams, according to one aide, meant he "would chop off the rest of the world if he could."[3] John F. Kennedy had considered the Dominican Republic a prime opportunity to demonstrate his reformist credentials; Johnson saw it as an obstacle to his goals. The status quo Mann Doctrine mirrored Johnson's ambitions for the region.[4] The administration's interpretation of the communist menace in the Dominican Republic reinforced its approach. In early 1964, a CIA analysis concluded that Dominican security forces "can control any subversive activities likely to occur during the next few months." Later that year a State Department intelligence report asserted that Dominican communists "have had little opportunity to develop an influential movement." With no looming danger, the White House believed it could ignore the Dominican Republic.[5]

While Washington looked elsewhere, troubles mounted in Santo Domingo. The brutal dictator Rafael Trujillo's thirty-one-year reign had ended in a hail of bullets in 1961. Trujillo's puppet president, Joaquín Balaguer, managed to hold power until he was exiled in early 1962. At the end of that year, the democratic-leftist Juan Bosch won the presidency in the first free elections in decades, and his Dominican Revolutionary Party (PRD) dominated the national legislature. Bosch, however, proved to be a better candidate than president. In September, 1963, right-wing military officers drove him from office. The PRD, fragmented by Bosch's policies, watched passively. The new military-backed civilian Triumvirate had little success ending military corruption and easing unemployment. Political discontent grew. By early 1965, the Triumvirate tottered on the brink of collapse. Support from the United States Embassy propped up the government, but even the State Department had begun to reconsider its status quo policy. On April 24, soldiers sympathetic to exiled President Bosch attempted to overthrow the government.[6]

The Triumvirate fell and a struggle emerged in Santo Domingo between right-wing "loyalist" generals and pro-Bosch political activists allied with "constitutionalist" junior officers. Loyalists controlled San Isidro on the eastern edge of Santo Domingo, the nation's most powerful army and air force base. Constitutionalists dominated downtown Santo Domingo, the heart of the country's political and economic life. The loyalist generals possessed an overwhelming advantage in military hardware, but their tanks and other heavy weapons faltered in the city's narrow streets when confronted with highly motivated squads of ordinary soldiers and citizens.

The United States reaction to the coup centered on Cold War concerns. The U.S. Embassy in Santo Domingo and the Central Intelligence Agency focused on the three small communist-oriented parties in the Dominican Republic,[7] neglecting the rebel military and civilian leadership.[8] The failure of the embassy to develop ties with disgruntled activists and the institutional bias in U.S. intelligence gathering handicapped the White House when the crisis hit. Policy makers had little information on the motives or goals of the rebel leadership. Imbued with the fear of a second Cuba, U.S. officials in both Santo Domingo and Washington emphasized the evidence of leftism in the intelligence they received, which, in turn, had come from sources that focused on communism. A reinforcing cycle had been established. Dominican communists indeed had attempted to take advantage of the chaotic situation, but they were such a small, divided bunch that they had nowhere near the influence attributed to them. Reflecting a Cold War mentality and inadequate information, Washington began working to prevent a "second Cuba" within twenty-four hours of the start of the coup. To the White House, that meant supporting the loyalist military against the constitutionalist rebels.[9]

Loyalist propaganda worked to cement these ties to Washington. San Isidro's generals designed their statements as much for Washington officials as for the Dominican people. The loyalists intended to create a political climate in the United States that made accommodation with the rebels impossible. Loyalist Radio San Isidro repeatedly charged that "Fidelista communist elements" and "Moscow" controlled the rebels. Radio broadcasts urged patriots to join "in the fight against communism."[10] More significant, San Isidro sent a plane to fly Jules Dubois, a rabidly anticommunist *Chicago Tribune* Latin America correspondent, to the Dominican Republic before any other foreign reporter. Dubois served as a mouthpiece for the loyalists, whom he called the "anti-communist forces." He repeated loyalist claims that "Bosch is a communist sympathizer" and that "this country [had come] within 12 hours of a communist takeover." Using Dubois and other sympathetic journalists, San Isidro conducted a propaganda offensive aimed in part at the United States.[11]

These charges reinforced the information in U.S. intelligence reports, confirming Washington's bias toward the loyalists. On the evening of April 28, President Johnson ordered more than four hundred marines ashore, ostensibly to protect the embassy and to facilitate the evacuation of foreign nationals. Although the troops avoided combat with Dominicans, U.S. officials intended the intervention to influence the course of the civil war. Ambassador W. Tapley Bennett cabled Washington: "I hope this action will give some heart to loyal forces." Later in the evening, Bennett repeated his political motives: "San Isidro Radio . . . [is] taking liberties with our landing and expanding its terms of reference. We cannot control that and I do not really mind too much on local grounds if it can have a psychological effect." Undersecretary of State Thomas Mann agreed, telling Secretary of Defense Robert McNamara that the landing "had been a shot in the arm to the loyalist junta."[12]

President Johnson, however, did not publicly commit the United States to either side in the fighting. Instead, he sought to keep his options open while winning approval for the troop landing. In Washington the president built a consensus around his decision, first in a meeting with his top advisers and then in a session with congressional leaders.[13] Johnson told legislators "that there was no alternative to the actions being taken by the United States in view of the unanimous recommendations received from all responsible officials." Johnson later told *New York Times* columnist Arthur Krock that he deliberately avoided giving this group "a scare story about communists."[14] The president's brief speech to the nation that evening also contained no reference to communism. Yet at Johnson's behest, top State Department officials privately informed journalists that communists had been active among the rebels.[15] These leaks helped win conservative support for the intervention, but they also lent credibility to fears of communists in Santo Domingo.[16]

In a bid to soothe liberals at home, the president further complicated matters by privately denying that the communist issue influenced his decision to send in troops. In an off-the-record conversation with Arthur Krock, Johnson asserted that "it was hopeless to think that anyone would ever believe him but that he had not landed marines to put down a communist threat." The president dismissed CIA claims that some rebel leaders were communists. He concluded "that no one on earth knew if this was a pro-Castro or Communist affair." Instead of acting to prevent a second Cuba, Johnson maintained he sent the marines when the ambassador reported that American lives were in danger: "Johnson said he would not have acted except for that reason, but that he would always act to save lives in any similar situation." In effect, the president told politicians and journalists what he thought they wanted to hear, ignoring the disparity between his justifications for the intervention. The internal contradiction within White House explanations soon would haunt U.S. policy. Consensus, already beginning to crumble on Vietnam, would be hard to construct around the Caribbean intervention as the president's manipulations became known.[17]

The embassy, too, faced increasing difficulties. Unlike congressional leaders, loyalist military officers failed to fall into line behind U.S. policy. Not only did the generals use the intervention for propaganda purposes, but many loyalists also believed that Washington had assumed responsibility for defeating the rebels by landing the marines. Ironically, the intervention had made the generals more capable, but less motivated, to fight successfully. The loyalists preferred to hoard their military resources and to try to manipulate Washington into defeating the constitutionalists.[18]

The arrival of the marines also affected the rebels. The constitutionalists generally expected the U.S. troops immediately to join the loyalist side. Some rebels deserted the movement; others prepared for a U.S. attack. When it became clear that the marines would not participate in the struggle directly, rebel morale revived. The rebels' centralized location in Santo Domingo gave them distinct tactical advantages. Although the situation remained chaotic, the leadership under Colonel Francisco Caamaño Deño began to improve its military organization. The strong new external threat to the rebellion reinforced this centralizing tendency, bringing the diffuse constitutionalist leadership into sharper focus. In a conflict that had taken sudden turns in the past, the rebels appeared to be gaining significant, perhaps decisive, momentum on April 29.[19]

Recognizing the new situation, the embassy asked for additional troops, and President Johnson approved the deployment of 1,400 more marines. Like the men landed the previous day, the marines would facilitate evacuations and defend U.S. property. Once again, U.S. forces would not be involved in combat, but technical assistance, advice, and even food were provided to encourage San Isidro.[20] However, State Department officials feared indirect aid to the loyalists would not be decisive, cabling the embassy: "We cannot afford to permit the situation to deteriorate to the point where a Communist takeover occurs." Ambassador Bennett replied to the message by all but asking for a full-scale military intervention.[21]

Shortly after Washington received the ambassador's cable on the evening of April 29, President Johnson ordered thousands more troops into the Dominican Republic. The Pentagon's plan called for troops from the 82d Airborne Division to take up positions just east of Santo Domingo, near San Isidro and on the opposite side of the city from where the marines had deployed. Although the orders stated that "the mission continues to be to protect American lives," few U.S. citizens lived in the vicinity. Instead of protecting Americans, the U.S. troops at San Isidro were intended to create a military cordon around the rebels in downtown Santo Domingo. Marines already in the west of the city and the airborne forces in the east would move together to trap the constitutionalist military, preventing a loyalist defeat. The final instruction to initiate the cordon had not been issued by the White House, but commanders "expect[ed] that loyal[ist] forces as available will be willing to patrol the area between [U.S.] army and marine forces along the line" until the order came. The loyalist generals, however, failed to respond as the Pentagon predicted. Loyalists withdrew to San Isidro, allowing the constitutionalists to operate freely in the gap between the airborne force and the marines. The loyalists again proved willing to let the U.S. fight for them.[22]

Despite sending in thousands of soldiers, President Johnson had not determined yet how to resolve what he perceived to be conflicting political and military goals. At a meeting on the morning of April 30, the president complained of being in a bind. He feared a communist takeover in Santo Domingo if he failed to act decisively, but he worried the United States would be isolated in the hemisphere if he ordered an assault on the rebels. Johnson said he wanted neither a communist victory nor a U.S. offensive but insisted he could not permit a second Cuba. In handwritten notes at the end of the meeting, White House aide Jack Valenti commented that "One thing is clear: A Castro victory in D.R. would [be] the worst domestic political disaster we could possibly suffer." With the stakes so high, the fear in Washington of a communist takeover in Santo Domingo encouraged Johnson to act decisively.[23] Johnson's top foreign policy advisers, who focused more on the Dominican situation and less on domestic pressures, tried to persuade the president to limit the intervention. An impatient Johnson snapped that anything was preferable to a second Cuba. He instructed McNamara to "find out what we would have to have to take that island" and told Secretary of State Dean Rusk to "find out what we have to do to make it look good. We'll get a cloak of international approval if we can get it before the baby dies." Johnson concluded: "But I'm not going to sit here with my hands in my pockets." Despite the bluster, the president resisted political pressures and did not order an immediate attack on the rebels.[24]

In response to Johnson's concerns, officials asked John Bartlow Martin to serve as a presidential emissary in the Dominican Republic. A liberal friend of John Kennedy and the U.S. ambassador during Bosch's presidency, Martin had been ignored by the Johnson White House after he resigned in early 1964. The crisis, however, drew administration attention to Martin's Dominican contacts and domestic political credentials. National Security Adviser McGeorge Bundy privately told Martin, "the president really wanted to be able to say that we had sent a good Kennedy liberal down there." Johnson also expected Martin would reassure his friends in Washington of the president's good intentions. Therefore, a top White House aide asked Martin to carry a special message from the president to Ambassador Bennett, ordering the embassy to downplay the communist danger and to emphasize that troops had landed only to save American lives. More efficient means of relaying this order were at the president's disposal, but giving the job to the gossipy Martin guaranteed that liberals would hear Johnson's spin from an apparently independent source. Once again, Johnson stressed to liberals his humanitarian goals.[25]

The White House also worked to gain Latin American support to lend credibility to the unilateral intervention. Only after President Johnson announced the initial marine landings on the evening of April 28 did the administration mount a coordinated campaign to involve the Organization of American States (OAS). McGeorge Bundy bluntly told the president: "We are going to have to use the OAS as a cloak for whatever we're going to do." Secretary Rusk concurred, assuring Johnson that "We can move thru [*sic*] the OAS and achieve what you want."[26]

With thousands of U.S. troops on the ground and the White House committed to winning hemispheric support for the intervention, the dynamics of U.S. policy changed. Armed intervention made a sudden communist takeover extremely unlikely; the fear of a second Cuba could be tempered by longer-term political aims. The goal remained a rebel defeat, but U.S. tactics now could be more flexible. The State Department sent the embassy a cable to clarify the new approach. Rather than urging the loyalists to crush the rebellion, as policy had dictated previously, the department instructed the embassy to "use your influence to persuade [loyalist] Junta forces that no useful purpose will be served by rash or ill-advised military action." San Isidro should rest its soldiers and capitalize on its position as "the only existing organized authority in the Dominican Republic" to guarantee that OAS mediation would not produce a communist victory. Embassy actions should "be designed to support the Junta in the achievement of this objective." Despite the bias, the administration noted that "it is essential that we maintain an outward attitude of impartiality as between the Junta and rebel forces." This façade had two goals. First, it would help the White House sell its intervention to domestic and international audiences. Second, the State Department feared the presence of U.S. troops at San Isidro would lead loyalists to assume incorrectly that Washington intended to settle the conflict militarily. The embassy was told to emphasize the error in this view to the junta and simultaneously to work toward an OAS-sponsored cease-fire.[27]

Like the Johnson administration, top constitutionalist leaders quickly changed their tactics. Juan Bosch led this shift from exile in Puerto Rico. To communicate with the White House, Bosch relied on telephone conversations with Abe Fortas, an unofficial Johnson adviser with extensive Puerto Rican contacts. After the military intervention began, Bosch promised Fortas he would broadcast a cease-fire appeal. Bosch and his advisers recognized that the constitutionalists could not launch a military attack against the loyalist camp without risking a direct confrontation with the United States. Rather than toying with certain destruction, Bosch and his advisers decided to conserve their armed strength and to fight a political battle with San Isidro's unpopular generals. This brought the conflict back into the propaganda arena, where Bosch excelled.

The constitutionalists traded a weakening military position for a strong political foundation by agreeing to accept a cease-fire.[28]

Bosch's commitment to halt the fighting matched Johnson administration policy, but it created a new problem for Washington. The White House worried that any bloodshed after Bosch's broadcast would be blamed on San Isidro. Therefore, the State Department instructed the embassy to "immediately inform Junta officials . . . of foregoing and recommend to them that Junta make a similar appeal." Washington also, with the admonition "This is URGENT," ordered the U.S. military to supplement embassy efforts to convince San Isidro to accept a cease-fire. The Defense Department told its commander in Santo Domingo to send his best officer to advise the junta on tactics, to supply San Isidro with whatever it needed, and to strengthen communication between loyalists and the U.S. military. Pressure on the generals quickly led them to acquiesce to a cease-fire. Washington previously had lamented San Isidro's reliance on the United States, but now it sought loyalists' compliance by further deepening their dependence.[29]

Although the intervention's size gave the United States influence over the loyalists, its scale complicated Johnson's situation at home. Carl Rowan, head of the U.S. Information Agency (USIA), told the president "it will be well nigh impossible to justify the presence of 16,000 American troops simply on the grounds that we are protecting Americans and other foreigners."[30] Presidential media adviser Jack Valenti urged Johnson to explain his action to the American people as a stark choice between victory for Castro or U.S. intervention. Valenti insisted the White House must provide "facts, figures, names and addresses" to support its case: "We must leave *NO DOUBT* as to our evidence." Valenti suggested the president conduct a nationally televised briefing. If the voters bought Johnson's pitch, Valenti asserted, the president would have turned a potential disaster into a resounding political victory.[31]

The available intelligence, however, failed to establish the sharp distinctions demanded by Valenti's proposed media campaign. The administration possessed extensive evidence of communist and leftist participation in the revolt, yet no communists held positions of authority in the constitutionalist movement. Rather than a firm foundation of facts, the White House case rested on the abdication of moderate political leadership in Santo Domingo. U.S. officials feared that communists would fill the vacuum. An April 29 CIA memo mentioned 45 communist-trained extremists who "can be presumed to be active in the current fighting." An April 30 CIA report listed "58 identified, prominent Communist and Castroist leaders." This document laid out the subversive background of 54 Dominicans (4 names were duplicated) and mentioned only 7 as active in the fighting, one of whom it failed to include among the original list of 58. Despite a flood of CIA reports, embassy cables, and alarmist messages from military officers, the administration did not have concrete evidence of communist domination of the rebellion. The quantity of intelligence data may have given a false impression of substance, but it failed to deliver the quality of information needed to make a solid case. Thomas Mann later noted: "Other things being equal, we would have preferred to have waited two or three days longer before speaking publicly of this issue."[32]

But Johnson carefully played the communist card in an April 30 evening statement. In his brief speech, Johnson described the turmoil in Santo Domingo and praised the recent cease-fire. Halfway through his remarks he stated that "there are signs that people trained outside the Dominican Republic are seeking to gain control." He did not elaborate. Instead, he stressed the importance of rapid inter-American action through the OAS to thwart an "international conspiracy." Johnson never uttered the words communism or Cuba, but his meaning was unmistakable. As he had with congressional leaders two nights before, the president sought to use hints and implications to win domestic support without producing evidence to back his claims.[33]

Most Americans backed the intervention, but Johnson's veiled comments did not win him overwhelming support. A number of congressional liberals and prominent members of the press had become skeptical of Johnson's foreign policy, and some were unwilling to accept intimations about communist rebels as reason for the growing U.S. force in Santo Domingo. Pressure built in the White House to satisfy these concerns before liberals opposed the intervention, perhaps presaging a larger split over Vietnam. USIA Chief Rowan, however, argued against attempting to satisfy liberals through leaks of specific intelligence on extremists. "[That would be] a huge mistake," Rowan said, "we can produce 45 names—17,000 troops against 45 men." The White House ignored Rowan's warning and plunged ahead with its behind-the-scenes emphasis of communist domination of the rebellion. On May 1, McGeorge Bundy leaked details to journalists, including the claim that 58 communists leaders were involved in the movement. Leaks of incomplete and inconclusive data only discredited the administration's position among skeptics in the press and Congress.[34]

On May 2 Johnson escalated the damage in a rambling national address. TelePrompTer problems forced the president twice to repeat sections of his text and then to ad lib: "And what began as a popular democratic revolution, committed to democracy and social justice, very shortly moved and was taken over and really seized and placed into the hands of a band of Communist conspirators."[35] The speech was a disaster. It alienated many liberals with its exaggerated claims about communism in Santo Domingo, while it angered some conservatives by proclaiming neutrality in what it presented as a classic Cold War struggle. The administration stumbled by trying to appeal to everyone. Controversy over the intervention threatened Johnson's policy in Vietnam and, more importantly, the Great Society legislation in Congress. Johnson told an AFL-CIO conference on May 3: "There never was a period in our national history when unity, understanding, perseverance, and patriotism would pay larger dividends than it would pay now." The president nearly had attained his ambitions for domestic reform, but now the Santo Domingo crisis had distracted the country. In his effort to refocus the nation on reform, he undercut his own position with a contradictory explanation of the intervention. As Theodore Draper has written, Johnson's Dominican problem "was, if ever there was one, a self-inflicted wound."[36]

Loyalist propaganda and actions further complicated the U.S. position. Radio San Isidro played the U.S. national anthem, "Stars and Stripes Forever," and, in honor of President Johnson, "The Yellow Rose of Texas." The songs so annoyed the State Department that it instructed the embassy to tell the chief loyalist general "it is neither in his interest nor ours for him to become over-identified with the U.S. at this point." Another leading loyalist, General Antonio Imbert, took a more subtle and effective approach to cementing his ties to the embassy. He not only met extensively with his old friend John Martin, but he also told officials lurid stories of rebel extremism. Ambassador Bennett called Imbert's stories "another example of Castro influence among the rebels."[37]

Embassy opposition to the constitutionalist movement, however, no longer translated into automatic support for the loyalist junta. Washington began to explore options for a nonconstitutionalist and nonloyalist regime, and, alternately, for a expansion of the loyalist junta to include prominent civilians. Officials drew up a list of potential political leaders, with former president Joaquín Balaguer singled out for special attention. Secret talks began with Balaguer; these discussions had little immediate impact, although they established the foundation for a later settlement. The State Department also considered forming several independent provisional councils to govern areas outside of Santo Domingo until the conflict could be resolved. The administration looked beyond San Isidro for a solution in the long run, but it had not yet settled on an alternative for the immediate crisis.[38]

Despite the negotiations and pledges of neutrality, U.S. forces conducted several moves intended to weaken the constitutionalists. The USIA and the U.S. Army jammed rebel radio broadcasts and established a black propaganda radio station to impersonate and discredit the rebels. More significant, General Bruce Palmer, the U.S. commander in Santo Domingo, ordered preparations for a "line of communication" (LOC) linking U.S. troops through rebel-held areas of downtown Santo Domingo. A patrol from the 82d Airborne twice scouted possible LOC routes through the constitutionalist zone, in a clear violation of the cease-fire. Two American soldiers were killed and two wounded, confirming, in Palmer's words, "that hostile forces control the gap and 'own' the bulk of the city." Late on May 2, the U.S. military established a four-block-wide ground connection between soldiers at San Isidro and the marines near the embassy. U.S. officials insisted publicly the LOC permitted humanitarian aid to be delivered more effectively while making evacuations and military coordination easier, but the LOC was created largely to trap most of the constitutionalist military between U.S. troops and the sea.[39]

Colonel Caamaño quickly adapted to the new situation. His success surprised not only his enemies but also many of his allies. The increasing scope of the U.S. military presence had demoralized the rebels. While some constitutionalists withdrew, Caamaño and others saw an opportunity. Early on May 4, the rebels declared Caamaño acting president. Since the constitutionalist stronghold had been isolated militarily by the U.S. LOC, Caamaño realized that the core of the rebellion now could not be attacked without overt U.S. complicity, although smaller rebel forces in northern Santo Domingo remained vulnerable. Washington inadvertently had given the constitutionalists the chance to transform the civil war from a military to a political conflict. Once again, Dominicans surprised the White House by refusing to follow the U.S. script.[40]

The rebel gambit stunned the Johnson administration. "We believe fast action is essential to counter," Bennett told Washington. "We have therefore decided to suggest the formation of a broad-based junta including responsible civilians representing important sectors." Bennett and Martin agreed that Antonio Imbert should head the new regime.[41] Rather than risk Caamaño's victory, Washington accepted the chance that Imbert would become, in Martin's words, "another Trujillo." The White House enthusiastically but covertly aided Imbert's new Government of National Reconstruction (GNR). Johnson ordered the transfer of $4.5 million to the GNR to pay for two weeks of the regime's expenses.[42] Washington also gave the GNR substantial political assistance. The embassy spearheaded a campaign to purge the Dominican military of its most unpopular leaders while the USIA continued to jam rebel Radio Santo Domingo. And U.S. special forces crippled the country's commercial telephone system, cutting a primary rebel communication link. Washington even used its ties to Dominican labor leaders to orchestrate a break between certain unions and the constitutionalist movement, with "every precaution being taken to insure American hand does not . . . show." This comprehensive program of aid and advice helped the GNR fortify its position.[43]

Imbert attempted to maximize the assistance he received from the United States while preserving his own interests. The GNR represented a paradox for the ambitious general. Imbert finally had attained the position he had sought for years, yet both the Caamaño government, by its very existence, and the United States, by its refusal to formally recognize the GNR, substantially limited his authority. Imbert consolidated his power only by making himself invaluable to the White House and by eliminating his rivals. Thus he expressed willingness to talk with the rebels while simultaneously preparing for a military offensive. A successful assault would guarantee his supremacy by defeating the constitutionalists and securing the Dominican military's loyalty. Despite embassy protests, Imbert told a U.S. official that Washington "'is not preventing . . . and will not prevent' [me] from attacking Caamaño." Imbert understood he had some independence from the White House. The United States needed him to counter the constitutionalist movement as much as he needed the United States to prop up the GNR. And some U.S. officials, including top members of the diplomatic and military staff in Santo Domingo, advocated an attack on the rebels. Imbert would risk being abandoned by the United States if he ignored Washington's ambivalent pleas for restraint, but the potential payoff was the Dominican presidency. Imbert, one of Trujillo's assassins, had earned his position by making high-stakes gambles.[44]

Political developments gave Imbert added incentive to launch an offensive. Emboldened by the presence of U.S. troops, the loyalist military regained its will to fight. Embassy cables describe San Isidro's leaders as "nervous and jumpy" but "ready to attack."[45] Imbert ordered military moves in places where he retained some flexibility, in the air above the city and in the rebel areas outside of the U.S. cordon around downtown Santo Domingo. On May 13, five San Isidro planes attacked Radio Santo Domingo, silencing the rebel broadcasts. The timing of the raid surprised the embassy, although Washington had permitted its execution.[46] Senior U.S. military officers attempted to dissuade San Isidro's leaders from further air attacks, doing everything, according to General Palmer, "short of physically blocking taxiways." However, embassy officials were pleased with the destruction of Radio Santo Domingo. Bennett noted: "It is hard to rap GNR for having taken an action to remove installation which was poisoning whole body politic."[47]

While San Isidro's planes struck, Imbert began a ground offensive against constitutionalists in northern Santo Domingo. Imbert's offensive may not have had the overt blessing of the United States, but it undoubtedly had the tacit approval of the embassy. U.S. forces even coordinated military moves with the GNR. On May 14 General Palmer wrote: "Operations are presently planned on a unilateral US basis, taking cognizance of disposition and known plans of

GNR forces. US special forces operations are also being planned and when approved, executed. In addition, certain GNR special operations are being planned and conducted with our knowledge but not repeat not under direction or with US participation." With the U.S. military and Imbert's troops acting against the constitutionalists, Washington was not neutral. Instead, the Johnson administration continued to use armed force to destroy the rebellion.[48]

Like the fighting, the intensity of negotiations escalated dramatically in mid-May. On May 12, Abe Fortas flew to Puerto Rico to meet with Juan Bosch.[49] Fortas asked Bosch to agree that "active Communists and Trujillistas" would be identified, interned, and perhaps deported after a new provisional government took power. Bosch refused. Fortas emphasized the White House would accept nothing less on communism. He hinted that if Bosch were willing to compromise on this, an agreement meeting most rebel demands might be possible because President Johnson privately summed up his bottom line: "Constitution, *Sí;* Communism, *No.*" Bosch then accepted Fortas's proposal, clearing a significant hurdle toward settlement. They drafted a short statement to be issued publicly by the White House as a step toward peace. Fortas used this rather bland document, with its bow to constitutionalism, to build momentum in the talks. A possible solution began to emerge, nicknamed the "Guzmán formula" after Bosch's hand-picked presidential favorite, Antonio Guzmán. According to this plan, the controversial Bosch would remain in exile while the United States supported a constitutionalist regime in Santo Domingo with Guzmán serving as president.[50]

Progress in the negotiations, however, conflicted with Fortas's desire to remain anonymous. The White House had to find someone else to move things forward. The president realized that neither the OAS nor U.S. officials in Santo Domingo could handle the delicate task. Johnson even contemplated conducting "Belly-to-Belly" talks himself with Guzmán. At the urging of his top advisers, Johnson decided to send a high-level committee to negotiate with all players simultaneously. Late on May 14, McGeorge Bundy, Thomas Mann, Deputy Secretary of Defense Cyrus Vance, and Assistant Secretary of State for Inter-American Affairs Jack Vaughn flew to the Caribbean. Bundy and Vance went to Puerto Rico to talk with Bosch and Guzmán, while Mann and Vaughn headed for the loyalist base in Santo Domingo.[51]

Speaking for the loyalists, Imbert resisted a compromise settlement. He told Mann and Vaughn that the GNR could take control of Santo Domingo after a few more days of fighting. If the United States persisted with the Guzmán talks, Imbert threatened to denounce the White House for abandoning him to the communists, hitting Johnson where he was most sensitive, in domestic politics. Imbert complained Washington was double-crossing him by building up the GNR only to destroy it. He also insisted Guzmán would be nothing more than a Bosch puppet who inevitably would permit the resurgence of the radical left. Imbert's arguments failed to persuade Mann and Vaughn. They told the White House that while Imbert deserved credit for rallying his forces, he probably could not capture Santo Domingo without dangerously weakening the military. Mann and Vaughn also considered him too conservative to be politically palatable in the United States. Imbert's resistance to the Guzmán formula neither surprised nor gravely worried the State Department officials. If the White House chose to, as both Imbert and the Johnson administration understood, it could pull the rug out from under the GNR. But until an agreement had been reached, Imbert remained useful to the United States as a counter to Caamaño.[52]

To induce Guzmán and the constitutionalists to compromise, Bundy offered at least $20 million in assistance to the Dominican government over the next three months, in addition to the $9 million already committed since the crisis began. Despite the pressure, Bundy and Guzmán reached an impasse over who would control the military, the loyalist generals or the rebellious junior officers. Guzmán also demanded U.S. troops enforce an effective cease-fire in Santo Domingo. The continued offensive by GNR soldiers outraged the constitutionalists. Because the United States had not committed entirely to a negotiated settlement, military moves against the GNR were not seriously contemplated. Failing to clear these crucial hurdles, the Bundy mission stalled.[53]

Back in Washington on May 17, President Johnson weighed his options. Johnson noted: "agreement [on the] control of Armed Forces [has] broken down. . . . [We] have reached a point of critical decision." Apparently to reassure himself, he wrote: "not going to lose Island." Johnson then listed two options. He could support San Isidro, or he could continue to play the political game. Johnson seemed hesitant to abandon negotiations, perhaps because he felt a solution still was close and because Abe Fortas apparently told him, as the president put it, "Bosch willing and eager" to broadcast an appeal for people to cease fire. Additionally, Johnson continued to hope the OAS could help settle the crisis. Johnson concluded: "Restrain fighting tonight. . . . [agreement] Done and announced as soon as possible." The president had not abandoned the Guzmán formula, although he recognized time was running short.[54]

Yet as a settlement seemed to grow nearer, powerful Dominicans worked to prevent a deal. Loyalists loudly protested to the U.S. Embassy and to journalists that their country was being surrendered to the communists. The GNR accelerated its offensive in a bid to win a military victory before a compromise could be reached. Meanwhile, sniping at U.S. troops from the rebel zones became more frequent. Opponents of negotiations on both the right and the left sought to destroy any chance for peace. At the same time, journalists in Santo Domingo wrote stories about the rumored Guzmán formula that complicated the president's domestic political position. Jules Dubois of the *Chicago Tribune,* reflecting his ties to the Dominican right, warned his readers the Bundy mission threatened to create "a second Bay of Pigs." Tad Szulc of the *New York Times,* who had many rebel sources, panicked the White House with his report that the Guzmán talks marked a sharp turn in administration policy away from the earlier concern about communists in the rebellion. Opinion began to polarize around the Guzmán formula, making compromise even more difficult for both Dominicans and the White House.[55]

On the morning of May 18, Bundy's team gathered to reevaluate the situation. In a cable to Washington, they complained that despite the massive U.S. armed presence, they still did not control the Dominican Republic: "each side, like a Chinese warlord, has true military force and can and has used that force to disrupt every political move we have attempted if it thought disruption was to its advantage." To eliminate this problem and to improve the climate for negotiations, they suggested the United States "physically interpose our military forces between the contending Dominican military factions." This maneuver would enhance U.S. power, create a less volatile climate for talks, and demonstrate Washington's neutrality. The operation also would meet one of Guzmán's crucial conditions for a settlement, an end to the GNR offensive in northern Santo Domingo.[56]

Despite the recommendation by the top U.S. officials in Santo Domingo, the fragile consensus within the administration about the Guzmán formula had begun to disintegrate. Abe Fortas had been wary of Guzmán from the start, and his opinions became more popular as the talks progressed. Kennedy Crockett, the State Department's director of Caribbean affairs, worked hard to kill a gambit that he believed undercut the Dominican military. Thomas Mann initially supported the negotiations and tried to contain Crockett's opposition, but his views shifted after Guzmán refused to back down on rebel control of the military. On the afternoon of May 18 Bundy wrote: "[Mann] thinks. . . . In event of mushy agreement danger of rise of Commie influence is considerable." Ambassador Bennett believed most U.S. officials in the Dominican Republic now doubted the practicality of the Guzmán formula: "everybody but Mac [Bundy] thought it wouldn't work." With both domestic politics and many administration policy makers arguing against the Guzmán formula, chances for a compromise acceptable to President Johnson declined.[57]

Events also began to overtake the negotiations in Santo Domingo. Continued GNR military advances in the north of the city reduced San Isidro's willingness to deal. Bundy and Bennett used the loyalist successes to ask again for permission to interpose U.S. soldiers between the combatants, warning that if the GNR were "permitted to take all of area north of LOC, Imbert will be increasingly difficult to deal with." President Johnson refused to issue the order, apparently fearing the domestic fallout of an operation that could be portrayed by conservatives as protecting communists. The embassy told Washington that the GNR advances and the death of a leading rebel "may well have effect of hardening approach by both sides to negotiations for compromise settlement." Indeed, an angry Colonel Caamaño for the first time refused to meet with Bundy on May 20, in part to placate rebels who demanded vengeance for their comrade's death. Caamaño averted a futile rebel offensive against U.S. troops, but compromise became more difficult politically for constitutionalist leaders.[58]

The Johnson administration's credibility problems further complicated the Guzmán formula. Rather than pursuing talks on May 20, several top U.S. officials focused their energy on the skeptical press corps in Santo Domingo. During a news conference, officials insisted the United States was impartial in the fighting, providing details and explanations to clear up what they saw as common misperceptions. Some reporters badgered the administration spokesmen about incidents of apparent U.S. support for GNR troops, while others demanded to know how restrictions on the loyalist military fit with claims of neutrality. Vague answers, complimented by a brief power outage that plunged the gathering into darkness, did nothing to salvage relations with the media. The administration's sinking credibility now undermined the negotiations as the press filed stories challenging U.S. policies, fueling the fires of criticism at home.[59]

Despite the mounting pressure against a settlement, Bundy and Guzmán neared a final deal on May 20–21. If the GNR's military advances raised the specter of a conservative backlash in Washington against a sell-out to the rebels, in Santo Domingo Imbert's success made a compromise more likely between Bundy and Guzmán. Moderate constitutionalists feared their impending defeat in the northern *barrios* would weaken their overall standing, so they became more willing to make concessions. Guzmán even agreed to accept a United States–backed candidate as minister of the armed forces, a substantial retreat. Still, Bundy and Vance told the White House a final package with Guzmán "will probably obtain acquiescence but not [repeat] not acceptance from Imbert forces and San Isidro leaders. There will be wounds and loud complaints to non-liberal press. Damage to whole structure of armed forces will probably be less than seemed likely [earlier] because of increased morale in recent days. But complaint against us will be more vocal. And we could meet flat refusal." Bundy and Vance hoped private guarantees to loyalist leaders of comfortable positions overseas and a U.S. pledge to accept what the GNR called "final responsibility" for the Guzmán formula would "soften up both Imbert and Service Chiefs." The State Department even promised to arrange for Imbert's "financial security" in exile. With Guzmán willing to deal and Washington capable of acting whether or not the loyalists agreed, Caamaño's rebels were the last hurdle to a compromise. If Caamaño and his advisers would leave the country, as the United States demanded, the pact could be sealed. If they refused, Bundy and Vance warned the White House that loyalist commanders might not give in quietly.[60]

Late on May 21, the constitutionalist military chiefs informed Bundy they would not accept any agreement that required the "heroes of the revolution" to leave the country. Guzmán concurred, saying he would be unable to govern if, in Bundy's words, he appeared to have "sold out to the Americans." Rebel leaders apparently concluded that Imbert's advance through northern Santo Domingo had not significantly weakened their position. Loyalist forces could not attack the rebel stronghold without crossing the LOC, clearly violating Washington's pledge of neutrality. Ironically, military pressure on the constitutionalists decreased after the GNR's successful offensive, making the rebels less likely to compromise.[61]

U.S. officials in Santo Domingo and the White House seriously debated the rebel demand. When Bundy outlined the case for and against accepting the continued presence of the constitutionalist leaders while still forcing Imbert and the generals to depart, domestic politics shaped the president's thinking. A summary of a telephone conversation between Johnson and George Ball revealed his conclusions:

> President said if [Guzmán] doesn't have will or power or the desire to agree to it, it is obvious we have pig in poke and that he would not do it later—therefore, we could not survive at home. President said let Bundy know that he is coming into Lion's den—he better realize he will be facing [Senators] Fulbright, Russell, Long, etc. . . . President referred to Mac Bundy and said that he probably will say that "I had a formula and you guys busted it up." But President feels that if he goes to Hill to face the Russells, Longs, etc. he will really get a beating.

The State Department repeated Johnson's concerns in its cable instructing Bundy to insist on the departure of Caamaño and his advisers: "Anything less would be impossible to explain and justify to Congress and the American people." Domestic politics prohibited the White House from giving any ground.[62]

Late on May 23, Bundy relayed the president's position to Guzmán. The Dominican said he could not participate in a government under these conditions. With neither side willing to concede, the Guzmán formula collapsed. Johnson's anticommunism and political calculations led the president to reiterate a demand Guzmán already had rejected. And Guzmán refused to take the final step that would have given him the provisional presidency, but which might also have destroyed his credibility with his supporters. In the end, the domestic politics of both the United States and the Dominican Republic doomed the Guzmán formula.[63]

The collapse of the Guzmán formula did not produce a dramatic shift in Johnson administration policy. Rather, the White House continued to pursue negotiations while ceding more responsibility to the OAS. The State Department prepared to hand over some authority even as the Guzmán discussions fell apart. In the cable instructing Bundy to refuse concessions, Secretary Rusk concluded: "if your efforts to reach an understanding should in fact meet a dead end we would propose that. . . . the OAS should now carry on from there."[64] The OAS quickly created a three-member negotiating team headed by U.S. Ambassador to the OAS Ellsworth Bunker.[65] Although the commission would not follow Bunker blindly, it would navigate along a course charted by the Johnson administration. Washington had no intention of loosening its grip, even though it sought to involve the OAS more directly. The embassy on June 2 submitted to the State Department a plan for media relations "In view of our attempts to create the *public image* of the OAS gradually beginning to assume primary responsibility for political-military solution of the Dominican crisis." The new mediating team flew to the Dominican Republic and began a slow effort to negotiate a compromise.[66]

The Johnson administration exploited the lull in Santo Domingo and the drift in public attention to shore up support for the president's policies. Popular opinion continued to back the intervention, but critical sniping troubled Johnson. The delicate Guzmán negotiations had kept policy makers from answering some of the critics' charges previously. After the Guzmán formula collapsed, Johnson's renewed campaign for public backing failed primarily because the president and his advisers could not keep their story straight.[67] The president's exaggerations again were worse than any of his advisers' miscues. For instance, Johnson told an audience that in the days before the intervention "Some fifteen hundred innocent people were murdered and shot and their heads cut off." After this claim, White House aides and embassy personnel frantically searched for any examples of beheading. The president phoned Ambassador Bennett, demanding: "For God's sake, see if you can find some headless bodies." A month later, following what Bennett called "a great deal of time and effort," officials produced "at least two confirmations of this ghoulish subject." Johnson's tall tales continued to undermine his credibility.[68]

Despite the barbs of a few conservatives, liberals monopolized the criticism of Johnson's policy.[69] Even some within the administration complained. Ambassador to the United Nations Adlai Stevenson told George Ball, "This is the worst since Bay of Pigs by far," and John Martin privately expressed doubts about policies he had helped shape. Major newspapers echoed these worries. James Reston of the *New York Times,* for example, took his concerns directly to the White House. Reston informed McGeorge Bundy of a "deep-seated distrust" of the administration developing in the country, particularly after LBJ's recent public statements. Bundy reassured Reston that rumors of disarray at the White House were false. Nevertheless, questions persisted about the handling of the Dominican crisis.[70]

Later that year these doubts erupted in a conflict between the president and the powerful chair of the Senate Foreign Relations Committee, J. William Fulbright (D-Ark.). The two had been close friends and allies in the Senate, but Johnson's move to the White House strained their relationship. Fulbright's concerns about Vietnam deepened the divide. They publicly broke when Fulbright critiqued Johnson's Dominican policies in a speech in September, 1965. Fulbright criticized U.S. actions for being inconsistent and lacking candor, arguing that facts had been misrepresented in order to defend mistakes by American officials in Santo Domingo. Fulbright pinned the blame for the failures on "faulty advice given to the President by his representatives." The senator drew limited parallels with Vietnam but concluded by emphasizing the need for Washington to support noncommunist reform in Latin America.[71] In an attempt to keep channels open to the president, Fulbright had sent an advance copy of his speech to the White House. He told Johnson in his cover letter: "Public—and I trust, constructive—criticism is one of the services that a Senator is uniquely able to perform. . . . It is in the sincere hope of assisting your Administration . . . and of advancing the objective of your policy in Latin America, that I offer the enclosed remarks."[72] To further soften the blow, Fulbright carefully avoided directly condemning Johnson. The cautiousness of Fulbright's critique underlined his hesitancy in breaking with the White House. The address represented, from Fulbright's perspective, a warning shot across the administration's bow.[73]

Johnson and his allies, however, responded fiercely to the speech. The day before Fulbright spoke, McGeorge Bundy offered Johnson several options: "Do you want us to have an answer ready for Fulbright, and if so, should we pick someone . . . who would do it with enthusiasm? Or should we try to find someone more 'liberal'? Or should we ignore Fulbright?" The president favored attack. Johnson may have feared that Fulbright's words would be seen as a trial balloon for a new American policy. To distance himself from Fulbright, the president would have to respond. But the venom of the assault on the senator indicates that this was more than a policy squabble. Johnson, who rarely took dissent well, lashed out at Fulbright for what the president perceived to be a betrayal of trust. Additionally, Johnson's aides and allies, eager for the president's pleasure, may have taken the assault even further than the Texan expected.[74] As soon as Fulbright finished his address, several senators criticized him for naively supporting communist aims in Latin America and Asia. The strongest barrage came the next day in a speech conceived at the White House and delivered in the Senate by Thomas Dodd (D-Conn.). Internal White House memos described Dodd's attacks on Fulbright as "pretty hot." An assistant told Bundy that the draft of Dodd's speech "could probably be defended by a skilled debater, [but it] is a little much." The aide recommended certain charges against Fulbright be deleted. Bundy disagreed, scribbling, "Let it ride" in the memo's margins. A draft letter from the president to the senator had a similar tone. In a note to Johnson about the letter, Bundy admitted, "I have tried to hit [Fulbright] with everything but the kitchen stove." Although the letter was never sent, it reflected White House anger with Fulbright's public dissent.[75]

The harshness of the administration's reaction to Fulbright's speech, more than anything else, cemented the division between the senator and the president.[76] Even after the initial attacks in the Senate subsided, Fulbright encountered hostility from White House allies. Rumors reached him that the administration "is sharpening its knives" in preparation for further stabs at his reputation. Three months later, still facing a White House that barred him from state ceremonies and denied him use of a jet for a flight to New Zealand, Fulbright finally acknowledged the divorce. He led televised Foreign Relations Committee hearings on Vietnam that helped legitimize antiwar dissent and secured his position as a leading critic of the war. The break had become complete. Although Fulbright remained in close contact with top administration officials on the Dominican Republic and other issues, the senator's personal relationship with the president had ended.[77]

Had the White House not reacted so strongly to Fulbright's Dominican speech, the gap between the senator and the president might not have grown so wide so soon. Yet some separation was unavoidable because fundamental differences existed on Vietnam. President Johnson's reaction, however, pushed Fulbright more quickly into the leadership of the Vietnam dissenters. Fulbright's Dominican address may indeed have been, as Daniel Yergin has argued, the first crack in the Cold War consensus,[78] but Johnson, not Fulbright, bears most of the responsibility for the emergence of that fracture. Once again, Johnson bungled his efforts to contain dissent.

Well before the Johnson-Fulbright divide, the slow pace of events in the

Caribbean and the dramatic escalation of the Vietnam War took the Dominican Republic off American front pages. Still, the intervention continued. The mid-summer creation of the OAS ad hoc committee marked a turning point in the Dominican conflict. Ambassador Ellsworth Bunker served as the committee's spokesman and leader. Bunker dominated but did not control the trio of OAS diplomats. Bunker also represented President Johnson like no previous emissary had because he could bypass the official hierarchy to dictate policy, and Johnson consistently followed his lead. Bunker controlled both the overall direction and the specific implementation of American actions.[79] Johnson gave Bunker what Bundy called "a free hand" largely because the president recognized the need to focus White House attention elsewhere. Vietnam and the Great Society remained Johnson's preoccupations. The president had little time for the Dominican Republic after the crisis had passed. With Bunker's ascendance, the center of U.S. policy making shifted from Washington to Santo Domingo.[80]

In June the ad hoc committee privately developed a program. It incorporated goals trumpeted by the United States and the OAS, yet it most closely resembled a proposal made earlier in Washington by Joaquín Balaguer. In secret talks with State Department officials, the exiled former president suggested the OAS create an apolitical provisional government. The temporary regime would guide the country through a six-to-twelve-month political cooling-off period, followed by OAS-supervised elections. Balaguer's plan also called for the restructuring and reduction in size of the armed forces. Balaguer expected to be the victor in the elections, and he advocated a schedule that would most benefit his Reformist Party.[81]

Balaguer's proposal appealed to U.S. officials. Ambassador Bunker considered the Dominican's scheme sensible and in line with the ad hoc committee's thinking. The White House particularly liked the successful U.S. exit strategy included in the plan. Secret CIA polls taken shortly before the April coup indicated Dominican voters favored Balaguer by a two-to-one margin over Bosch, his closest competitor. Some in Washington doubted the accuracy of the polls, but the attractiveness of an electoral solution outweighed the fear that Bosch might triumph. Although the Kennedy and Johnson administrations previously had not favored Balaguer, he was a known quantity with a firm anticommunist record. After the recent turmoil, the White House would be hard pressed to imagine a more optimistic scenario than peaceful elections won by a conservative U.S. friend. Johnson's intervention would be vindicated. Washington quickly adopted the Balaguer proposal. "My own feeling is that [Balaguer's] solution is very near to what we should come out with," Bundy told Johnson. "My object will be to leave [Caamaño's forces] as the dogs in the manger while the country goes about its business." The president, however, sought to avoid public identification with Balaguer and hoped, in Bundy's words, to not have a "Made in the USA" label on the settlement.[82]

The OAS ad hoc committee's June 18 "Proposal for a peaceful solution of the Dominican crisis," which closely followed Balaguer's secret plan, initiated the process that ended the civil war. The proclamation forced the combatants to state their intentions. A critical struggle emerged between two groups within the constitutionalist leadership for control of rebel political strategy. The moderates inclined toward compromise and free elections, which they believed they would win. Their opponents among the rebels were an assortment of radicals, nationalists, and communists who favored confrontation, arguing concessions would betray both their principles and the memory of their fallen comrades. After the mid-June battle in Santo Domingo, many rebels considered further fighting to be suicide. The moderates exploited these feelings. They persuaded the majority of the leaders of the Caamaño government to support a favorable response to the ad hoc committee's proposal.[83]

The rebel announcement guaranteed the GNR would respond affirmatively. Throughout the negotiations, Imbert walked a razor's edge. He opposed any compromise that would limit his power, yet he understood his survival depended on the goodwill of the United States. Therefore, he could not reject mediation outright. Rather than opposing talks, Imbert continued to portray himself as the moderate and nationalist alternative to the extremist rebels. Despite his posturing, Imbert's political position was nearly untenable. He would lose authority if the negotiations succeeded, yet he could do little to undermine the talks without endangering his backing from the United States. Additionally, Bunker and his associates knew they could force Imbert to accept a settlement by cutting off GNR funding and by dealing separately with loyalist military chiefs, who always had been suspicious of Imbert. The ad hoc committee wanted to make concession as easy as possible for Imbert, to ease the transition to a new government and to calm the waters in Washington, where Imbert's staunch anticommunism won him allies. The United States guaranteed the GNR's survival as the negotiations progressed, but the regime continued to be primarily a tool, albeit an independent one, to counter the rebels. The crucial talks would be among the ad hoc committee, the rebel negotiating team, and the loyalist military chiefs.[84]

After all sides accepted in principle the OAS panel's proposal, detailed discussions began. The mediators decided first to name the leadership of the provisional government. They expected this to be a relatively simple task when compared with the tricky disputes surrounding the military. They also concluded their effort would gain substantial momentum if they could attach a prominent Dominican face to their plan. After interviewing several possible candidates, the committee gave Héctor García Godoy what Bunker called "[our] complete backing." García Godoy, a diplomat who had served in both Trujillo's and Bosch's governments, had the support of many conservatives, moderate rebels, and, reluctantly, the loyalist military chiefs. Radical constitutionalists refused to accept him, and the GNR opposed him as an unacceptable alternative to Imbert.[85]

The ad hoc committee then prepared to force the GNR to compromise. The diplomats reluctantly concluded, in Bunker's words, that it seemed "likely considerable pressure will have to be used to get [Imbert] out." The committee could cut off OAS and U.S. funding to the GNR, but "this club" would strike too heavy a blow, because it would prevent the GNR from continuing to check the constitutionalists. The panel first would try to split the loyalists from the GNR. If this separation could be made, the committee could force Imbert to concede without eliminating a balance to the rebels. The most controversial of the loyalists, General Elías Wessin, would be removed, but other changes would be postponed. By abandoning military reform in the short term the ad hoc committee hoped to secure the necessary support for its plan in the armed forces. Washington accepted the strategy: "Restructuring of military establishment and changes in armed forces leadership desirable but agree that it is not practicable to achieve this now. We would hope provisional government could make a start but this is a problem for resolution later." With the tactic approved by Washington, Bunker had what he called a "lengthy and satisfactory meeting" with the loyalist military chief who pledged the military's "full support." The ad hoc committee, with loyalist backing, had overcome one obstacle. Imbert could be ignored.[86]

The moderates on the rebel negotiating commission, led by Antonio Guzmán, broke the jam on the constitutionalist side. Guzmán and his allies secretly approached the ad hoc committee, breaking an internal rebel pact not to negotiate separately. The moderates expressed their support for García Godoy and blamed radicals for blocking a settlement. To overcome the opposition, Guzmán proposed a coordinated approach with the OAS panel.[87] The ad hoc panel agreed. Bunker reported that in a meeting with the rebel negotiators: "In accordance with script previously suggested by Guzmán, I first went through the rebel list name by name. . . . Rebel reply (again according to Guzmán script) was to ask what we would suggest by way of candidates. . . . [I] said we considered García Godoy the man who best met the requirements. . . . If rebels continue to follow Guzmán script, they will indicate acceptance of our proposal in one manner or another." The next day the rebels held a meeting as Guzmán had predicted. The debate focused on the likely result if they refused to approve García Godoy. When the votes were counted, the constitutionalist leaders agreed to accept García Godoy, with only the most radical opposing. According to Bunker, the gambit had worked just as Guzmán had intended: "Finally Caamaño and PRD served notice on extreme left if they didn't go with [García] Godoy, Caamaño and PRD would break away."[88]

The ad hoc committee then worked closely with García Godoy to devise an institutional act that would serve as the basic law under the provisional government. The debate over the institutional act quickly centered on what Bunker called the "hard essentials, i.e., composition of armed forces' high command, future of constitutionalist military and amnesty/disarmament procedures." The rebels demanded the document explicitly remove the current armed services chiefs. The loyalist leaders claimed the right to stay in their positions until an elected government took office. Because control of the armed forces meant de facto control of the country, both sides resisted concessions. García Godoy resolved the issue by making qualified promises to each group. He assured the generals they could remain in power at least until he took office, and he guaranteed he would not appoint communists to his administration. The generals had little to lose by accepting García Godoy's offer, as they would retain their posts temporarily and, with their concession, would earn the gratitude of the United States. If García Godoy's presidency failed, as many expected, they would still be on top. To the constitutionalists, García Godoy pledged to allow their leaders to stay in the country. He also promised to reform the military. Caamaño and his associates had few alternatives but to accept the offer. If they remained intransigent, the García Godoy solution might collapse. They believed the majority of Dominicans supported their movement, so they concluded García Godoy or his elected replacement could carry out real reform. With Caamaño's approval on the institutional act in early August, García Godoy had secured the crucial deal. The institutional act now possessed sufficient backing to move forward.[89]

Parallel secret negotiations also took place between Bunker and García Godoy on plans for communists in the Dominican Republic. The White House considered these talks even more significant than those on the institutional act. As a final settlement neared, the president asked Bunker, "Has he agreed to get rid of Communists?" The diplomat responded that García Godoy "Wants our assistance" and "Agrees to controlling Communists." Rather than deporting leftists, which permitted them to receive foreign training, Bunker said García Godoy intended to "Send them to a rocky island off the coast. [He] is well aware of the problem of Communists." The White House had refused to accept such a plan from Guzmán in May, but Bunker reassured Johnson that García Godoy was different. After Bunker vouched for García Godoy, Johnson approved the deal.[90]

Under intense pressure from the United States, on August 30 Imbert resigned. Members of the GNR refused to sign the settlement, yet by stepping aside they permitted the formation of García Godoy's provisional government. Caamaño then publicly approved the plan, resigned as president, and proclaimed victory. The chiefs of the armed forces also put their stamp on the compromise. On September 3, García Godoy took office, formally ending the conflict. The ad hoc committee did not attend García Godoy's inauguration ceremony, according to its report to the OAS, "because it was essentially a Dominican act."[91] Although the ad hoc committee, and particularly Bunker, had influenced the evolution of the García Godoy settlement, Dominicans laid its main foundations. Balaguer drafted the plan that established its structure. Guzmán scripted the critical confrontation within the constitutionalist camp. García Godoy closed the final deals on both military reform, with Dominicans, and control of communists, with Washington. Bunker and the ad hoc committee wielded significant power during the talks, but fundamentally they served more as facilitators than architects of the settlement. The White House had little impact, as the president ceded nearly complete control to Bunker. In the end, Dominicans built the central pillars of the García Godoy regime.

The Dominican character of the compromise made the García Godoy settlement profoundly different from the earlier Guzmán formula. Had the Guzmán talks not stalled, Bosch's PRD would have triumphed through direct negotiations with the White House. Instead, García Godoy's provisional regime marked a victory for Balaguer and, to a lesser extent, for the loyalist armed forces. The military chiefs remained in office under a president who owed his position, in part, to their cooperation. And although García Godoy did not actively assist Balaguer during his tenure, Bosch's failure to carry the rebellion to victory damaged his prospects in the upcoming elections. Ironically, the White House had gained its initial goal in the intervention, the defeat of the rebels, by giving up its control of policy to Bunker and, indirectly, to conservative Dominicans.

Once in office, García Godoy balanced the competing factions while struggling to revive the nation's economy. His efforts to win the goodwill of the moderate rebels worried Washington. Bunker and Bennett came to his defense, establishing a pattern that would endure through the provisional regime. The embassy tried to influence García Godoy's decisions, but the interim president always had the final say. Bennett later recalled García Godoy "was by no means putty in the hands of Bunker." The White House continued to follow Bunker's lead.[92]

The cooperation between García Godoy and the United States was most seriously tested in January, 1966. The provisional president had ordered military leaders from both sides of the civil war to accept posts abroad. Rebel commanders, seeing the political advantage of leaving first, quickly departed.[93] The loyalist chiefs still refused to budge. Santo Domingo became a riot of antimilitary demonstrations. U.S. officials told the loyalist generals "frankly and directly" that they should obey the government's orders. García Godoy even offered a written guarantee that he would make no further changes in the military leadership. The chiefs continued to resist. Dismayed, García Godoy privately told the ad hoc committee he might resign. García Godoy's apparent despair forced Bunker's team to commit to using the Inter-American Peace Force (IAPF), the occupying army of U.S. and OAS troops, to eject the chiefs. Bunker cabled the White House to say the committee planned to take this step to save García Godoy's regime. Typical of the relationship that had developed between Bunker and President Johnson, the ambassador stated his position rather than asking for permission.[94] After several days of delay, the newly replaced loyalist minister of defense agreed to depart if García Godoy promised to maintain the present service chiefs. The president reluctantly and secretly accepted this condition, against the advice of the ad hoc committee. A White House memo noted: "Bunker has doubts about García Godoy's wisdom in allowing the Army and Air Chief to remain, but he says that this is a matter which García Godoy has to decide for himself." García Godoy then decided to meet the intransigent generals halfway. He promoted both remaining loyalist officers to powerless new positions as vice ministers of defense.[95]

Once the military leadership crisis subsided, Dominicans focused on the upcoming presidential election. The major candidates were familiar names: Juan Bosch and Joaquín Balaguer. Bosch had won the last elections and was a hero to many Dominicans, but Bosch's brief presidency had fractured his once dominant party, the PRD. His alleged cowardice during the civil war further damaged him. Balaguer, on the other hand, lacked Bosch's charisma and electoral experience, yet he appealed to conservatives and peasants who had suffered during the recent turmoil. Balaguer's ties to Trujillo even won favor with some Dominicans who looked back fondly on the stability during the dictator's reign.[96]

As the candidates entered the stretch run, the U.S. Embassy considered the race too close to call.[97] Washington's secret polls consistently showed Balaguer in the lead, but the embassy concluded that turnout would be decisive. Election day fell in the middle of the rainy season, and bad weather could prevent many peasants from casting their ballots for Balaguer. Also, with the surveys counting many undecided voters, the embassy expected a large number of people to jump on the bandwagon of whoever seemed to be ahead. Momentum appeared to swing behind Balaguer in mid-May, with Bosch's campaign peaking early. On election eve, a White House memo concluded: "It is still very much a horse-race, with Balaguer having the edge if the weather holds out, the turnout is large, and the silent vote breaks the way we think it is [*sic*]."[98]

Despite Washington's hopes for Balaguer, the United States prepared for victory by either of the leading candidates, indicating some officials considered the election's outcome in doubt. In mid-May, Ambassador Bunker and Assistant Secretary of State Lincoln Gordon privately informed Johnson that Bosch might win. "[Johnson] looked at me with a kind of glare as if he wanted to murder the messenger," Gordon recalled. "But then he nodded very, very slowly and said, in effect . . . 'I wouldn't like it but you're also right we'd have to live with it.'" Documents were drafted on the strategy and timing for approaching the president-elect, with basic policy being identical for Balaguer and Bosch. The administration then waited apprehensively.[99]

Only scattered clouds filled the sky on election day, June 1, allowing voters to flock to the polls. The turnout of 1.3 million, or 75 percent of those eligible, surpassed the total from the previous election, in 1962, by nearly 300,000. Reports by international observers emphasized the orderliness of the balloting. The OAS monitoring team immediately proclaimed the elections fair. A committee of U.S. liberals, led by Bayard Rustin and Norman Thomas, also concluded the polling had been free. Although some of the defeated protested, the PRD's secretary general called the process "honest" and an editorial in the pro-Bosch newsmagazine *Ahora* stated: "'fraud' definitely was not decisive in altering the results of the elections."[100] The final results showed Balaguer victorious with 57 percent of the vote, followed by Bosch with 39 percent. Balaguer's Reformist Party swept twenty-two of the nation's twenty-six provinces, beating the PRD in eighteen that Bosch had won four years earlier. Balaguer won by a landslide.[101]

Bosch admitted in late June he could not prove sufficient fraud had occurred to alter the election's outcome. Allegations of intimidation, however, proved harder to dismiss. The threat of a military coup hung over Bosch's candidacy. Even those who supported his program may have decided to vote against him to avoid further turmoil. Continuing occupation of the country by foreign troops also must have weighed on voters' minds. Again, abandoning Bosch may have seemed the rational choice to those favoring a rapid end to the intervention. Bosch emphasized the Yankee role in his explanation of the election results. But despite these protests, Bosch lost for primarily domestic reasons. Balaguer ran a far stronger campaign than had Bosch's 1962 opponent, winning the support of peasants and Trujillistas who previously had flocked to the PRD. Bosch also had more enemies and a less cohesive party in 1966 than four years earlier. Perhaps most important, Bosch had announced he did not want to be president. His lethargic campaign seemed to reinforce that message. Voters simply may have taken him at his word.[102] Although Balaguer earned his victory, his win lacked moral legitimacy in the eyes of many Dominicans because the entire process had been tarnished by foreign occupation. Doubts about his triumph would linger unless he could demonstrate his commitment to democracy. All elected leaders must prove their fitness for the next round of voting. Balaguer had the added burden of showing he deserved credit for his victory in the past election.[103]

Balaguer's inauguration signaled the beginning of the end of foreign occupation. Both major presidential candidates had called for the immediate withdrawal of the Inter-American Peace Force. Yet privately, Balaguer and Bosch wanted the international brigade to remain to restrain the military. After the election, Balaguer and Bosch quietly asked the IAPF to stay indefinitely, but both men refused to state their preference publicly. The United States, the OAS, and García Godoy, on the other hand, now wanted the troops removed. With neither Balaguer nor Bosch willing to take a stand, the process moved ahead. On June 28, a U.S. contingent departed, beginning "Operation Well Done."[104]

The removal of international troops did not mark the end of foreign intervention. Many nations remained active in Dominican affairs, but none rivaled the continuing U.S. presence. The embassy in Santo Domingo, already the largest in the region, added economic development staff. U.S. diplomats offered Balaguer additional aid of $25 million for 1966 and advised how $40 million in outstanding credits could be used more efficiently. After repeated demands by the embassy, in August the White House also granted the Dominican Republic permission to fill the year's U.S. sugar quota shortfalls, worth about $9.5 million. Agricultural interests throughout the Americas complained, but Johnson gave Balaguer this gift to demonstrate his stake in the regime's success. The two-month delay in approving the sugar deal, however, illustrated how Santo Domingo had slipped as a U.S. priority. Ambassador-designate John Hugh Crimmins already complained of "business as usual" attitudes at the State Department. With the occupation coming to a close and with major problems elsewhere, Washington had resumed its traditional inattention to Dominican affairs.[105]

Still, Washington did not totally disengage. The Johnson administration quietly attempted to bolster moderates in the Dominican Republic. After working to prevent the PRD from gaining power, Washington decided to help the party's conservative wing regain stature. The embassy also encouraged Balaguer to cultivate rather than disregard the opposition and to rebuild his own party's organization. Most of all, the White House wanted Balaguer to keep the lid on the incipient turmoil in his country. Administration estimates consistently stressed the uncertainty of Balaguer's presidency. A September, 1966, analysis concluded, "the chances are somewhat better than even that he will survive in office" over the next six months. The savvy Dominican understood his value to Washington, and milked the embassy for aid while playing to nationalists by rejecting Yankee demands. Similarly, the Johnson administration considered the Dominican armed forces the last bastion against communism, so military funding kept up even as the embassy admitted that "we are essentially limited to instruction, example and moral suasion" to influence the generals. Ironically, the United States supported the two primary rivals for power in Santo Domingo, in part because the Dominicans manipulated Washington and in part because top foreign policy makers neglected the Dominican Republic after mid-1966. Soon assistance began to be scaled back and the size of the embassy shrunk, but Dominican rulers could do as they pleased without fear that the aid would stop altogether.[106]

As Washington looked elsewhere, politics polarized in the Dominican Republic, and Balaguer turned farther to the right. To stay in power the president needed to prevent an alliance between the armed forces and conservative plotters. Paramilitary violence against the left continued, spearheaded by a group called *"la banda"* that had close ties to the police. Through such organizations the armed forces remained the most powerful force in the country.[107] Balaguer shuffled military chiefs to prevent any officer from gaining dominance, but he permitted the armed forces to have nearly everything it sought. In exchange for these favors, the military allowed Balaguer to be president. Balaguer provided a stable "democratic" front for relations with Washington. By emphasizing his ties to the United States and by preventing the emergence of any single rival for power, Balaguer guaranteed the military needed him as much as he needed them. The symbiotic arrangement between the National Palace and the armed forces kept up a façade of legitimacy that smoothed relations with the United States, but only the most rudimentary mechanics of democracy continued to operate. In the elections of 1970 and 1974, Balaguer beat token opposition while many Dominicans lived in fear of *la banda*. Ironically, the 1966 election, although conducted under occupation, was procedurally more free than the two that followed. Had the White House worked conscientiously to reinforce the positive trends in Dominican affairs after 1966, perhaps the intervention could have had more positive, lasting results.[108]

The Johnson administration paid a relatively low price for the intervention. Twenty-seven U.S. soldiers died in combat. Washington supplied perhaps $150 million more in assistance to Santo Domingo than it would have otherwise. The Pentagon's operational costs added another $75 million. These amounts paled in comparison with expenses in Vietnam. The larger battle in Southeast

Asia also overshadowed the intervention's political impact. Popular opinion initially supported the occupation, then most people forgot about it. The crisis catalyzed a division within the Democratic Party and widened the credibility gap, but again only the fighting in Vietnam magnified these into substantial liabilities. Most of the political cost for the administration resulted from its own bungling statements, not from the details of the intervention. The crisis could have taxed the White House substantially less had Johnson managed his public relations policy more effectively.[109]

The intervention achieved Johnson's main goal: a relatively democratic transition to stable, pro-Washington government in Santo Domingo. Johnson was successful largely because he held to a consistent and broadly defined policy throughout the intervention. Although he worried about the political implications of his actions, he never permitted domestic concerns to determine his policy. Instead, the president allowed others, both administration officials and Dominicans, the freedom to shape the course of events within the parameters established by the White House. Johnson's willingness to let others control the details of Dominican affairs led to his ultimate success in Santo Domingo.

NOTES

1. The quotation can be seen in U.S. Army MP37 Staff Film Report 66-19A, April, 1966, Lyndon Baines Johnson Presidential Library, Austin. [Unless otherwise noted, all documents cited below are from the LBJ Library.]
2. Robert J. McMahon makes a similar argument for South Asia in *The Cold War on the Periphery* (New York: Columbia University Press, 1994).
3. Quoted in Brian VanDeMark, *Into the Quagmire* (New York: Oxford University Press, 1991), p. 213.
4. H. W. Brands, *The Wages of Globalism* (New York: Oxford University Press, 1995), p. 46; Joseph S. Tulchin, "The Promise of Progress," pp. 219–24, in *Lyndon Johnson Confronts the World* (New York: Cambridge University Press, 1994), edited by Warren I. Cohen and Nancy Bernkopf Tucker; William O. Walker III, "Mixing the Sweet with the Sour," pp. 59–63, in *The Diplomacy of the Crucial Decade* (New York: Columbia University Press, 1994), edited by Diane B. Kunz.
5. Special National Intelligence Estimate [hereafter SNIE] 86.2-64, Jan. 17/64, 1, 5–7, "Dominican Republic," [hereafter DR] box 9, National Intelligence Estimates, National Security File [hereafter NSF]; Opportunities for Communist Exploitation in Latin America [hereafter LA], Department of State [hereafter DOS] Bureau of Intelligence and Research, Apr. 7, 1964, 4–6, "Vol. 1," box 1, Country File, National Security File [hereafter CF]. See also: Outline Guide to Communist Activities in LA, DOS Director of Intelligence and Research, Oct. 20, 1964, "Vol. 2," box 1, CF.
6. For a detailed account of these events, see the author's 1995 Ph.D. dissertation, "The 1965–1966 United States Intervention in the Dominican Republic" (University of Texas at Austin).

7. The three parties were: the (Castroist) Fourteenth of June Action Group, or 1J4; the (Moscow-oriented) Popular Socialist Party, or PSP; and the (Maoist) Dominican People's Movement, the MPD.

8. TDCS-314/05403-65, TDCS-314/05415-65, Apr. 25, 1965, "CIA Reports," box 5, National Security Country Histories, National Security File [hereafter NSCH]; "Presence in the National Palace," CIA Cable, Apr. 25, 1965, "Vol. 1," box 38, CF, NSF. For the strongest statement of the CIA's case, see: CIA Memo 1120, 1965, May 7, 1965, 5–8, "Communism in the DR," box 2 + 3, Files of Gordon Chase, National Security File [hereafter FGC]. For a critique of the CIA case, see: John Prados, *Keepers of the Keys* (New York: William Morrow Publishers, 1991), p. 143. PSP leaders later admitted to have been "unprepared for the uprising"; J. I. Quello and N. Isa Conde, "Revolutionary struggle in the Dominican Republic and its lessons," *World Marxist Review* (December, 1965), p. 97.

9. DOS Telegram [hereafter DEPTEL (unless otherwise noted, from DOS to Embassy in SD)] 633, Apr. 25, 1965 (1255), "Vol. 1," box 38, CF; Cole Blaiser, *The Hovering Giant* rev. ed. (Pittsburgh: University of Pittsburgh Press, 1985), pp. 248–49; Matthew James Burns III, "Managing Regional Crises," (Master of Public Affairs Report, University of Texas at Austin, 1993), pp. 106, 121, 146–47; Theodore Draper, "The Dominican Intervention Reconsidered," *Political Science Quarterly* 86 (March, 1971): 23; Abraham Lowenthal, *Dominican Intervention* (New York: Harvard University Press, 1970), pp. 70–73; Howard J. Wiarda, *Dictatorship, Development and Disintegration* (Ann Arbor: Xerox University Microfilms, 1975), p. 893. See also: Piero Gleijeses, *Dominican Crisis* (Baltimore: Johns Hopkins University Press, 1978), p. 383, n. 14; notes on telephone conversation with Connett, Apr. 25, 1965 (0945), State Operations Center Log, "Chronology [Tabs 1–31]," box 8, NSCH.

10. Embassy Telegram [hereafter EMBTEL (unless otherwise noted, from SD to DOS)] 1085, Apr. 26, 1965 (1349), and EMBTEL 1094, Apr. 26, 1965 (2027), "Incoming State Cables," box 4, NSCH; "Foe of Revolution," *New York Times,* Apr. 30, 1965, p. 14; Gleijeses, *Dominican Crisis,* pp. 223–24.

11. Articles by Dubois appear in the *Chicago Tribune* daily during this period: "Loyal Forces Tell Winning Domingo Fight," Apr. 28, 1965, p. 2; "Planes Strike at Strongholds of Rebels," Apr. 29, 1965, pp. 1–2; "Tells Role in Dominican Revolt," Apr. 30, 1965, pp. 1, 3; "Dubois Again Man on Scene for Tribune," Apr. 30, 1965, p. 2. See also: Brigette Lebens Nacos, *The Press, Presidents, and Crises* (New York: Columbia University Press, 1990), p. 58; Wiarda, *Dictatorship,* pp. 915–16. Ambassador Bennett, in July 16, 1965, testimony, cited Dubois and Hal Hendricks (of Scripps-Howard) as examples of U.S. journalists with strong loyalist sympathies; *Executive Sessions of the Senate Foreign Relations Committee Together with Joint Sessions with the Senate Armed Services Committee (Historical Series)* 17, 1965 [hereafter SFRC'65], p. 866.

12. EMBTEL 1155, Apr. 28, 1965 (1952), and EMBTEL 1167, Apr. 29, 1965 (0354), "Incoming State Cables," box 4, NSCH; Section E, Chapter 6, box 2, Administrative History of the Department of State, Volume I.

13. Memo of chat with Johnson, Apr. 29, 1965, p. 1, and memo on backgrounder luncheon with Moyers, May 10, 1965, 4–6, box 1, Arthur Krock Papers, Seeley G. Mudd Library, Princeton University; Chronology of Dominican Crisis, Apr. 28, 1965 (1645–1801), 12, "Chronology [Tabs 1–31]," box 8, NSCH; Dominican Crisis: Presidential Decisions, n.d., 2, "Bowdler to Rostow Memo," box 8, NSCH;

memo, Chase to Roberts, July 3, 1965, 2, and handwritten memo, [Mann] to Chase, n.d., 3–5, "Vol. 9, 7, 1965," box 42, CF; David C. Humphrey, "NSC Meetings during the Johnson Presidency," *Diplomatic History* 18 (Winter, 1994): 35, 38.

14. Minutes: Meeting with congressional leadership, Apr. 28, 1965 (1930), "Important Documents," box 4, FGC; memo on chat with Johnson, Apr. 29, 1965, 1, 3, box 1, Krock Papers. See also: Dean Rusk, oral history, 17–18; A. Krock, "The Larger Stake in Santo Domingo," *New York Times,* May 2, 1965, p. E11.

15. *Public Papers of the President: Lyndon Baines Johnson, 1965* [hereafter *PPP: LBJ*], I, 461; memo of chat with Johnson, Apr. 29, 1965, 1, box 1, Krock Papers; teleconference, Johnson and Ball, Apr. 29, 1965 (1425), "DR," box 3, George W. Ball Papers [hereafter GWBP]. For a news story based in part on administration leaks, see: J. W. Finney, "Talks Tomorrow," *New York Times,* Apr. 30, 1965, p. 1. See also: Lowenthal, *Dominican Intervention,* 104–106.

16. Telecon, president and Ball, Apr. 29, 1965 (1425), "DR," box 3, GWBP. For a journalist's comment on leaks from Ball and Mann, see: memo of chat with Johnson, Apr. 29, 1965, 1, box 1, Krock Papers.

17. Memo of chat with Johnson, Apr. 29, 1965, 1–2, box 1, Krock Papers.

18. EMBTEL 1176, Apr. 29, 1965 (1351), "Incoming State Cables"; EMBTEL 1187, Apr. 29, 1965 (1713), "Incoming State Cables"; box 4, NSCH. See also: EMBTEL 1173, Apr. 29, 1965 (1057), and EMBTEL 1178, Apr. 29, 1965 (1433), "Incoming State Cables," box 4, NSCH; "Plans of anti-rebel troops," CIA Intelligence Info Cable, Apr. 29, 1965, "Vol. 1," box 38, CF; TDCSDB-315/01413-65, 2, "CIA Reports," box 5, NSCH.

19. EMBTEL 1173, Apr. 29, 1965 (1057), and EMBTEL 1178, Apr. 29, 1965 (1433), "Incoming State Cables," box 4, NSCH; EMBTEL 1190, Apr. 29, 1965 (2304), "Incoming State Cables," box 4, NSCH; TDCSDB-315/01413-65, Apr. 29, 1965, and TDCS-314/05783-65, Apr. 30, 1965, "CIA Reports," box 5, NSCH; Gleijeses, *Dominican Crisis,* pp. 256–58. See also: "Opinions of Colonel Miguel Angel Hernando Ramirez," CIA Intelligence Information Cable," Apr. 28, 1965, "Vol. 1" box 38, CF; transcript, second telephone interview between Juan Ortiz Jiménez of Radio El Mundo, San Juan, Puerto Rico, and Colonel Francisco Caamaño, Apr. 29, 1965 (0745), "Vol. 3," box 39, CF; José A. Moreno, *Barrios in Arms* (Pittsburgh: University of Pittsburgh Press, 1970), pp. 34, 154–55.

20. Teleconference, President and Ball, Apr. 29, 1965 (1425), "DR," box 3, GWBP; EMBTEL 1187, Apr. 29, 1965 (1713), "Incoming State Cables," box 4, NSCH.

21. EMBTEL 1187, Apr. 29, 1965 (1713), "Incoming State Cables," box 4, NSCH. See also: EMBTEL 1178, Apr. 29, 1965 (1433), "Incoming State Cables," box 4, NSCH; Department of Defense Telegram [hereafter DODTEL (unless otherwise noted, from SD to Department of Defense)] Apr. 30, 1965 (0247), "Department of Defense [hereafter DOD] Messages," box 6, NSCH.

22. DODTEL, Apr. 29, 1965 (2140), and DODTEL, Apr. 29, 1965 (2315), "DOD Messages," box 6, NSCH; DODTEL, n.d. [Apr. 30, 1965], "DOD Messages," box 6, NSCH; DEPTEL 689, Apr. 29, 1965 (2311) and DODTEL, Apr. 30, 1965 (0618), "Vol. 1," box 38, CF; DODTEL, Apr. 30, 1965 (0739), "Chron. [Tabs 142–169]," box 9, NSCH; chronology, n.d., pp. 16–18, "Chronology [Tabs 111–41]," box 9, NSCH. See also: Major Lawrence M. Greenberg, *United States Army Unilateral and Coalition Operations in the 1965 Dominican Republic Intervention* (Washington, D.C.: U.S. Army Center for Military History, 1987), pp. 36–40; General Bruce Palmer, *Intervention in the Caribbean* (Lexington: University Press

of Kentucky, 1989), pp. 30–36; Herbert J. Schoonmaker, *Military Crisis Management* (New York: Greenwood Press, 1990), pp. 42, 47 (note 28), pp. 68–69; Lawrence A. Yates, *Power Pack* (Fort Leavenworth: Combat Studies Institute, 1988), pp. 55–73.

23. Meeting in Cabinet Room, Apr. 30, 1965 (0830), 11 and 14, "Meeting Notes (Handwritten)," box 13, Office Files of the President; transcripts from dictated notes, X3, 3–5, June 1, 1965, folder 2, box 273, Book File, John Bartlow Martin Papers, Library of Congress Manuscripts Division [hereafter JBMP]. Valenti repeated his ideas in an April 30 memo to the president in "ND 19/CO 62," box 201, White House Central File. See also: memo on backgrounder luncheon with Moyers, May 10, 1965, 6, box 1, Krock Papers; Philip Geyelin, *Lyndon B. Johnson* (New York: Frederick B. Praeger, 1966), p. 254. Johnson repeated his complaints of being in a bind later: congressional briefing, May 2, 1965 (1845), p. 37, "Meeting Notes (Handwritten)," box 13, Office Files of the President File.

24. Transcripts from dictated notes, X3, 3–5, June 1, 1965, folder 2, box 273, Book File, JBMP; meeting in Cabinet Room, Apr. 30, 1965 (0830), "Meeting Notes (Handwritten)," box 13, Office Files of the President. See also: John B. Martin, oral history, 23–27.

25. Transcripts from dictated notes, X1, 1–2, and X4, 1–2, 4, June 1, 1965, folder 2, box 273, Book File, JBMP; teleconference, Martin and Ball, Apr. 30, 1965 (1145), "DR," box 3, GWBP; John B. Martin, oral history, 21–22, 24–25, 27; memo on backgrounder luncheon with Moyers, May 10, 1965, 6, box 1, Krock Papers; Rusk's May 21, 1965, testimony in *SFRC'65*, p. 595; John Bartlow Martin, *Overtaken by Events* (Garden City, N.J.: Doubleday, 1966), p. 640; John B. Martin, "Struggle To Bring Together Two Sides Torn by Killing," *Life*, May 18, 1965, p. 28.

26. Transcripts from dictated notes, X3, 5–6, June 1, 1965, folder 2, box 273, Book File, JBMP; meeting in Cabinet Room, Apr. 30, 1965 (0830), 9, "Meeting Notes (Handwritten)," box 13, Office Files of the President. See also: Chronology of Contacts with Latin Americans, n.d., Overseas Contacts with Latin Americans, n.d., and Summary of Circulars sent as guidance to field posts, n.d., "Vol. 4," box 39, CF. V. Shiv Kumar, *U.S. Interventionism in Latin America* (New York: Advent Books, 1987), pp. 31–32.

27. DEPTEL 695, Apr. 30, 1965 (1135), "Outgoing State Cables," box 5, NSCH; DODTEL, Apr. 30, 1965 (0618), "Vol. 1," box 38, CF; list of assignments, May 1, 1965, 3–4, "Background Docs.," box 7, NSCH; chronology, n.d., 18, "Chronology [Tabs 111–141]," box 9, NSCH; Lowenthal, *Dominican Intervention,* pp. 118–20.

28. Memo, Read for Bundy, Apr. 30, 1965, "Vol. 2," box 38, CF; note, mf to the President, Apr. 30, 1965 (1120), box 16, Appointment File (Diary Backup); TDCS-314/05783, Apr. 30, 1965, "CIA Reports," box 5, NSCH. See also the teleconferences between Mann and Ball, Apr. 30, 1965 (1320), Fortas and Ball, Apr. 30, 1965 (1330), and McNamara and Ball, Apr. 30, 1965 (1340), in "DR," box 3, GWBP; Moreno, *Barrios in Arms,* p. 33; Juan Bosch, "A Tale of Two Nations," *The New Leader,* June 21, 1965, pp. 3–4.

29. DEPTEL 698, Apr. 30, 1965 (1218), DEPTEL 704, Apr. 30, 1965 (1342), and EMBTEL 1214, Apr. 30, 1965 (2052), "Vol. 1," box 38, CF.

30. Memo, Rowan to Johnson, May 1, 1965, "Vol. 3," box 39, CF.

31. Memo, Goodwin to Johnson, Apr. 29, 1965, "Valenti File Re: DR," box 8, Name File, NSF; memo, Mansfield to Johnson, Apr. 30, 1965, "Vol. 2," box 38, CF; memo, Moyers to Johnson, n.d. [probably Apr. 29, 1965], "Vol. 3," box 39, CF;

memo, Valenti to Johnson, Apr. 30, 1965, "ND 19/CO 62," box 201, White House Central Files [hereafter WHCF]; memo on backgrounder luncheon with Moyers, May 10, 1965, 6, box 1, Arthur Krock Papers.

32. OCI No. 1208, 1965, Apr. 29, 1965, "Communism in the DR [Folder 1]," box 2+3, FGC; memo: Communist Participation in the Current Dominican Rebellion, Apr. 30, 1965, "Communist Participation," box 49, CF; Mann for the record, July 12, 1965, "Background Documents," box 7, NSCH. On Caamaño, see: EMBTEL 1216, Apr. 30, 1965 (2236), "Vol. 1," box 38, CF. For an example of embassy bias in cables, see: EMBTEL 1191, Apr. 29, 1965 (2355), "Incoming State Cables," box 4, NSCH. See also: Addenda Concerning Communist Participation, n.d. [May 1, 1965], "Communist Participation," box 49, CF; Summary of CIA Publications, May 12, 1965, "CIA's Role," box 52, CF; Communist Propaganda Activities and Communist Propaganda , n.d., "Vol. 1," box 290, CF; OCI No. 1116, 1965 and Annex I, n.d., "Communism in the DR," box 2+3, FGC; weekly Cuban summary, May 5, 1965, 1–2, "Vol. 2," box 36, CF; EMBTEL 1429, May 7, 1965 (0421), "Incoming State Cables," box 4, NSCH. Many CIA cables for this period are in "CIA Reports," box 5, NSCH, and "Vol. 1," box 38, CF. For the DOS position, see Mann's May 3, 1965, and Rusk's May 21, 1965, testimony in *SFRC'65,* pp. 482–517, 574–96. For U.S. military intelligence on the rebels, see: DODTEL, May 2, 1965 (0437), and DODTEL, May 3, 1965 (1025), "DOD Messages," box 6, NSCH. On divisions among LA communists in April, 1965, see: memo: Chinese Communist Activities in LA, CIA Directorate of Intelligence, Apr. 30, 1965, "Vol. 3," box 2, CF. See also: Draper, *Dominican Revolt,* pp. 138–43; Prados, *Keepers of the Keys,* pp. 142–43. For an analysis of two rebel "commando" units, see: Moreno, *Barrios in Arms,* pp. 46–64.

33. *PPP: LBJ,* Apr. 30, 1965, pp. 465–66; Apr. 30, 1965 (1940–2004), box 3, Daily Diary. See also: memo, Valenti to Johnson, Apr. 30, 1965, "President Johnson April 1965 (Notes, instructions, doodles)," box 7, Handwriting File; memo on backgrounder luncheon with Moyers, May 10, 1965, 4–5, box 1, Krock Papers.

34. Memo, Rowan to Johnson, May 1, 1965, "Vol. 3," box 39, CF; memo, Bundy to Johnson, May 1, 1965, "Vol. 10," Memos to the President, National Security File [hereafter MTP]; EMBTEL 1274, May 2, 1965 (1707), "Vol. 2," box 38, CF. See also: May 3, 1965, comments by Senators Wayne Morse and Frank Church in *SFRC'65,* pp. 485–87, 492–95, 512–13, 516–18; Nacos, *Press, Presidents, and Crises,* pp. 60–63. For an example of the unfavorable reaction to the leaks, see: Dan Kurzman, *Santo Domingo* (New York: G. P. Putnam's Sons, 1965), pp. 21, 194–98. For examples of information leaked, see: "Dominican Civil War," *Wall Street Journal,* Apr. 30, 1965, p. 2,; J. Dubois, "Shaky Truce Is Not Respected," *Chicago Tribune,* May 3, 1965, p. 2; T. Szulc, "2,500 Men Fly In," *New York Times,* Apr. 30, 1965, p. 1.

35. *PPP: LBJ,* May 2, 1965, pp. 469–74. For a copy of Johnson's May 2, 1965, speech, including his repetitions, see: Text of Johnson's Address, May 3, 1965, "Footnoted Text of President Johnson's Speech 5/2, 1965 [Folder 1]," box 4, FGC. See also: Paul K. Conkin, *Big Daddy from the Pedernales* (Boston: Twayne, 1986), p. 199; Robert Dallek, *American Style of Foreign Policy* (New York: Oxford University Press, 1983), p. 242; Geyelin, *Lyndon B. Johnson,* pp. 19, 237; Hugh Sidey, *A Very Personal Presidency* (New York: Atheneum, 1968), pp. 177–79; Kathleen J. Turner, *Lyndon Johnson's Dual War* (Chicago: University of Chicago Press, 1985), p. 135.

36. *PPP: LBJ,* May 3, 1965, p. 481; Draper, *Dominican Revolt,* p. 1.
37. DEPTEL 753, May 2, 1965 (1949), EMBTEL 1224, May 1, 1965 (0542), EMBTEL 1233, May 1, 1965 (1421), EMBTEL 1235, May 1, 1965 (1332), and EMBTEL 1245, May 1, 1965 (2017), "Vol. 2," box 38, CF; draft cable, "Martin's third report [not sent]," n.d., folder 5, box 272, Book File, JBMP; transcript of dictated notes, X8, 2, June 1, 1965, folder 2, box 273, Book File, JBMP. Martin's May 4, 1965, report on the rebel leadership used Imbert as its primary source, see: EMBTEL 1335, May 4, 1965 (0322), "Incoming State Cables," box 4, NSCH.
38. EMBTEL 1284, May 2, 1965 (2244), DEPTEL 721, May 1, 1965 (1657), and EMBTEL 1281, May 3, 1965 (0154), 1, "Vol. 2," box 38, CF; DEPTEL 756, May 2, 1965 (2219), "Outgoing State Cables," box 5, NSCH; list of assignments, May 1, 1965, 4–5, and check list, May 2, 1965, 2–3, "Background Documents," box 7, NSCH; DODTEL, May 1, 1965 (2010), "DOD Messages," box 6, NSCH. For the CIA report on Balaguer, see: TDCSDB-315/01506-65, May 4, 1965, "CIA Reports," box 5, NSCH.
39. Sitrep, May 1, 1965 (2300), 1, "Task Force Sitreps," box 49, CF; check list, May 2, 1965, 4, and check list #3, May 3, 1965, 4–5, "Background Documents," box 7, NSCH; DODTEL, May 2, 1965 (0314), "DOD Messages," box 6, NSCH; DODTEL, May 2, 1965 (0641), 1, "Chronology [Tabs 170–209]," box 9, NSCH; DEPTEL 742, May 2, 1965 (1912), EMBTEL 1267, May 2, 1965 (1851), EMBTEL 1269, May 2, 1965 (2124), EMBTEL 1283, May 2, 1965 (2111), EMBTEL 1284, May 2, 1965 (2244), and EMBTEL 1315, May 3, 1965 (1833), "Vol. 2," box 38, CF; memo, Bundy to Johnson, May 2, 1965 (1830), "Vol. 10," box 3, MTP; EMBTEL 1301, May 3, 1965 (1125), "Vol. 1, Memos and misc.," box 38, CF; USIA cable, Rowan to SD, May 3, 1965 (1152), "Vol. 3," box 38, CF. See also: EMBTEL 1253, May 2, 1965 (0146), "Vol. 2," box 38, CF; Greenberg, *U.S. Army,* pp. 44–47; Palmer, *Intervention in the Caribbean,* pp. 43, 47–48, 51; Yates, *Power Pack,* pp. 87–88, 94–96. See also Mann's May 3, 1965, testimony in *SFRC'65,* 482. For examples of minor military moves that could have been viewed as provocative by the rebels, see: EMBTEL 1284, May 2, 1965 (2244), 3, "Vol. 2," box 38, CF, and CIA Report No. 71, n.d. [May 2, 1965], "Vol. 10," box 3, MTP. For U.S. propaganda efforts, see: USIA, 24th Report to Congress, Jan. 1–June 30, 1965, pp. 16–19, "Doc. #59 89/2 1/26, 1966," box 7, SEN89A-F9, Communications and Reports, Foreign Relations Committee, National Archives; memo, Rowan to Johnson, May 1, 1965, "CO 62," box 8, Confidential File; memo, Rowan to Johnson, May 1 and 4, 1965, "ND 19/CO 62," box 70, Confidential File; memo, Rowan to Johnson, May 1 and 3, 1965, "Vol. 3," box 39, CF; memo, Rowan to Johnson, May 2, 1965, "Valenti File Re: DR," box 8, Name File, NSF; EMBTEL 1274, May 2, 1965 (1707), and EMBTEL 1300, May 3, 1965 (1604), "Vol. 2," box 38, CF. For sociological details on the barrios effected by the LOC, see: Moreno, *Barrios in Arms,* pp. 92–95.
40. EMBTEL 1253, May 2, 1965 (0146), and EMBTEL 1281, May 3, 1965 (0154), "Vol. 2," box 38, CF; CIA Report No. 71, n.d. [May 2, 1965], 2, "Vol. 10," box 3, MTP; TDCS-314/05983-65, May 3, 1965, "CIA Reports," box 5, NSCH; DODTEL, May 3, 1965 (1025), May 3, 1965 (1853), May 4, 1965 (0206), May 4, 1965 (2300), "DOD Messages," box 6, NSCH; EMBTEL 1335, May 4, 1965 (0322), "Incoming State Cables," box 4, NSCH; Gleijeses, *Dominican Crisis,* p. 259; Moreno, *Barrios in Arms,* pp. 40–41, 154–55. See also: EMBTEL 1321, May 3, 1965 (2051), "Vol. 2," box 38, CF.

41. Martin eagerly backed Imbert's scheme, although the former ambassador previously had not trusted the general. See: Notes from personal file, Dec. 30, 1965, 11, folder 2, and ambassador's journal, Feb. 23, 1963, 3, folder 3, box 44, Ambassador File, JBMP; Martin, *Overtaken by Events,* p. 681; transcripts of dictated notes, XI, 5, June 1, 1965, folder 2, box 273, Book File, JBMP. See also: memo for the files, Nov. 4, 1962, 1, 4–6, 14, and ambassador's journal, Nov. 25, 1962, 6, folder 2, box 44, Ambassador File, JBMP.

42. EMBTEL 1417, May 7, 1965 (0005), EMBTEL 1437, May 7, 1965 (1104), EMBTEL 1497, May 8, 1965 (2247), EMBTEL 1503, May 8, 1965 (2306), EMBTEL 1505, May 9, 1965 (0000), and EMBTEL 1506, May 9, 1965 (0037), "Vol. 3," box 38, CF; memo: Summary of Present Economic Situation, May 9, 1965, EMBTEL 1615, May 12, 1965 (0036), DEPTEL 992, May 12, 1965 (1920), and EMBTEL 1673, May 13, 1965 (1748), "Vol. 4," box 39, CF. See also: memo, Read to Bundy, May 10, 1965, "Vol. 4," box 39, CF; sitrep, May 7, 1965 (0500), 2–3, sitrep, May 9, 1965 (0500), 2–3, sitrep, May 10, 1965 (0500), 1, sitrep, May 12, 1965 (0500), 2–3, and sitrep, May 13, 1965 (0500), 2, "Task Force Sitreps," box 49, CF.

43. Sitrep, May 8, 1965 (0500), 1, and sitrep, May 9, 1965 (0500 and 1900), "Task Force Sitreps," box 49, CF; EMBTEL 1523, May 9, 1965 (1343), DEPTEL 919, May 9, 1965 (1426), EMBTEL 1544, May 9, 1965 (2224), EMBTEL 1551, May 9, 1965 (2123), DEPTEL 934, May 10, 1965 (1600), EMBTEL 1575, May 10, 1965 (1856), EMBTEL 1580, May 10, 1965 (2033), DEPTEL 946, May 10, 1965 (2206), and EMBTEL 1599, May 11, 1965 (1450), "Vol. 3," box 38, CF; DODTEL, May 9, 1965 (0254), 2, DODTEL, May 10, 1965 (0635), and DODTEL, May 13, 1965 (0134), "DOD Messages," box 6, NSCH; memo, Rowan to Johnson, May 9, 1965 (1500), and memo, Rowan to Johnson, May 11, 1965 (1700), "ND 19/CO 62," box 70, Confidential File; EMBTEL 1688, May 14, 1965 (0105), "Vol. 4," box 39, CF; Gleijeses, *Dominican Crisis,* p. 260; Palmer, *Intervention in the Caribbean,* p. 55; Yates, *Power Pack,* pp. 129–40.

44. EMBTEL 1516, May 9, 1965 (1035), EMBTEL 1543, May 9, 1965 (2133), EMBTEL 1576, May 10, 1965 (1954), EMBTEL 1580, May 10, 1965 (2033), EMBTEL 1590, May 11, 1965 (0149), EMBTEL 1593, May 11, 1965 (0823), EMBTEL 1606, May 11, 1965 (2125), EMBTEL 1612, May 11, 1965 (2209), and EMBTEL 1615, May 12, 1965 (0036), "Vol. 3," box 38, CF; sitrep, May 9, 1965 (1900), sitrep, May 10, 1965 (0500), and sitrep, May 11, 1965 (1200), "Task Force Sitreps," box 49, CF; DODTEL, May 10, 1965 (0244), DODTEL May 10, 1965 (0635), and DODTEL, May 13, 1965 (0525), "DOD Messages," box 6, NSCH. See also: J. Dubois, "Imbert Calls Corruption a Major Enemy," *Chicago Tribune,* May 8, 1965, p. 3.

45. EMBTEL 1440, May 7, 1965 (1225), EMBTEL 1460, May 7, 1965 (2318), EMBTEL 1477, May 8, 1965 (1023), EMBTEL 1508, May 9, 1965 (0214), EMBTEL 1515, May 9, 1965 (0813), EMBTEL 1576, May 10, 1965 (1954), EMBTEL 1593, May 11, 1965 (0823), and EMBTEL 1606, May 11, 1965 (2125), and EMBTEL 1612, May 11, 1965 (2209) "Vol. 3," box 38, CF; EMBTEL 1460, May 7, 1965 (2318), "Incoming State Cables," box 4, NSCH; DODTEL, May 10, 1965 (0635), and DODTEL, May 10, 1965 (0801), "DOD Messages," box 6, NSCH; sitrep, May 10, 1965 (0500), sitrep, May 11, 1965 (0500), 1, "Task Force Sitreps," box 49, CF.

46. Ironically, U.S. troops guarding the embassy apparently shot down one of the planes when it flew too close to their positions.

47. EMBTEL 1674, May 13, 1965 (1831), EMBTEL 1690, May 14, 1965 (015-), and EMBTEL 1697, May 14, 1965 (0817), "Vol. 4," box 39, CF; sitrep, May 14, 1965

(0500), and sitrep, May 14, 1965 (1600), "Task Force Sitreps," box 49, CF; Department of State Circular Telegram [hereafter DEPCIRCTEL] 2224, May 14, 1965 (1802), 1, "Chronology [Tabs 274–299]," box 11, NSCH; DODTEL, May 14, 1965 (2304), 2, "DOD Messages," box 6, NSCH. See also: EMBTEL, American Embassy Lisbon to White House, Nov. 5, 1968 (2050), "Bowdler to Rostow Memo," box 8, NSCH; Martin, *Overtaken by Events;* Szulc, *Dominican Diary,* p. 199; Yates, *Power Pack,* p. 114.

48. DODTEL, May 14, 1965 (2304), 1, "DOD Messages," box 6, NSCH. See also: DODTEL, May 14, 1965 (1800), "DOD Messages," box 6, NSCH; Gleijeses, *Dominican Crisis,* p. 264; Greenberg, *U.S. Army,* pp. 50–51; Slater, *Intervention and Negotiation,* p. 56; Yates, *Power Pack,* pp. 116, 129–30, 132.

49. To keep the talks secret, Fortas used the alias "C. J. Davidson." Kalman, *Abe Fortas,* pp. 237–38; Murphy, *Fortas,* pp. 150–51.

50. Handwritten memo [n.d.] with attachment [dated May 20, 1965], "Dictated by Mr. Davidson," May 13, 1965, and "The President of the United States," May 13, 1965 (1620), "Vol. 10," box 3, MTP; handwritten notes, Bundy, May 14, 1965 (1750), 1, "Chronology [Tabs 274–299]," box 11, NSCH; Fortas, oral history, 25–30. Kalman, *Abe Fortas,* pp. 238–39, 453 n. 66. See also: H. Bigart, "U.S. and Bosch: A Middleman's Story," *New York Times,* May 6, 1965, pp. 1, 15; Vance, oral history, 26–27.

51. Handwritten notes, Bundy, May 14, 1965 (1730, 2020 and 2200), "Chronology [Tabs 274–299]," box 11, NSCH; Valenti notes of lunch meeting, May 21, 1965 (1445), 22, "Meeting Notes (Handwritten)," box 13, Office Files of the President File; W. Tapley Bennett telephone interview by author, June 16, 1993; Fortas, oral history, 30; Kalman, *Abe Fortas,* p. 239; Murphy, *Fortas,* pp. 153–55; Charles Roberts, *L.B.J.'s Inner Circle* (New York: Delacorte Press, 1965), p. 79. See also: M. Frankel, "Bundy is Unable to Appear," *New York Times,* May 16, 1965, p. 1; Prados, *Keepers of the Keys,* p. 140; Rusk, oral history, 24; Harry Shlaudeman telephone interview by author, June 7, 1993. Caamaño told a CBS interviewer on May 14 that he would prefer to negotiate with a special U.S. envoy, not Bennett: *Face the Nation,* 1965, Vol. 8, 121–22.

52. Cable, Mann and Vaughn to White House, May 16, 1965 (0749), 2, and EMBTEL 1756, May 17, 1965 (1530), 1–3, "Bundy Mission," box 2, FGC; *SFRC'65,* 1066; Shlaudeman interview; Vance, oral history, 23–24; Thomas C. Mann, *Be There Yesterday* (unpublished manuscript, 1980), excerpts, p. 2. See also: Martin, *Overtaken by Events,* p. 696. On May 21 Rusk told an executive session hearing that Imbert "is not a man that ought to run that country"; *SFRC'65,* 592.

53. Handwritten notes, Bundy, May 17, 1965, May 17, 1965, and n.d. [May 17, 1965], and document 109, n.d., 2, "Davidson," box 51, CF; teleconferences, Ball and Davidson, May 17, 1965 (1800), and President and Ball, May 18, 1965 (1035), "DR," box 3, GWBP. For U.S. documents on the details of the Bundy-Guzmán negotiations, see: draft statement of the position of Antonio Guzmán, May 18, 1965, Communism, n.d, and declaración de la posición de Antonio Guzmán, n.d., "Vol. 4," box 39, CF; statement of the position of Antonio Guzmán, May 19, 1965, memo: Communism, n.d., and talking paper: referendum for Constitutional Amendment, n.d., "Davidson," box 51, CF.

54. "Pocket Cleaned," May 17, 1965, "President Johnson," box 7, Handwriting File; Palmer, *Intervention in the Caribbean,* p. 58.

55. Evening situation report, Bennett to the President, May 17, 1965 (2325), 1–3, "Misc. Reports," box 48, CF; J. Dubois, "Writer Sees Bay of Pigs," *Chicago Tribune,* May 18, 1965, p. 7; Szulc, *Dominican Diary,* p. 233; Szulc, "Junta is Defiant," *New York Times,* May 18, 1965, p. 1; Wicker, "U.S. Policy Change Denied," *New York Times,* May 18, 1965, p. 18, and "Reversing the Gears," p. 38; teleconferences, Moyers and Ball, May 17, 1965 (1610 and 1645), and teleconference, Wicker and Ball, May 17, 1965 (1715), "DR," box 3, GWBP.

56. EMBTEL 1776, May 18, 1965 (1343), "Bundy's mission," box 2, FGC; teleconference, President and Ball, May 18, 1965 (1035), "DR," box 3, GWBP. See also: handwritten notes, Bundy, May 19, 1965, "Davidson," box 51, CF.

57. Handwritten notes, Bundy, May 18, 1965 (0930), 3–4, "Davidson," box 51, CF; Kennedy Crockett interview by author, Oct. 13, 1993, author's collection; Bennett interview; Mann, oral history, 23–24; Vance, oral history, 23–24; DEPTEL 1181, May 21, 1965, "Bundy Mission," box 2, FGC; teleconference, Ball and the President, May 23, 1965 (1400), "DR," box 3, GWBP; Martin, *Overtaken by Events,* p. 699; Palmer, *Intervention in the Caribbean,* pp. 58, 62; Slater, *Intervention and Negotiation,* pp. 88–89; Szulc, *Dominican Diary,* pp. 242–43, 251; Yates, *Power Pack,* pp. 96, 102, 116.

58. EMBTEL 1805, May 19, 1965 (1105), "Bundy's Mission," box 2, FGC; evening sitrep of president, May 18, 1965 (2245), 1, and morning sitrep for president, May 20, 1965 (1020), "Misc. Reports," box 48, CF. See also: sitrep, May 19, 1965 (0500), 1, sitrep, May 20, 1965 (0500), 1, and sitrep, May 20, 1965 (1600), 1–3, "Task Force Sitreps," box 49, CF; EMBTEL 1801, May 19, 1965 (1045), and EMBTEL 1809, May 19, 1965 (1340), "Bundy's Mission," box 2, FGC; memo, Rowan to president, May 19, 1965 (1230), "ND 19/CO 62," box 70, Confidential File; memo [document #82], May 20, 1965, "Davidson," box 51, CF; report: J. B. Martin and the 1965 Dominican Crisis, n.d., 3–4, folder 5, box 5, Richard Rovere Papers, Archive Division, State Historical Society of Wisconsin; Martin, *Overtaken by Events,* pp. 697–98; *SFRC'65,* 579; Shlaudeman interview; Szulc, *Dominican Diary,* pp. 247–49, 253.

59. Handwritten notes, Bundy, May 20, 1965 (0810 and 1040), "Davidson," box 51, CF; teleconference, Ball and Vance, May 20, 1965 (1105), and teleconference, Bundy and Ball/Rowan, May 20, 1965 (1145), "DR," box 3, GWBP; EMBTEL 1809, May 19, 1965 (1340), "Bundy's Mission," box 2, FGC; Vance's statement, May 20, 1965 and EMBTEL 1854, May 21, 1965 (0041), "Vance Press Conference," box 51, CF; Szulc, *Dominican Diary,* pp. 201–202, 243–46. See also: handwritten notes, Bundy, May 20, 1965, "Davidson," box 51, CF; *SFRC'65,* 883–84; commentary by Paul Niven, *Face the Nation,* 1965 Vol. 8, pp. 119, 122.

60. EMBTEL 1835, May 20, 1965 (1223), EMBTEL 1855, May 21, 1965 (0030), and DEPTEL 1209, May 23, 1965 (1656), "Bundy's Mission," box 2, FGC; sitrep, May 20, 1965 (1600), "Task Force Sitreps," 1, box 49, CF; Gleijeses, *Dominican Crisis,* pp. 266–67. See also: *SFRC'65,* 574–75, 587, 592; Vance, oral history, 23–24.

61. Handwritten notes, Bundy, May 21, 1965, p. 3, and May 22, 1965 (0815), "Davidson," box 51, CF; Szulc, *Dominican Diary,* pp. 257, 260; Szulc, "Mediators and Rebels Ask," *New York Times,* May 22, 1965, p. 1.

62. EMBTEL 1896, May 22, 1965 (1358), EMBTEL 1925, May 23, 1965 (1445), and DEPTEL 1208, May 23, 1965 (1632), "Bundy's Mission," box 2, FGC; memo, Smith to president, May 22, 1965, "Vol. 10," box 3, MTP; teleconference,

McNamara and Ball, May 23, 1965 (1345), and teleconference, Ball and president, May 23, 1965 (1400), "DR," box 3, GWBP; Vance, oral history, 26–27. See also: E. W. Kenworthy, "Closure is Asked," *New York Times,* May 22, 1965, p. 1; Slater, *Intervention and Negotiation,* pp. 91–93; teleconference, Ball and Moyers, May 22, 1965 (1245), "DR," box 3, GWBP. Congressional comment on the Guzmán formula was almost nonexistent while the talks progressed; however, Senator Frank Lausche (R-Ohio) expressed his "grave apprehensions" about Guzmán on May 24, 1965; *Congressional Record,* 11358 [hereafter *CR*].

63. Memo by Wicker on conversation with Bundy, May 28, 1965, box 1, Krock Papers; Gleijeses, *Dominican Crisis,* pp. 267–68; Vance, oral history, 24–25. See also: Draper, *Dominican Crisis,* pp. 183–84; Quinten Allen Kelso, *The Dominican Crisis of 1965* (Ann Arbor: University Microfilms International, 1980), 199; *SFRC'65,* 882, 1067–68, 1071; Slater, *Intervention and Negotiation,* pp. 94–95; Wiarda, *Dictatorship,* p. 1792.

64. DEPTEL 1208, May 23, 1965 (1632), 2, "Bundy's Mission," box 2, FGC; memo on talk with Bundy, May 28, 1965, box 1, Krock Papers. See also: memo of conversation, Rusk and Sapena Pastor, May 28, 1965, 3, "Memorandum of Conversations," box 49, CF; Vance, oral history, 28.

65. DEPCIRCTEL 2403, June 2, 1965 (1046), and DEPCIRCTEL 2411, June 2, 1965 (1821), "Vol. 7," box 40, CF. Other members were Ilmar Penna Marinho (Brazil) and Ramón de Clairmont Dueñas (El Salvador).

66. [emphasis added] EMBTEL 1958, May 24, 1965 (1155), "Davidson," box 51, CF; EMBTEL 2065, May 28, 1965 (1838), and EMBTEL 2125, May 30, 1965 (1853), "Vol. 6," box 40, CF; EMBTEL 2184, June 2, 1965 (0353), "Vol. 7," box 41, CF.

67. For example, Dean Rusk twice alleged the initial decision to land troops was made as armed rebels terrorized U.S. citizens waiting to be evacuated from the Embajador Hotel. In fact, this incident occurred more than twenty-four hours *before* the marines had been landed. Although the inaccuracy of Rusk's story was apparent, the president embellished it further in a June 1 news conference. Secretary Rusk's News Conference, May 26, 1965, and Secretary Rusk's Television Discussion, May 28, 1965, Senate Committee, *Background Information,* 76–87; *PPP: LBJ,* June 1, 1965, 617.

68. News conference, June 1, 1965, "Excerpts from News Conference," box 8, NSCH; *PPP: LBJ,* June 1, 1965, 617, and June 17, 1965, 678; letter, Bennett to Bundy, July 31, 1965, "Vol. 13," box 4, MTP; Dean Rusk as told to Richard Rusk, *As I Saw It* (New York, 1990), p. 374. For two mentions of beheading incidents, see: EMBTEL 1217, Apr. 30, 1965 (2313), "Vol. 1," box 38, CF; Martin, "Struggle To Bring Together," p. 29.

69. From the right, for example see the *National Review:* "Will LBJ Crumble?" June 1, 1965, p. 447; "Focus on Washington" and "Caribbean Blind Alley," June 15, 1965, pp. 493 and 495.

70. Teleconference, Stevenson and Ball, May 15, 1965 (1250), "DR," box 3, GWBP; report: John Bartlow Martin and the 1965 Dominican crisis, n.d., 2–4, folder 5, box 5, Richard Rovere Papers; memo, Bundy to Johnson, June 3, 1965 (1825), "Vol. 11," box 3, MTP See also: memo, Goodwin to Johnson, June 1, 1965, "President Johnson," box 7, Handwriting File; letter, Mansfield to Johnson, June 1, 1965, "ND 19/CO 62," box 202, WHCF; Wicker, "Johnson Policies," pp. 1, 14; Nacos, *Press, Presidents, and Crises,* p. 73.

71. *CR* 1965, 23855–61.

72. Letter, Fulbright to LBJ, Sept. 15, 1965, "Answer to Fulbright," box 53, CF.

73. Pat Holt, Oral History Interview (1980), 173–77, Senate Historical Office, Washington; memo, Seth Tillman to Senator Clark, Sept. 17, 1965, folder 7, box 31, series 71, J. William Fulbright Papers, Special Collections, University of Arkansas Library, Fayetteville [hereafter JWFP]; memo, Tillman to Clark, Sept. 17, 1965, "Senator Clark" folder, box 1, Senate Foreign Relations Committee, 89th Congress, National Archives. See also: Eugene Brown, *J. William Fulbright* (Iowa City: University of Iowa Press, 1985), pp. 69–73; J. William Fulbright, *The Arrogance of Power* (New York: Random House, 1966), pp. 83–92; J. William Fulbright with Seth Tillman, *Price of Empire* (New York: Pantheon Books, 1989), p. 115.

74. Memo, Bundy to LBJ, Sept. 14, 1965 (6:30 P.M.) "Vol. 14," Box 4, MTP; Randall Bennett Woods, *Fulbright* (New York: Cambridge University Press, 1995), pp. 337, 385–87.

75. *CR* 1965, 23861–63, 24168–73; memo, Chase/Bowdler to Bundy, Sept. 7, 1965 and Sept. 8, 1965, "Vol. X, Memos and Misc.," box 43, CF; memo, Bundy to LBJ, Sept. 17, 1965 (12:45 A.M.), "Vol. 14," Box 4, MTP; memo, G. C. to Bundy, Sept. 15, 1965, "Vol. XI, Memos and Misc.," box 44, CF; draft letter, LBJ to Fulbright, n.d., and memo, Bundy to LBJ, Sept. 18, 1965 (4:45 P.M.), "Answer to Fulbright," box 53, CF. See also: teleconference, Ball and Bundy, Oct. 2, 1965 (12:15 P.M.), "Congress, etc. III," box 2, GWBP; Haynes Johnson and Bernard M. Gwertzman, *Fulbright* (New York: Curtis Books, 1968), pp. 258–59; Lee Riley Powell, *J. William Fulbright and His Time* (Memphis: Guild Bindery Press, 1996), pp. 262–63; Yergin, "Fulbright's last frustration," p. 14.

76. Memo, Pat Holt to Senator Clark, Sept. 20, 1965, "Senator Clark," box 1, Senate Foreign Relations Committee, 89th Congress, National Archives.

77. Memo, CM [Carl Marcy] to Senator, Oct. 15, 1965, unprocessed January, 1990, accession, JWFP; Fulbright, Oral History Interview, March 5, 1987, p. 21, Former Members of Congress Oral History Project, Library of Congress Manuscripts Division; memo, Pat Holt to Senator Clark, Sept. 20, 1965, "Senator Clark," box 1, Senate Foreign Relations Committee, 89th Congress, National Archives. See also: letter, Ellsworth Bunker to Senator Fulbright, Sept. 17, 1966, "OAS," box 36, Subject File, NSF; Charles DeBenedetti, "Lyndon Johnson," pp. 28, 38, in *Johnson Years, Volume Two* (Lawrence: University Press of Kansas, 1987), ed. Robert A. Divine; Larry Berman, "Johnson and the White House Staff," pp. 193–94, in *Johnson Years, Volume One* (Lawrence: University Press of Kansas, 1987), ed. Robert A. Divine; Turner, *Lyndon Johnson's Dual War*, p. 156; Powell, *Fulbright and His Time*, pp. 264–66; Woods, *Fulbright*, pp. 385, 391–414; Yergin, "Fulbright's last frustration," pp. 78–82.

78. Yergin, "Fulbright's last frustration," p. 78.

79. Although Ambassador Bennett remained in place, he now "was definitely playing second fiddle," according to Palmer, *Intervention in the Caribbean*, pp. 79, 84–87.

80. Sitrep, June 4, 1965 (0500), "Task Force Sitreps," box 49, CF; memo, Bundy to USUN, June 5, 1965, 2, and memo, Bundy to Johnson, June 11, 1965, "Vol. 11," box 3, MTP; Holt, oral history, 172. See also: George W. Ball, *The Past Has Another Pattern* (New York: W. W. Norton, 1982), pp. 329–30; Audrey Bracey, *Resolution of the Dominican Crisis, 1965* (Washington, D.C.: Institute for the Study

of Diplomacy, Georgetown University, 1980), p. 45; Lyndon Baines Johnson, *The Vantage Point* (New York: Holt, Rinehart & Winston, 1971), p. 204; Kalman, *Abe Fortas,* pp. 239–40; Murphy, *Fortas,* pp. 155–56; Slater, *Intervention and Negotiation,* pp. 97–98.

81. Sitrep, May 20, 1965 (1600), "Task Force Sitreps," box 49, CF; memo, Read to Bundy, June 5, 1965, "Vol. 6," box 40, CF; DEPTEL 1374, June 5, 1965 (1803), "Vol. 7," box 41, CF; EMBTEL 2332, June 11, 1965 (2111), 2, "Bunker Activities," box 3, FGC; *SFRC'65,* 784–85, 787. For Crockett's summary of Balaguer's plan, see: "Balaguer Views as of June 4, 1965," attached to memo, Bundy to Johnson, June 7, 1965 (1915), "Vol. 11," box 3, MTP. For partial evidence of the evolution of Balaguer's plan among his allies in the DR, see: "Prospects for Formation of 'Third Force,'" May 29, 1965, "Important Documents," box 4, FGC; DODTEL, May 29, 1965 (0046), 2, "DOD Messages," box 6, NSCH.

82. Teleconferences, Johnson and Ball, June 3, 1965 (1420 and 1555), "DR," box 3, GWBP; EMBTEL 4872, USUN to DOS, June 5, 1965 (0152), 1, memo with attachment, Bundy to Johnson, June 7, 1965 (1915), and draft telegram for Bunker, June 11, 1965, "Vol. 11," box 3, MTP; DEPTEL 1374, June 5, 1965 (1803), and EMBTEL 2323, June 10, 1965 (1325), "Vol. 7," box 41, CF; draft telegram for Amb. Bunker, n.d. [approx. June 10, 1965], "Vol. 6," box 40, CF; draft telegram for Bunker, June 11, 1965, "Planning Group," box 2, FGC; DEPTEL 1445, June 15, 1965 (1249), "Vol. 8" box 42, CF; Shlaudeman interview.

83. EMBTEL 2496, June 18, 1965 (1247), EMBTEL 2500, June 18, 1965 (1923), EMBTEL 2513, June 19, 1965 (1506), EMBTEL 2515, June 19, 1965 (1953), EMBTEL 2522, June 20, 1965 (1648), 2, EMBTEL 2530, June 21, 1965 (0307), 3, EMBTEL 2532, June 21, 1965 (0753), EMBTEL 2540, June 21, 1965 (1821), EMBTEL 2542, June 21, 1965 (2104), EMBTEL 2549, June 22, 1965 (0454), and EMBTEL 2552, June 22, 1965 (1144), "Vol. 8," box 3, FGC; EMBTEL 2517, June 20, 1965 (0311), EMBTEL 2568, June 23, 1965 (2029), and EMBTEL 2585, June 24, 1965, "Ad hoc committee proposal," box 4, FGC; EMBTEL 2564, June 23, 1965 (0905), and EMBTEL 2565, June 23, 1965, "Meetings with the President," box 2, FGC; EMBTEL 2628, June 27, 1965 (0250), "Task Force Meeting," box 2, FGC; EMBTEL 2, July 1, 1965 (0818), "Vol. 9," box 42, CF; "Especulan sobre propuesta de OEA," and "Una contrapropuesta," *La Nación,* June 23, 1965, pp. 1, 2; "Acogida a una proposición práctica," *La Nación,* June 25, 1965, p. 2; Gleijeses, *Dominican Crisis,* pp. 270–71.

84. EMBTEL 2497, June 18, 1965 (1648), EMBTEL 2515, June 19, 1965 (1953), 2, and EMBTEL 2531, June 21, 1965 (0455)2, "Vol. 8," box 42, CF; EMBTEL 2517, June 20, 1965 (0311), EMBTEL 2577, June 24, 1965 (0819), and EMBTEL 2585, June 24, 1965, "Ad hoc committee proposal," box 4, FGC; sitrep, June 23, 1965 (0500), and EMBTEL 2564, June 23, 1965 (0905), "Meetings with the President," box 2, FGC; EMBTEL 2617, June 26, 1965 (1826), "Task Force Meeting," box 2, FGC; OEA/Ser. F/11.10 Doc. 251, July 17, 1965, 18–21, "Chronology [Tabs 300–320]," box 11, NSCH; "Frente a la formula de la OEA," *La Hoja,* June 21, 1965, p. 3; *SFRC'65,* 879; Gleijeses, *Dominican Crisis,* p. 272. For the GNR response to the OAS proposal, see: EMBTEL 2574, June 24, 1965 (0248), "Ad Hoc Committee Proposal," box 4, FGC.

85. EMBTEL 2612, June 26, 1965 (0412), "Vol. 8," box 42, CF; EMBTEL 2618, June 26, 1965 (1854), "Task Force Meeting," box 2, FGC; EMBTEL 5, July 1, 1965 (1712), EMBTEL 10, July 1, 1965 (2251), EMBTEL 18, July 2, 1965 (1910), EMBTEL 30, July 3, 1965 (2057), EMBTEL 121, July 11, 1965 (2303), "Vol. 9," box 42, CF;

OEA/Ser. F/11.10 Doc. 251, July 17, 1965, 22, "Chronology [Tabs 300–320]," box 11, NSCH; "Proponen candidatos a presidencia," *Patria,* July 2, 1965, p. 1. See also: EMBTEL 2651, June 28, 1965 (2244), "Vol. 8," box 42, CF; Slater, *Intervention and Negotiation,* pp. 119–20.

86. EMBTEL 2628, June 27, 1965 (0250), 1–2, "Task Force Meeting," box 2, FGC; DEPTEL 1542, June 28, 1965 (2156), "Vol. 8," box 42, CF; EMBTEL 5, July 1, 1965 (1712), EMBTEL 49, July 6, 1965 (0247), 2–3, and EMBTEL 115, July 11, 1965 (1110), 2, "Vol. 9," box 42, CF; *SFRC'65,* 1071–72. See also: "Alocución dirigida al pueblo," *Reconstrucción,* distributed July 1, 1965; EMBTEL 13, July 2, 1965 (0435), "Vol. 9," box 42, CF. See also: Palmer, *Intervention in the Caribbean,* pp. 91, 93–94; Slater, *Intervention and Negotiation,* pp. 124–26. Washington's response to the ad hoc committee's proposal went through a series of drafts; see: "Task Force Meeting," box 2, FGC, and "Vol. 6," box 40, CF.

87. EMBTEL 2618, June 26, 1965 (1854), "Task Force Meeting," box 2, FGC; EMBTEL 49, July 6, 1965 (0247), and EMBTEL 76, July 8, 1965 (0410), "Vol. 9," box 42, CF. See also: Gleijeses, *Dominican Crisis,* pp. 273–74. On a earlier meeting between Bunker and a rebel negotiator, see: EMBTEL 2396, June 13, 1965 (1445), "Bunker Activities," box 3, FGC.

88. EMBTEL 76, July 8, 1965 (0410), 3–4, EMBTEL 88, July 9, 1965 (0131), EMBTEL 100, July 9, 1965 (2237), EMBTEL 106, July 10, 1965 (1742), and EMBTEL 107, July 10, 1965 (091-), "Vol. 9," box 42, CF; notes from cabinet room, July 16, 1965 (1800), 1, "Meeting with foreign policy advisors," box 1, Meeting Notes File; OEA/Ser. F/11.10 Doc. 251, July 17, 1965, 22–26, "Chronology [Tabs 300–320]," box 11, NSCH; Gleijeses, *Dominican Crisis,* pp. 274–75, 408–409. For a transcript of the meeting, see: *Caamaño frente a la O.E.A.* (Santo Domingo: Editora Universitaria—UASD, 1985), pp. 79–113. See also: "Gobierno no objeta" and "No objeción," *La Nación,* July 11, 1965, pp. 1–2,; "No objetan García-Read," *Patria,* July 11, 1965, p. 1; Moreno, *Barrios in Arms,* pp. 41–42, 44; Slater, *Intervention and Negotiation,* pp. 122–24.

89. EMBTEL 58, July 6, 1965 (2218), EMBTEL 96, July 9, 1965 (1834), EMBTEL 115, July 11, 1965 (1110), EMBTEL 131, July 13, 1965 (0039), DEPTEL 148, July 29, 1965 (1619), EMBTEL 392, July 30, 1965 (1907), EMBTEL, American Embassy Rio de Janeiro to DOS, July 30, 1965, 4–5, DEPTEL 164, July 31, 1965 (1311), and DEPTEL 165, July 31, 1965 (1620), "Vol. 9, Cables," box 42, CF; basic settlement issues, July 12, 1965, "Background Documents," box 7, NSCH; notes from cabinet room, July 16, 1965 (1800), "Meeting with foreign policy advisors," box 1, Meeting Notes File; EMBTEL Aug. 1, 1965 (1555), and memo, Bundy to Johnson, Aug. 16, 1965 (1800), "Vol. 13," box 4, MTP; OEA/Ser. F/11.10 Doc. 374, Sept. 24, 1965, 4–9, "Chronology [Tabs 321–331]," box 11, NSCH; Gleijeses, *Dominican Crisis,* pp. 376, 409 n. 102; Palmer, *Intervention in the Caribbean,* p. 98; Slater, *Intervention and Negotiation,* pp. 133–34.

90. Notes from cabinet room, June 16, 1965 (1800), "Meeting with foreign policy advisors," box 1, Meeting Notes File; memo, Bundy to Johnson, Aug. 2, 1965 (1915), "Vol. 13," box 4, MTP; memos, Chase to Bundy, Sept. 1, 1965 and Sept. 2, 1965, "Vol. 10," box 43, CF; EMBTEL 616, Sept. 3, 1965 (1731), "Vol. 10," box 43, CF. See also: Bundy Committee Meeting, Aug. 31, 1965, "Vol. 18," box 48, CF; Slater, *Intervention and Negotiation,* pp. 127–28.

91. Memo, Smith to Johnson, Aug. 30, 1965 (2045), and memo, briefing officer to Johnson, Sept. 2, 1965 (0700), "Vol. 10," box 43, CF; EMBTEL 563, Aug. 30,

1965 (2127), EMBTEL 581, Aug. 31, 1965 (2215), EMBTEL 584, Sept. 1, 1965 (0154), EMBTEL 612, Sept. 3, 1965 (1817), and EMBTEL 630, Sept. 4, 1965 (0114), "Vol. 10," box 43, CF; OEA/Ser. F/11.10 Doc. 374, Sept. 24, 1965, 14–15, 70–95, "Chronology [Tabs 321–331]," box 11, NSCH; "El presidente Caamaño renuncia," *La Nación,* Sept. 3, 1965, pp. 1, 4, 8, and "García Godoy asume presidencia," *La Nación,* Sept. 4, 1965, p. 1; "Discurso de Caamaño," *Patria,* Sept. 3, 1965, pp. 1–2,; "Instalan García Godoy," and "Discurso de García Godoy," *La Hoja,* Sept. 4, 1965, pp. 1, 2, 4.

92. Memo, Bundy to Johnson, Sept. 11, 1965 (1030), EMBTEL 722, Sept. 14, 1965, and EMBTEL 723, Sept. 14, 1965, "Vol. 14," box 4, MTP; EMBTEL 717, Sept. 13, 1965 (1719), "Vol. 10," box 43, CF; EMBTEL 730, Sept. 14, 1965 (2255), and EMBTEL 780, Sept. 22, 1965 (2035), "Vol. 11," box 44, CF; Bunker report, Oct. 12, 1965, 1, "Vol. 15," box 5, MTP; "Presidente designa primeros," *La Nación,* Sept. 2, 1965, p. 1; "Presidente designa nuevos," *La Nación,* Sept. 6, 1965, p. 1; and "Suprema corte de justicia," *La Nación,* Sept. 10, 1965, p. 1,; Bennett interview; Slater, *Intervention and Negotiation.*

93. EMBTEL 1643, Jan. 12, 1966 (0211), 2, EMBTEL 1648, Jan. 12, 1966 (1832), EMBTEL 1652, Jan. 12, 1966 (2024), EMBTEL 1724, Jan. 22, 1966 (1327), and EMBTEL 1725, Jan. 22, 1966 (1619), "Vol. 14," box 46, CF; Caamaño press conference, Jan. 26, 1966 (1910), "Vol. 15," box 46, CF; "Envoy Bennett," *Washington Post,* Jan. 11, 1966; See the following in *El Caribe:* "Seis militares," Jan. 12, 1966, p. 1; R. Berrellez, "Creen indicos saldrán," Jan. 17, 1966, p. 1; M. J. Torres, "Se ausenta hoy," Jan. 21, 1966, p. 1, "Militar considera," Jan. 22, 1966, p. 1; and "Se ausentan," Jan. 24, 1966, p. 1. See also: EMBTEL 1122, Oct. 28, 1965 (0438), "CO 62," box 8, Confidential File; memo, Marvin to Johnson, Dec. 29, 1965 (1652), "Vol. 13," box 45, CF.

94. EMBTEL 1623, Jan. 10, 1966 (1603), EMBTEL 1624, Jan. 10, 1966 (1700), EMBTEL 1643, Jan. 12, 1966 (0211), and EMBTEL 1646, Jan. 12, 1966 (0051), "Vol. 13," box 45, CF; EMBTEL 1732, Jan. 24, 1966 (2034), EMBTEL 1781, Jan. 31, 1966 (1349), "Vol. 14," box 46, CF; EMBTEL 1794, Feb. 1, 1966, memo with attachment, Bundy to Johnson, Feb. 3, 1966, "Vol. 19," box 6, MTP; See *El Caribe* for "El presidente recomienda," Jan. 26, 1966, p. 1; "Reunión de militares," Jan. 27, 1966, p. 1; "Dicen será confidencial," Jan. 28, 1966, p. 1; R. Berrellez, "Sigue estancada," Jan. 31, 1966, p. 1; R. Berrellez, "Estima actitud," Feb. 1, 1966, p. 1; and "Se espera," Feb. 3, 1966, p. 1. See also: "Huelga," *El Caribe,* Jan. 15, 1966, p. 1A.

95. Memo for Johnson, Feb. 9, 1966, "Vol. 4," box 2, CF; EMBTEL 1856, Feb. 9, 1966 (2001), EMBTEL 1858, Feb. 10, 1966 (0155), EMBTEL 1872, Feb. 11, 1966 (1745), EMBTEL 1886, Feb. 11, 1966 (2222), EMBTEL 1897, Feb. 13, 1966 (1425), EMBTEL 1899, Feb. 13, 1966 (1457), EMBTEL 1901, Feb. 13, 1966 (2108), EMBTEL 1907, Feb. 15, 1966 (0043), memo, Bowdler to Bundy, Feb. 18, 1966, EMBTEL 1971, Feb. 22, 1966 (2131), memo, Bundy to Johnson, Feb. 24, 1966 (1200), EMBTEL 2009, Feb. 26, 1966 (190-), and memo, Bowdler to Johnson, Feb. 26, 1966 (1915), "Vol. 14," box 46, CF; memos, briefing officer to Johnson, Feb. 13, 1966 (1745) and Feb. 20, 1966 (1735), "Vol. 47," box 27, CF; memo, Bowdler to Johnson, Feb. 16, 1966 (0030), "Vol. 20," box 6, MTP; teleconferences, Sayre and Ball, Feb. 16, 1966 (1310), Ball and Bunker, Feb. 16, 1966 (1330), Ball and Vance, Feb. 16, 1966 (1635), and Crimmins and Ball, Feb. 17, 1966 (1010), "DR II," box 3, GWBP; See the following, all in *El Caribe:* "Sigue

estancada crisis," Feb. 7, 1966, p. 1; "Rumores insistentes," Feb. 8, 1966, 1; "Creen reunión," Feb. 9, 1966, p. 1, "Disturbois dejan," Feb. 10, 1966, p. 1; "Huelga sólo afectó," Feb. 11, 1966, p. 1; "Por segundo día," Feb. 12, 1966, p. 1; E. Deschamps, "Presta juramento nuevo," Feb. 12, 1966, p. 1; "Estiman decisivo día," Feb. 14, 1966, p. 1; "El presidente debe hablan," Feb. 14, 1966, p. 8; "Texto de alocución," Feb. 14, 1966, p. 11; "Comité huelga," Feb. 15, 1966, p. 1; "Actividades en capital," Feb. 15, 1966, p. 1; "Huelga crece," Feb. 16, 1966, p. 1; "Texto de alocución," Feb. 16, 1966, p. 14; "Ordenan vuelta trabajo," Feb. 17, 1966, p. 1; "Tras la huelga," Feb. 18, 1966, p. 1; "Deportarán inmigrantes," Feb. 19, 1966, p. 1, "Anuncian que expulsarán," Feb. 19, 1966, p. 1; and "Ejecutivo recibe," Feb. 26, 1966, p. 9; Bennett interview. See also: letter, Volman to Thomas, Feb. 27, 1966, folder 6, box 38, subseries 14, series 48, JWFP.

96. Letter, Tap [Bennett] to Tom [Mann], Nov. 20, 1965, and EMBTEL 1538, Dec. 28, 1965 (2344), 1, "Vol. 13," box 45, CF; EMBTEL 2416, May 9, 1966, "Vol. 2," box 7, MTP; "Balance de la política," *Ahora,* Dec. 27, 1965, pp. 34–35; *El Caribe* articles: "Forman comité," Dec. 20, 1965, p. 11; "Titular del PR dice," Feb. 21, 1966, p. 1; "La consulta electoral," Feb. 22, 1966, p. 8; "Expreso confianza," Mar. 1, 1966, p. 1, "Balaguer señala causa," Mar. 7, 1966, p. 12; "Balaguer," Mar. 24, 1966, p. 6; "Balaguer," Apr. 14, 1966, p. 15; "Reformista elige," Apr. 16, 1966, p. 1; V. A. Mármol, "Augusto Lora derrota," Apr. 18, 1966, p. 1; "El partido reformista," Apr. 18, 1966, p. 9; "Balaguer refuta," May 7, 1966, p. 1; and "Balaguer trata problemas," May 10, 1966, p. 7.

97. The embassy tried to keep a low profile during the campaign, but officials remained engaged in local affairs. Covert U.S. aid to Balaguer may have been provided. FBI director J. Edgar Hoover favored Balaguer and possessed the resources to support him, but no evidence demonstrates the FBI acted on its director's inclination. Other undocumented or still classified assistance to Balaguer may have occurred. Memo, Valenti to Johnson, Apr. 11, 1966 (1045), and memo, Rostow to Johnson, Apr. 25, 1966 (1710), "Vol. 14," box 46, CF; John Hugh Crimmins telephone interview by author, Aug. 18, 1993.

98. Letter, Tap to Tom, Nov. 20, 1965, "Vol. 13," box 45, CF; memo, Bowdler to Johnson, Mar. 25, 1966 (1330), "Vol. 14," box 46, CF; EMBTEL 2416, May 9, 1966, "Vol. 2," box 7, MTP; EMBTEL 2459, May 15, 1966 (1704), memo, Rusk to Johnson, n.d., and cable, Bunker and Crimmins to Johnson and Sayre, n.d., "D. Election," box 10, Intelligence File, NSF; memo with attachment, Rostow to Johnson, May 17, 1966 (1305), memo, Rostow to Johnson, May 24, 1966, and EMBTEL 2537, May 26, 1966, "Vol. 13," box 7, MTP; draft circular telegram to all ARA posts, n.d., EMBTEL 2586, May 30, 1966, and memo, Rostow to Johnson, May 31, 1966, "Vol. 15," box 46, CF; Crimmins interview; Lincoln Gordon telephone interview by author, May 27, 1993; Mann, oral history, 19; Mann, *Be There Yesterday* (excerpts), pp. 6–7; Palmer, *Intervention in the Caribbean,* p. 134; *SFRC'65,* 1858–59; Shlaudeman interview. See also: memo, Bundy to Johnson, Sept. 28, 1965 (2000), "Vol. 15," box 5, MTP; memo for files, Nov. 4, 1965, "Chron. File," box 568, W. A. Harriman Papers.

99. Gordon interview; teleconference, Ball and Fulbright, Apr. 21, 1966 (1650), "Brazil," box 1, GWBP; cable, Bunker and Crimmins to Sayre and Johnson, n.d., memo with attachment, to Rostow, May 23, 1966, contingency paper—Bosch victory, n.d., and negotiating paper for talks with Bosch, n.d., "D. Election," box 10, Intelligence File, NSF; memo, Rostow to Johnson, May 24, 1966, "Vol. 3," box 7,

MTP; memo, Rusk to Johnson, May 30, 1966, memo with attachment, Rostow to Johnson, May 31, 1966, and negotiating paper for talks with president-elect, n.d., "Vol. 5," box 8, MTP; Rusk, *As I Saw It,* p. 376; Slater, *Intervention and Negotiation,* pp. 170–71.

100. Election data sheet, n.d., EMBTEL 2618, June 2, 1966, memo, Rostow to Johnson, June 2, 1966 (0930), and memo, Rostow to Johnson, June 8, 1966 (1215), "Vol. 5," box 8, MTP; See *El Caribe* for "Reinó orden," June 2, 1966, p. 1; "Comisión OEA," June 2, 1966, p. 1; "Dice admitirían," June 3, 1966, p. 14; "Observadores de la OEA," June 4, 1966, p. 16; and "Comisión del reformista," June 7, 1966, p. 1; "Frente a la nueva situación," *Ahora,* June 20, 1966, p. 3. See also: summary report, Committee on Free Elections in the DR, Apr. 24, 1966, folder 6, box 38, subseries 14, series 48, JWFP; memo, Bowdler to Smith, May 26, 1966, "Vol. 15," box 47, CF; R. Berrellez, "Llegan primeros observadores," *El Caribe,* May 25, 1966, p. 1; William H. Chafe, *Never Stop Running* (New York: Basic Books, 1993), pp. 256–61; Slater, *Intervention and Negotiation,* p. 172; W. A. Swanberg, *Norman Thomas* (New York: Charles Scribner's Sons, 1976), pp. 468–70.

101. Memo, briefing officer to Johnson, June 2, 1966 (0705), "Vol. 55," box 33, CF; memo, Rostow to Johnson, June 2, 1966 (0705 and 1510), "Vol. 16," box 47, CF; memos, Rostow to Johnson, June 2, 1966 (0930 and 1530), "Vol. 15," box 8, MTP; memo, Rostow to Johnson, June 2, 1966 (1030), "June 2," box 35, Appointment File; See *El Caribe* articles "reformista lleva ventaja," June 2, 1966, p. 1; "Junta informa Balaguer," June 3, 1966, p. 1; and "Junta informa reformista," June 4, 1966, p. 1. Election totals from 1962 and 1966 are listed in *El Caribe* on June 4, 1966, p. 6, and June 22, 1966, p. 7. See also: Henry Wells, ed., *Dominican Republic Election Factbook June 1, 1966* (Washington, D.C.: Institute of Comparative Study of Political Systems, 1966).

102. "Tras fondo y perspectivas," *Ahora,* June 20, 1966, pp. 30–31; Jan Knippers Black, *Dominican Republic* (Boston: Allen and Unwin, 1986), pp. 40–42; Crimmins interview; Gleijeses, *Dominican Crisis,* p. 281; Slater, *Intervention and Negotiation,* pp. 173–74, 177–82; Wiarda, *Dictatorship,* pp. 1299, 1799–1801; Howard J. Wiarda and Michael J. Kryzanek, *Dominican Republic* (Boulder: Westview Press, 1992), p. 47. See also: Edward S. Herman and Frank Brodhead, *Demonstration Elections* (Boston: South End Press, 1984), pp. 3–53. On fraud, see *El Caribe:* "Gritan Bosch presidente," June 3, 1966, p. 9; "Bosch anuncia," June 4, 1966, p. 1; "El perredeísmo recusa," June 8, 1966, p. 1; A. Arvelo, "PRD y PRSC discuten," June 8, 1966, p. 1; and A. Arvelo, "Junta rechaza," June 11, 1966, p. 1.

103. Jonathan Hartlyn, "The Dominican Republic's Disputed Elections," *Journal of Democracy* 1 (Fall, 1990): 92–94.

104. DODTEL, May 5, 1966 (0315), "Vol. 15," box 46, CF; memo with attachment, Rostow to Johnson, May 11, 1966 (1915), "Vol. 2," box 7, MTP; EMBTEL 2616, May 23, 1966 (1659), "Vol. 15," box 47, CF; memo to Rostow, May 23, 1966, 2, "D. Election," box 10, Intelligence File, NSF; EMBTEL 2661, June 6, 1966, "Vol. 5," box 8, MTP; memo, Rostow to Johnson, June 7, 1966 (1100), memo, Bowdler to Rostow, June 24, 1966, CIA memo, Aug. 29, 1966, "Vol. 16," box 47, CF; memo, Rostow to Johnson, June 23, 1966 (1900), "Vol. 7," box 8, MTP; "¡Antes del 1 de julio!" *Ahora,* May 16, 1966, p. 3; M. A. Prestol, "¿Negativa de juramentación . . . ?" *Ahora,* May 16, 1966, pp. 5–6; *El Caribe* articles: "Gobierno proyecta," June 1, 1966, p. 1; "Predicen FIP dejará," June 3, 1966, p. 1; "Reitera

planea," June 15, 1966, p. 1; "Dice hay factores," June 23, 1966, p. 1; "Presidente declara," June 29, 1966, p. 1; "OEA adopta," June 25, 1966, p. 1; M. J. Torres, "Considera era necesario," June 27, 1966, p. 1; "La fuerza interamericana," June 29, 1966, p. 1, and "La evacuación total," Aug. 5, 1966, p. 1; Crimmins interview; Slater, *Intervention and Negotiation,* pp. 168–69, 184.

105. Negotiating paper, n.d., "Vol. 5," box 8, MTP; memo, Rostow to Johnson, June 15, 1966 (1755), "CO 62," box 8, Confidential File; memo, Bunker to Johnson, June 16, 1966, memo, Read to Rostow, June 30, 1966, memo of conversation, Humphrey and Balaguer, July 1, 1966 (1730), memo, Rusk to Johnson, July 29, 1966, memo, McPherson to Jacobson, Aug. 15, 1966, and EMBTEL 522, Aug. 19, 1966, "Vol. 16," box 47, CF; memo, Gaud to Johnson, June 16, 1966, "Vol. 6," box 8, MTP; memo of conversation, Harriman and Crimmins, June 22, 1966, "Chron. File," box 569, W. A. Harriman Papers; memo, Rostow to Johnson, June 30, 1966 (1700), "Vol. 7," box 8, MTP; memo, Rostow to Johnson, Aug. 1, 1966, and translated letter, Balaguer to Johnson, n.d., "Vol. 10," box 9, MTP; memo, Bowdler to Smith, Aug. 20, 1966, "Bowdler Memos," box 1, Name File, NSF; report on DR, Holt, Nov. 7, 1966, 8, folder 3, box 16, subseries 3, series 48, JWFP; See *El Caribe* for V. A. Mármol, "Dice tratará," June 4, 1966, p. 1; D. May, "EU ofrecen," June 4, 1966, p. 1; "Johnson declara," July 6, 1966, p. 1; and "EU estaán listos," July 9, 1966, p. 1; J. C. Estrella, "La lección que debemos aprender," *Ahora,* Aug. 29, 1966, pp. 5–7,; Crimmins interview; Crimmins, oral history, 38–39; Gordon interview.

106. Memo, WGB to Walt, June 14, 1966, June 14, 1966, "Vol. 6," box 8, MTP; memos, Rostow to Johnson, June 21, 1966 and June 23, 1966, "Vol. 7," box 8, MTP; memo, McPherson to Johnson, June 24, 1966 (1650), "CO 62," box 28, WHCF; memo, Rostow to Johnson, June 25, 1966 (1650), CIA report, Aug. 5, 1966, and SNIE 86.2-2, 1966, Sept. 19, 1966, 8, "Vol. 16," box 47, CF; memo, Rostow to Moyers, Sept. 13, 1966, "Vol. 15," box 47, CF; memo, Rostow to Johnson, Sept. 19, 1966, "Vol. 13," box 10, MTP; EMBTEL 1515, Nov. 1, 1966, EMBTEL 1542, Nov. 16, memo, Rostow to Johnson, Nov. 18, 1966, memo, Bowdler to Rostow, Nov. 29, 1966 (1430), memo, Gaud to Johnson, Apr. 14, 1967, and courses of action (short-term)—DR, May 5, 1967, 4, "Vol. 17," box 47, CF; National Intelligence Estimate [hereafter NIE] 86.2-67, 4/20/67, 10, "Vol. 5," box 3, CF; EMBTEL 1272, Dec. 7, 1967, EMBTEL 2317, Apr. 24, 1968, memos, Gaud to Johnson, Dec. 26, 1967, and June 18, 1968, and EMBTEL 4460, Dec. 13, 1968, "Vol. 18," box 46, CF. See also: Atkins, *Arms and Politics,* p. 30; Black, *Dominican Republic,* pp. 43–44; Wiarda, *Dictatorship,* pp. 1805–1808. For addresses on Dominican policy, written with White House help, in June, 1966: *CR,* 12958–59 (Long), 13339–40 (Boggs).

107. Martin to Moyers, Nov. 21, 1966, folder 13, box 35, General Correspondence, JBMP; memo, Rostow to Johnson, Dec. 14, 1966, EMBTEL 2326, Jan. 29, 1967 (1805), and EMBTEL 3665, May 23, 1966 (2231), "Vol. 17," box 12, MTP; NIE 86.2-67, Apr. 20, 1967, 6–10, "Vol. 5," box 3, CF; "En torno a las deportaciones," *Ahora,* Oct. 31, 1966, pp. 15–16; Black, *Dominican Republic,* pp. 48–49; Pedro Catrain, "Transición democratica, socialdemocracia y clases populares en la República Dominicana," *Ciencia y sociedad* 12 (April–June, 1987): 272–74. See also: *Arms and Politics,* pp. 25–26; Sherri Grasmuck and Patricia R. Pessar, *Between Two Islands* (Berkeley: University of California Press, 1991), pp. 33–50.

108. NIE 86.2-67, Apr. 20, 1967, 1–6, 9–10, "Vol. 5," box 3, CF; memo, Oliver to Rusk, Dec. 26, 1967, "Vol. 18," box 46, CF; "Some aspects of the human rights situation in the DR," Amnesty International, AMR 27/03/78, Mar. 29, 1978; Anderson, oral history, 109; Atkins, *Arms and Politics,* pp. 2–4, 18–19, 36–39, 42, 52–57; Richard S. Hillman and Thomas J. D'Agostino, *Distant Neighbors in the Caribbean* (New York: Praeger, 1992), p. 130; Kryzanek, "Diversion, Subversion and Repression," *Caribbean Studies* 17 (April–July, 1977): 86–103; Michael J. Kryzanek, "Political Party Decline and the Failure of Liberal Democracy," *Journal of Latin American Studies* (May, 1977): 124–43; Frank Moya Pons, *Manual de historia dominicana* (Santo Domingo: Editora Corripio, 1992), pp. 538–39; Wiarda, *Dictatorship,* pp. 1810–21, 1835–57; Howard J. Wiarda and Michael J. Kryzanek, "Dominican Dictatorship Revisited," *Revista/Review Interamericana* 7 (Fall, 1977): 417–35. See also: Catherine M. Conaghan and Rosario Espinal, "Unlikely Transitions to Uncertain Regimes?" *Journal of Latin American Studies* 22 (October, 1990): 554–55, 560–64; Larry Diamond and Juan J. Linz, "Introduction," pp. 1–58, in *Democracy in Developing Countries: Volume 4, Latin America* (Boulder: Lynne Reinner, 1989), Larry Diamond, et al., eds.; Jorge I. Domínguez, "The Caribbean Question," pp. 13–14, in *Democracy in the Caribbean* (Baltimore: Johns Hopkins University Press, 1993), Jorge I. Domínguez, et al., eds.; Howard J. Wiarda, "The Struggle for Democracy and Human Rights in Latin America," pp. 231–54, in *The Continuing Struggle for Democracy in Latin America* (Boulder: Westview Press, 1980), Howard J. Wiarda, ed.

109. Burns, "Managing Regional Crises," pp. 134–35; Greenberg, *U.S. Army,* p. 85; Lars Schoultz, *Human Rights and United States Policy toward Latin America* (Princeton: Princeton University Press, 1981), pp. 20–21; Yates, *Power Pack,* p. 171. Twenty U.S. military personnel died in noncombat situations, as did one Latin American member of the IAPF; Greenberg, *U.S. Army,* p. 85.

6

Nasser Delenda Est

Lyndon Johnson, the Arabs, and the 1967 Six-Day War

DOUGLAS LITTLE

During the first week of March, 1967, Lucius Battle, America's ambassador to Egypt, packed his bags, piled into the embassy's limousine, and headed for Cairo International Airport, where he boarded a plane bound for Washington and a better job as assistant secretary of state for Near Eastern Affairs. Before spring became summer, the Johnson's administration's new point man on the Middle East would see Israel defeat Egypt and its other Arab neighbors in just six days. Diplomatic historians have studied the three months between March and June, 1967, almost as carefully as they have studied the two months between June and August, 1914, and with good reason. Just as the world was forever changed by the guns of August, so too the Middle East has never been the same since the Six-Day War. Indeed, a generation after Yitzhak Rabin's army called Gamal Abdel Nasser's bluff by knifing across the Sinai, surging onto the West Bank, and storming the Golan Heights, memories of June, 1967, continue to haunt both Arabs and Israelis as they grope their way toward a lasting peace. And Nasser's allegations that President Lyndon Johnson did too little too late to prevent Israel from striking first have been echoed by anti-American Arab radicals for more than three decades.

Because so much of the archival record remains classified and because so many declassified documents remain ambiguous, long after the fact there is still no scholarly consensus about the Johnson administration's handling of the run up to the Six-Day War. Critics like Stephen Green, Donald Neff, and Edward Tivnan claim that LBJ's tilt toward Israel in June, 1967, was a case of interest-group politics, pure and simple. Neff in particular has argued that with so many Jews in such high places (the NSC staff, both houses of Congress, and the Democratic National Committee), Lyndon Johnson merely counted votes and collected campaign contributions.[1] Scholars as diverse as Steven Spiegel, David Schoenbaum, and H. W. Brands, on the other hand, present a more complicated story in which electoral algebra was overshadowed by the calculus of geopolitics. According to Brands, for example, although LBJ and his top aides were preoccupied with an increasingly unpopular war in Southeast Asia that had produced an acute case of "Tonkin Gulfitis," they nevertheless worked hard to restrain Israel before acquiescing in the Jewish state's preemptive strike against Ho Chi Minh on the Nile. In a variation on this interpretation, Richard Parker, who was serving as U.S. deputy chief of mission in Cairo when the shooting started on June 5, treats the Six-Day War as the unintended outcome of a series of miscalculations, some by the Americans, some by the Soviets, but mostly by the Arabs.[2]

Although the Israel lobby, the Vietnam quagmire, and multiple miscalculations certainly influenced American decision making on the eve of the Six-Day War, to a very great degree Lyndon Johnson's handling of the conflict reflected his profound mistrust of Gamal Abdel Nasser, whose pan-Arab aspirations were anathema not only for the United States and Israel but also for other American friends in the Middle East, such as Iran and Saudi Arabia. Warren Cohen recently provided a marvelous reconstruction of Washington's head-on collision with Nasser's Egypt. He showed that the highway was steep and winding, the lighting was bad, and the pavement was wet. A careful look at the accident scene, however, reveals that there were no skid marks. (Everyone remembers the old joke: "How do you tell the difference between a dead skunk and a dead lawyer in the middle of the road? There are skid marks in front of the skunk.") Nasser always believed that the United States was out to destroy him, a belief that Richard Parker and others have attributed mainly to an overactive Egyptian imagination. But even paranoids have enemies. And recently declassified documents confirm that on the eve of the Six-Day War, American officials were determined, in the words of National Security Adviser Walt Whitman Rostow, to see that Nasser was "cut down to size."[3] In short, by June 5, 1967, LBJ and his senior advisers had in effect embraced an unspoken motto that would have warmed the heart of Cato the Elder on the eve of the Second Punic War: "Nasser delenda est." Nasser must be destroyed.

Unlike Cato, Luke Battle embraced that motto with considerable regret. When the lanky Georgian paid his farewell call on March 4, 1967, on President Nasser, the Egyptian leader "launched into [a] thirty minute tirade of [the] most emotional character yet displayed in my meetings with him." Washington's recent attempts to use American economic leverage to silence Cairo's anti-Israeli diatribes and pan-Arab jeremiads by slashing economic aid to Egypt, Nasser thundered, were certain to backfire. "We must find [a] way to build

[the] lasting friendship" that "both sides really wanted," Battle retorted. Unmoved by this plea for understanding, Nasser made it clear that his government had other options. Should the Egyptians be unable to develop "satisfactory relationships . . . with [the] West," he snapped, "we will go on with other countries."[4] Because the Kremlin had been bankrolling development projects like the Aswan Dam and providing military hardware like MIG jet fighters for more than a decade, the American ambassador knew very well that the Soviet Union was at the top of Nasser's list. "Mr. President, I want you to remember one thing," Battle remarked sadly as he got up to leave, "you gave up before I did."[5]

By the time Battle arrived in Washington to assume his new duties later that month, few at Foggy Bottom (the State Department) doubted that Nasser would soon invite Moscow to play a greater role in the Middle East. To be sure, after Nasser had seized power in a bloodless coup in Cairo fifteen years earlier, many U.S. officials had hoped that he would bring modernization and westernization to a land badly in need of both. A postman's son, a career officer, and a straight arrow, Nasser was just thirty-four years old when he masterminded the overthrow of Farouk, Egypt's playboy king, and unveiled a reformist agenda in July, 1952. Once he acquired arms from the Kremlin in September, 1955, and wrested control of the Suez Canal from Britain and France ten months later, however, Nasser became America's bête noire in the Middle East. As the Suez crisis deepened during the last half of 1956, President Dwight Eisenhower branded him a Hitler on the Nile; Secretary of State John Foster Dulles labeled him a Soviet stooge; and Senate Majority Leader Lyndon Johnson dismissed him as an unreliable tin-pot colonel.[6]

Although the Eisenhower administration thwarted the tripartite military intervention against Egypt in November and forced the British, the French, and the Israelis to withdraw their troops, Nasser remained "an evil influence" in the eyes of the president and most other U.S. policy makers.[7] "Nasser has wide popular support throughout the Arab world as the symbol of the resistance of radical Pan-Arab Nationalism to Israel and Western 'imperialism,'" the CIA warned the White House in the autumn of 1957, which would probably mean "closer relations with the [Soviet] Bloc because it appears to be championing the Arab point of view."[8] Ike, who had been toying privately with the possibility of a "rapprochement" with Egypt, quickly concluded that "we don't want to be in the position of 'bootlicking a dictator.'" Dulles agreed, pointing out that "Nasser would be satisfied with nothing less than our willingness to treat him as the leader of the Arab world," something certain to antagonize Saudi Arabia and other conservative Muslim states.[9]

Notwithstanding such serious reservations high inside the Eisenhower administration, there was a gradual thaw in Egyptian-American relations during the late 1950s. The rapprochement between Egypt and America stemmed in part from changes in Washington, where Dulles lost his long battle with stomach cancer in May, 1959, and was succeeded by Christian Herter, who drew much clearer distinctions between Arab nationalism and international communism than his predecessor. It also stemmed from changes in Cairo, where throughout 1959 and into 1960, Nasser had grown ever more suspicious about the Kremlin's ties with Iraqi strongman Abdel Karim Qassim, who was rapidly emerging as a left-wing rival for leadership of the Arab world. Washington had begun to signal its good intentions toward Cairo as early as February, 1958, when the Eisenhower administration quietly acquiesced in Nasser's plans to merge Egypt and Syria into a single United Arab Republic (UAR). Hoping to draw the new UAR closer to the United States, Ike agreed during his last two years in office to provide the Nasser regime with $153 million in surplus American wheat under the auspices of Public Law 480 (PL-480), the Food for Peace Program. Not surprisingly, by the time that the two men sat down together for the first and only time on September 26, 1960, Eisenhower was "looking forward to better relations with the UAR" while, for his part, Nasser was insisting that he too wanted "good relations with the United States."[10]

Determined to broaden American ties with Nasser and other Third World neutralists, Ike's successor used another $500 million in surplus U.S. wheat and lots of lace curtain Irish charm to expand the rapprochement with the UAR. During the spring of 1961, John F. Kennedy offered to help Egypt preserve the great stone pharaohs at Abu Simbel from inundation by the backwash from the Aswan Dam, encouraged hundreds of Egyptian students to attend American universities, and opened a warm personal correspondence with Nasser himself. And when anti-Nasser officers in Damascus staged a coup in September and pulled Syria out of the UAR, JFK privately assured the Egyptian president that the CIA had not been involved. Nasser responded to all this by agreeing to put the Arab-Israeli dispute "in the icebox" and to focus his attention instead on social reform and economic development. By the summer of 1962, the Kennedy administration had approved a multiyear PL-480 aid package designed to meet 60 percent of Egypt's grain needs and was considering a multi-million dollar development program to strengthen Egypt's economic infrastructure. The blend of personal diplomacy and economic assistance seemed to have worked wonders in Cairo, White House Middle East expert Robert Komer assured JFK on July 30, leaving little doubt that "our desire for better relations with Nasser is understood and reciprocated."[11]

The view from Blair House, where Vice President Lyndon Johnson marked time, was considerably less rosy. Worried that Kennedy's flirtation with neutralism might alienate Israel, Iran, and the Arab conservatives, LBJ saw no reason to change his own earlier assessment of Nasser as untrustworthy, temperamental, and vulnerable to Soviet influence. The ten-day fact-finding trip to the Middle East that he undertook at JFK's request in late August, 1962, merely strengthened these doubts. Although Johnson spent time in Lebanon, Turkey, and Greece, it was his three-day stay in Iran that left the most lasting impression. Briefed in advance that "the Shah detests Nasser" and that he might "attempt to 'sell' the Vice President on the prevalence of Soviet influence in the United Arab Republic," LBJ arrived in Tehran expecting to find a kindred spirit. Mohammed Reza Pahlavi did not disappoint. He treated the Texas Democrat like Persian royalty and saw to it that huge cheering crowds lined the route of Johnson's motorcade, then privately hammered home the Soviet threat and the neutralist menace to the region.[12]

The postmortem that LBJ passed along to the White House in mid-September confirmed that the vice president had bought what the Shah was selling. Because "these rimland states"—Greece, Turkey, and Iran—"stand a lonely guard against communist expansion to the oil of the Middle East, to continuity with the chaotic Arab world, and the Dardanelles and the Mediterranean," he reminded JFK, the United States needed to provide enough economic and military aid to enable them "to maintain their armed forces along the underbelly of the [Soviet] Bloc." Washington must stand by its friends in Ankara and Athens, Johnson added, and "in Iran, we must accept the Shah, with his shortcomings, as a valuable asset." In short, LBJ believed that the Kennedy administration must do all that it could to assure the Turks, the Greeks, and the Iranians "that they are nearer our hearts than are the neutralist states they fear we are wooing at the expense of our friends."[13]

Before the year was out, LBJ's oblique criticism of Kennedy's rapprochement with Nasser would be dramatically borne out in Southwest Arabia. In late September, pro-Nasser officers seized power in Yemen, an archaic land at the mouth of the Red Sea whose ruling house had developed close ties with Saudi Arabia. When the House of Saud responded by bankrolling royalist guerrillas in the Yemeni highlands, Nasser sent an Egyptian expeditionary force to help the new regime restore order. By early 1963, some U.S. officials worried that UAR intervention in Yemen might well become "a hunting license to go after Saudi Arabia."[14] Later that spring, CIA director John McCone was buttonholed by nervous American oil company executives, who "expressed concern . . . that we were playing an increasingly close game with Nasir (which was understandable in the interest of keeping him away from the Soviet bloc), but there was a danger that in doing this we would complicate our problems with Saudi Arabia."[15] And once Saudi Crown Prince Faisal began to hint that it might be necessary to revise the Arabian-American Oil Company's mammoth oil concession, the Kennedy administration backpedaled furiously from its rapprochement with Egypt to avoid offending the House of Saud. When JFK and LBJ left for Dallas in November, 1963, relations between Washington and Cairo were far chillier than when the Massachusetts Democrat had first arrived at the White House a thousand days earlier.[16]

As he settled into the Oval Office, President Johnson must have been tempted to say "I told you so." Looking back on Kennedy's opening to Nasser, LBJ saw Egyptian duplicity colliding with American naiveté. Hoping that Nasser would stop "trying to dominate the Arab world" and start trying "to concentrate instead on improving the lot of his own people," Johnson recalled in his memoirs, "we gave substantial aid to Egypt, mainly wheat to feed the people of its teeming cities." Nasser, however, had "persisted in his imperial dream" and "sent troops to Yemen to support revolutionaries trying to take over that country." And this, LBJ emphasized, had made Egypt "increasingly dependent on Soviet arms," poisoning its relations with America. "Nasser's attitude toward the United States grew more and more hostile," Johnson concluded, "and his speeches more inflammatory."[17]

Holdovers from the Kennedy administration shared Johnson's mounting frustration with Nasser but nevertheless tried to preserve the Egyptian-American rapprochement. Ten days after JFK's death, for example, NSC staffer Robert Komer forecast "a time of trouble throughout the Middle East" largely because of Egyptian meddling in Yemen. Known affectionately as "Blowtorch Bob" because of his hyperbolic prose, Komer observed that "Nasser has the bear by the tail and the fool can't let go." But he cautioned the new president against relying on American economic leverage to curb Egyptian adventurism. "Nasser won't get out of Yemen just because we cut off aid; we'd have to push him out," Komer concluded on December 3, 1963. "And if we try, you know where he'll go for support." John Badeau, JFK's ambassador to the UAR, echoed Komer and reminded Washington in early 1964 that "Cairo is [the] mountain in [the] heart of [the] Arab world to which all Mohammeds must come." Emphasizing the "indispensable role Nasser plays" in the region, Badeau insisted that "to protect US interests in [the] Arab world at [the] present time involves us in maintaining good relations with [the] UAR and continuing to exert maximum influence in Cairo." Downplaying recent anti-Israeli and anti-Western outbursts on Radio Cairo, State Department Middle East experts praised Nasser in mid-February for his statesmanlike efforts "to reconcile the minimum demands of Arab public opinion with preservation of Arab ties with the West" and advised the White House that it was premature to scuttle "the U.S.-UAR policy of cooperation."[18]

Johnson and his top advisers, however, interpreted Nasser's actions during the spring of 1964 as proof that the UAR was more interested in confrontation than cooperation. Not only was Nasser "sending more troops into Yemen rather than withdrawing them," Secretary of State Dean Rusk informed the National Security Council in early April, he was also "exerting various types of pressure against the British" next door in Aden, a Crown Colony that was home to one of the Royal Navy's most important bases east of Suez. "If [the] British left Aden suddenly, what would result?" Rusk wondered out loud a month later. "Tensions, chaos and perhaps local war," he concluded, from which "only [the] USSR would ultimately benefit." The situation in North Africa was no better. Undersecretary of State Averell Harriman, for example, returned from a whirlwind tour of the Dark Continent gravely concerned about "the difficult situation we are facing in Libya which is responding to Nasser's influence." Radio Cairo's "Voice of the Arabs," Harriman told LBJ on April 3, was promoting "'super Arabism' and anti-Israeli sentiment in Libya," pressuring King Idris to revoke the U.S. Air Force's lease on Wheelus Field outside Tripoli, and demanding the cancellation of several lucrative American oil concessions in the Sahara Desert. Unhappy with continued UAR meddling from North Africa to Southwest Arabia, Washington instructed Ambassador Badeau to remind Nasser in early June that "Wheelus Field and Aden are part . . . [of a] Western defense system [that] remains important as a *cordon sanitaire* for the non-communist world," including neutralist states like Egypt.[19]

U.S. relations with the UAR deteriorated even more rapidly during the last half of 1964. The presence of seventy thousand Egyptian troops in Yemen and the radical diatribes that Radio Cairo launched against Saudi Arabia and Jordan persuaded many at Foggy Bottom by late August that the UAR now assumed "that its own survival depended upon promoting the collapse of the traditional tribal and monarchic regimes of the Arab world."[20] For its part, the CIA warned that "Nasir is clearly working and planning to fall heir to British power," especially in the Arabian Peninsula, where he was "undermining Western base areas, such as Aden, and reducing the West's power to react quickly to changes."[21] Nasser's "threatening tone" during the inter-Arab summit meeting he hosted at Alexandria in early September, particularly his promise to help the newly created Palestine Liberation Organization (PLO) fund and train a guerrilla army, worried U.S. diplomats in Egypt, who concluded that it was "inevitable that there will be an increase in tension in the area."[22] And in a gesture certain to rub Lyndon Johnson the wrong way, later that autumn Nasser condemned U.S. intervention in the Congo, where several hundred European settlers were threatened by African insurgents, as imperialism, pure and simple.[23]

Luke Battle, who replaced John Badeau as LBJ's man in Cairo in September, 1964, urged Washington not to overreact to Nasser's latest moves. "US-UAR relations are neither [a] football game nor [a] western movie with 'bad guys chasing good guys,'" the new ambassador insisted on November 19, but rather a game of finesse, full of ambiguity and filmed in shades of gray.[24] When African exchange students protesting American policy in the Congo stormed a U.S. Information Agency (USIA) library in Cairo a week later and burned it to the ground, however, even Battle agreed that tough talk was warranted. When no apology was forthcoming from Nasser, LBJ summoned Egyptian ambassador Mustapha Kamel to the White House and snapped: "How can I ask Congress for wheat when you burn our library?" Then to make matters worse, a flying boxcar owned by John Mecom, a Texas oil man and long-time "Friend of Lyndon," wandered across the Libyan border into Egyptian airspace three weeks later and was shot down by Nasser's MIGs, killing the Swedish pilot and an American geologist. Lyndon Johnson was extremely upset, Ambassador Battle warned Nasser in mid-December, because "first you burn his libraries, then you kill his friends."[25] Not surprisingly, when Ramses Stinno, Nasser's minister of supply, pressed for still more American wheat just before Christmas, Battle retorted that "it was impossible [to] discuss expansion [of the] PL-480 [program] in [the] tense atmosphere of today."[26]

Outraged by what he regarded as thinly veiled diplomatic blackmail, Nasser responded swiftly and sharply on December 23. "The American Ambassador says that our behavior is not acceptable," Nasser angrily informed a huge throng at Port Said on the banks of the Suez Canal. "Well, let us tell them that those who do not accept our behavior can go and drink . . ." Here he paused theatrically, asked the crowd "from where?" and heard them roar "from the sea!" Then, smiling at Soviet Deputy Premier Alexander Shelepin, who had accompanied him to Port Said, Nasser added that "if the Mediterranean is not enough to slake their thirsts," the Americans "can carry on with the Red Sea." Whether Lyndon Johnson liked it or not, Egypt would continue to support movements for national liberation in Palestine, in Algeria, in the Congo, and elsewhere. "We will cut the tongues of anyone who speaks badly about us," Nasser thundered. "We are not going to accept gangsterism by cowboys."[27]

If the postman's son meant to sting the cowboy in the White House, he succeeded. National Security Adviser McGeorge Bundy forwarded a CIA assessment of Nasser's speech to the LBJ Ranch on Christmas Eve with the observation that "no one is particularly interested in ostentatious feeding of the hand that bites." Terming the performance at Port Said "Nasir's bitterest attack on the US since 1956," the agency speculated that "he may have believed Shelepin was carrying an open checkbook." In any case, Nasser's message seemed quite clear to the CIA. "American aid will not control Egyptian policy," nor would it weaken the UAR's determination "to back 'national liberation' movements at whatever cost."[28] When he returned to Washington two weeks later, LBJ was in no mood to renew the PL-480 Food for Peace deal that his predecessor had struck with Nasser three years earlier. Anti-American incidents, "especially the burning of the USIA library in Egypt, are serious problems which make everyone very angry," Johnson told congressional leaders on January 22. "One way to react is to tell the heads of the states where the outrages take place to go to hell." Although he was not quite ready to go that far, his secretary of state did tell the assembled senators and congressmen that the time had come to send an unmistakable message to Cairo. "We should live up to the existing [PL-480] agreements, which do not expire until July," Dean Rusk insisted, "but [we] should discuss no new agreements with Nasser."[29]

The Johnson administration's obvious attempt to employ economic leverage against Nasser merely prompted him to undertake even more provocative actions during 1965. Not only did Nasser continue to denounce American imperialism in the Congo, he actually invited Che Guevara, who was in the process of injecting revolution Cuban-style into the heart of Africa, to come to Cairo in February. Although he evidently cautioned the Cuban revolutionary not to become "another Tarzan, a white man coming among black men, leading them and protecting them," the Egyptian president did agree to run guns to the Congolese insurgents who, with Guevara's help, sought to topple the pro-American regime in Kinshasa.[30] Nasser's African adventure deeply troubled U.S. officials, who "hammered home sometimes in words of one syllable" the message that "until [the] UAR stopped its arms traffic to [the] Congo we saw no prospect of advancing with PL-480 purchase authorities."[31] The Johnson administration was even more disturbed by the "Blueprint for the Liberation of Palestine" that Nasser unveiled later that spring. "The only force capable of liberating Palestine is Arab revolutionary action," he told a PLO gathering in Cairo on May 31. "If the Palestinians ever go back, it will be under the U.A.R. flag." Nor was Washington pleased a few weeks later when Nasser embraced the Front for the Liberation of South Yemen (FLOSY), a shadowy pro-Soviet group waging guerrilla war against British troops in Aden.[32]

By the autumn of 1965, America clearly seemed to be on a collision course with Nasser and the Arab radicals. "Winds of change," the State Department warned the White House in late September, "are beginning to erode the Near East's social anachronisms" with dangerous consequences for the West. "Feudalism, tribalism, and theocracy are no longer adequate to meet the minimum aspirations of the people," Foggy Bottom's Middle East experts pointed out. "Insofar as Western interests are keyed to these institutions, they are in jeopardy." For revolutionary nationalists like Nasser, "the West is the 'enemy,' while the Soviets are kindred spirits and purveyors of weapons unobtainable elsewhere." All this was cause for considerable concern for Lyndon Johnson, who must have muttered an expletive or two when he read that "the Near East is not yet at the Viet-Nam stage of anti-Western insurgency, but Soviet advisors have already infiltrated the inner circles of the Arab military in Egypt, Syria, and Yemen."[33]

Hoping to arrest the downward spiral in Egyptian-American relations and avoid driving the UAR farther into the Soviet orbit, LBJ invited Anwar Sadat, one of Nasser's most trusted colleagues, to the White House in early 1966. "The U.S. had contributed more than $1 billion of aid to the U.A.R. over the years," Johnson reminded his visitor on February 23, "yet in spite of this there were bad moments between us." Confessing that disagreements over matters like Yemen or Israel "were perhaps inevitable," the president nevertheless "hoped they could be discussed quietly among ourselves and not announced to the public over loudspeakers." Pointing out that it was extremely difficult to make foreign policy "in a goldfish bowl being watched by 200 million people," LBJ hinted that the Egyptians and the Americans might be able to work out a new economic aid package behind closed doors. "When your government has something to say to us, you just tell Ambassador Kamel to put on his hat and come on down here," Johnson told Sadat. "Let's not talk about it in public." Although Sadat's side of the conversation remains classified, LBJ seemed to feel that the meeting had gone reasonably well.[34]

The "Johnson treatment," however, failed to have the desired effect on Gamal Abdel Nasser, who persisted in policies that the White House found increasingly problematic. In late April, for example, the UAR permitted the Viet Cong to open a permanent office in Cairo, a gesture that confirmed the Nasser regime's "sympathy if not support for [the] insurgents whom despite all our efforts they continue [to] view as [a] progressive, nationalist and not necessarily communist movement."[35] A month later, LBJ learned that the Egyptians were stirring up trouble much closer to home. "Nasir has attacked the Shah directly in recent speeches," the CIA reported on May 21, and "is actively engaged in subversive activity in the Persian Gulf sheikdoms," something that might pose "a long-range threat to Iranian transit through the Strait of Hormuz." Before the month was out, the CIA also suspected that the Kremlin was "preparing to work somewhat more closely with [Nasser] than in the past in espousing his kind of Arab nationalism, socialism, and opposition to Western influence" from Saudi Arabia to Libya. While the agency thought it "most unlikely that the Russians gave Nasir anything like a blank check to engage in escapades that might involve the USSR in a serious confrontation with the West," there was little doubt that "Egypt remains the keystone of Soviet policies in the Middle East."[36]

Although Luke Battle was no happier than his superiors about Nasser's rapid swing to the left, the U.S. ambassador attributed the recent anti-American upsurge in Cairo at least in part to some recent anti-Egyptian actions in Washington. Despite frequent hints that the United States might resume PL-480 grain shipments, no wheat was in the pipeline, leading most Egyptian officials to conclude that the Johnson administration "was being less than forthright about aid to [the] UAR and [was] attempting [to] use aid as [a] political instrument." Furthermore, recent American military assistance for Nasser's adversaries— Skyhawk jets for Israel and early warning radar for Saudi Arabia—left little doubt among some of his advisers that the "USG [U.S. government] [was] prejudiced against them." In short, Battle believed that the Nasser regime was "in [the] midst of [an] agonizing reappraisal and that some factions were urging drastic action against us." A few inside Nasser's inner circle were saying that "early favorable consideration on [Egypt's] US wheat request" could reverse the downward spiral, but Ambassador Battle was not sanguine. "All of us should bear in mind that we are approaching [a] watershed in US-UAR relations," he concluded on May 25, 1966, "and that decisions [are] not entirely in our hands."[37]

Most U.S. policy makers, however, were inclined to write Nasser off as a lost cause. Walt Rostow, who had recently replaced McGeorge Bundy as national security adviser, gradually emerged as a particularly staunch critic of the UAR, less because of his private affection for Israel than because of his very public distaste for Soviet-backed wars of national liberation in the Third World. "The Egyptians asked us in March to negotiate a new one-year $150 million PL 480 agreement," Rostow told LBJ on June 18. Although "Nasser badly needs this food," both the State Department and the NSC staff opposed the resumption of low-cost surplus wheat shipments and preferred to sell Egypt grain "on fairly hard terms" at or near market price. "We recommend this line with some regret," Rostow explained. "But Nasser has left us little choice." The list of Nasser's sins was predictable. "He has almost dared us publicly not to renew our agreement. He has lambasted us on Vietnam. He continues to stir things up in Yemen and South Arabia," Rostow reminded LBJ. "In general, he has not picked you up on the suggestion you made to Sadat last winter to discuss our differences quietly and build a more constructive relationship." To be sure, rejecting the UAR's request for cheap wheat was "taking a calculated risk," because "Nasser may react violently." But Johnson's senior advisers felt that Nasser was only getting what he deserved. So did LBJ, who checked the "Approve" box on Rostow's memo.[38]

During the twelve months between June, 1966, and June, 1967, however, the Johnson administration's calculated risk taking in Egypt backfired and helped ignite the Six-Day War. Nasser's initial "low-key" response to the bad news about low-cost grain imports was good news in Washington. "We have managed to say 'no' to his PL 480 request," Rostow told LBJ on July 23, "without driving him off the deep end." But Egyptian Ambassador Kamel soon reported that his boss was very unhappy that UAR participation in the Food for Peace Program remained a political football. "Ending this aid would amount to telling Nasser," Kamel warned White House Middle East expert Harold Saunders on August 10, "that [you] are out to upset him." This line of reasoning revealed "a very real mistrust of US motives," Saunders replied testily, "which we do not believe is justified." Perhaps not, Kamel retorted, but "the history of our relationship since 1955 has offered enough examples of bad faith in the Egyptian view to make Nasser very sensitive to any imagined move to undercut him." When Nasser's man in Washington tried to make many of the same points in the Oval Office two days later, sparks flew. "Kamel was very long-winded," one NSC staffer remarked immediately afterward, "the President was in a hurry," and neither he nor his visitor left smiling.[39]

As the Egyptian-American stalemate deepened, the Johnson administration watched a powerful wave of radical Arab nationalism batter U.S. friends and allies in the Middle East during the last half of 1966. In Syria, where the anti-Western and pro-Soviet Ba'ath party had seized power in February, fiery young officers like Hafez al-Assad challenged Nasser for leadership of the Arab world and encouraged the PLO to step up its hit-and-run war inside Israel. Throughout the autumn of 1966, LBJ recalled in his memoirs, "a new radical government in Syria increased terrorist raids against Israel, sending Arab guerrillas across the borders . . . in flagrant violation of international law." Drawing implicit parallels between the Syrians and the North Vietnamese and between the PLO and the Viet Cong, Johnson insisted that "every state is as responsible legally for irregular forces of armed bands attacking a neighbor as it is for attacks made by its own army." Not surprisingly, when LBJ requested "a special study of Soviet penetration in the Middle East" in September, his advisers confirmed "a pattern of serious Soviet advances," not only in Cairo, where Nasser was busily substituting rubles for dollars, but also in Damascus.[40]

Complicating the already complex situation in the Middle East still further was Britain's impending departure from the region. Rather than become mired down in a no-win war against pro-Nasser guerrillas armed with Soviet weapons, Whitehall (the British foreign office) confirmed in November, 1966, that it would relinquish its naval base at Aden and turn power over to the pro-Western South Arabian Federation within eighteen months. Many U.S. officials regarded the British decision as premature, precipitous, and pusillanimous.

Convinced that Whitehall was about to "abandon the friendly South Arabian Government to the tender mercies of its enemies," the American consul in Aden warned Washington that by pulling out of the Crown Colony, "the UK will be throwing the Federation to the wolves." With FLOSY guerrillas poised to take over in Aden and with the Egyptian army and air force still firmly entrenched next door in Yemen, White House Middle East experts Howard Wriggins and Harold Saunders agreed on December 1 that "we've reached a crossroads in US-UAR relations:"

> *The Kennedy experiment is over.* We gambled that a three-year food deal, personal correspondence, and a certain amount of human respect for Nasser might moderate his revolutionary policies. We probably went too far too fast, but we have been frankly disappointed in results. He continued clandestine organization against the more moderate, oil-rich monarchies; he ventured into the Congo rebellion; more recently, his army has become increasingly Draconian in the Yemen; Radio Cairo continues to agitate Arab "nationalism"; [and] his policy often parallels Moscow's.[41]

Easy answers were in short supply, but Wriggins and Saunders believed that the Johnson administration would have to work hard during the new year to prevent Nasser, the Arab radicals, and the Soviet Union from making more trouble for America and its Middle Eastern friends like Israel and Saudi Arabia. Neither those who dwelt in the House of David nor those who dwelt in the House of Saud disagreed. Nor were they prepared to stand idly by while Nasser or his trouble-making allies in Syria stirred the pot. By March, 1967, the Israelis had unleashed a series of brutal retaliatory raids against Syrian-backed Palestinian groups on the West Bank while the Saudis had stepped up their aid to the royalist guerrillas battling Nasser's army fifteen hundred miles to the south in the mountains of Yemen. Matters began to escalate rapidly in mid-April after Israeli jets shot down six Syrian MIGs over the Golan Heights. Later that same month, Yemeni secret police ransacked the Agency for International Development (AID) office in the port city of Taiz and arrested four Americans as spies while Egyptian military advisers looked the other way.[42]

With war clouds looming, Walt Rostow sent Harold Saunders to Tel Aviv and several Arab capitals to assess the prospects for peace. Saunders's report makes gloomy reading even thirty years after it landed on LBJ's desk. "I went to the Middle East with this question," he explained: "Why should the President care about the Middle East?" Although Saunders did not use the word, his answer was "credibility":

The "war of national liberation" as a technique has come to the Middle East—on Israel's borders and now in South Arabia. President Johnson in Vietnam has invested much of himself in demonstrating that we will not tolerate this brand of aggression. His friends in the Middle East are asking how he can stand against terrorist attackers in Vietnam and not in Israel or South Arabia? We must find a way to contain them or risk losing the respect the President has won for his courage in Vietnam.[43]

What troubled Saunders most were *"the deepening political cleavages"* in the region, not just between Arabs and Israelis, but also "between moderate (Saudi Arabia, Jordan, Lebanon) and pro-Nasser states." Both sets of cleavages intersected in Cairo. For the Israelis and their friends on Capitol Hill, Nasser was little more than Hitler on the Nile. And for Saudi Arabia's King Faisal, "Nasser is the agent of Communism and is out to topple moderate regimes throughout the area" with Soviet help. On May 16 Saunders concluded, "What this adds up to is great pressure on us to join a confrontation with Nasser and [the] prediction that the US will lose its stature in the area if we refuse and fail to stop him, the USSR and the liberation armies. . . . The great temptation . . . is to conclude with our friends that Nasser is a lost cause and throw in the sponge on trying to deal with him."[44]

Even as Saunders was putting the finishing touches on this grim forecast, Nasser was taking steps in the Sinai Desert that would prompt Lyndon Johnson to reach for the sponge sooner rather than later. On May 11, Moscow had informed Cairo that the Israelis were rapidly mobilizing for an invasion of Syria. Acting on what was in retrospect misinformation and perhaps even disinformation, Nasser sent his army across the Sinai on May 16 and demanded the evacuation of a series of observation posts that the United Nations had set up in the no man's land between Egypt and Israel a decade earlier. Once UN Secretary General U Thant complied with Nasser's demand, Egyptian troops moved into Sharm el-Sheikh, which overlooked the Straits of Tiran at the mouth of the Gulf of Aqaba, the narrow waterway connecting the Israeli port of Eilat with the Red Sea. Then on May 22, Nasser announced that the straits would be closed to all Israeli shipping, something that the Jewish state regarded as an act of war. Stunned by Egypt's unilateral action, at least one White House aide drew a historical analogy likely to be well received inside Johnson's inner circle. "I confess that I look on the Israelis as Texans," presidential speechwriter John P. Roche told his boss late that night, "and Nasser as Santa Ana."[45]

Like the Texan in the Oval Office, the Israelis remembered the Alamo very well, and they had no intention of sharing the fate of Davy Crockett. Once the

Santa Ana of the Sinai took steps to make good on his threat to shut off Israeli access to the Red Sea, Prime Minister Levi Eshkol and his cabinet accelerated their contingency planning for military action against Egypt. "The last thing Israel wanted would be a war," Israeli diplomat and long-time LBJ crony Ephraim "Eppie" Evron told State Department officials as news of Nasser's action spread. But because "the Arabs felt that the United States would not act," war might soon be Eshkol's only option.[46] The Gulf of Aqaba "was where all the oil from Iran came in," investment banker, Democratic bigwig, and outspoken friend of Israel Abraham Feinberg remembered telling LBJ as the crisis deepened. Should Eshkol permit Nasser to sever that petroleum lifeline, Feinberg concluded in words that must have made Lyndon Johnson wince, "Israel would be economically castrated."[47] In short, in the vernacular of the Lone Star State, Israel's balls were on the line, and Nasser held the knife.

On May 24, 1967, LBJ and his National Security Council discussed how best to persuade Nasser to resheath his weapon. In background materials delivered to the Oval Office the previous day, NSC Adviser Walt Rostow had emphasized that the stakes were extremely high, not just for Israel but for America's other friends in the region as well. "The main issue in the Middle East today is whether Nasser, the radical states and their Soviet backers are going to dominate the area," Rostow observed with characteristic bluntness. "A related issue is whether the US is going to stand up for its friends, the moderates, or back down as a major power in the Near East" at a time when the Kremlin was probing for weak spots. "Two weeks ago, we expected South Arabia to provide that test," Rostow concluded. "The current Arab-Israeli crisis has brought the test sooner than we expected."[48]

Like Rostow, the other participants in the NSC review of the Middle East crisis believed that passing the test meant reopening the Straits of Tiran. When Secretary of State Dean Rusk suggested that the United Nations might broker a compromise, LBJ was not optimistic. "I want to play every card in the UN," he snapped, "but I've never relied on it to save me when I'm going down for the third time." Irritated by second-guessing in Congress, where some in the upper house were suggesting "that the U.S. could not manage two crises at once" and that "we ought to withdraw from Vietnam" in order to assume a higher profile in the Middle East, Johnson told Rusk to advise these nervous Nellies "that this kind of music in the Senate is just what [Soviet premier Alexei] Kosygin wants to hear." Unwilling to make a Sophie's Choice between Saigon and Tel Aviv, Johnson authorized the Pentagon to begin mobilizing a U.S. naval show of force, either alone or in conjunction with America's North Atlantic Treaty Organization (NATO) allies, to ensure Israeli access to the Red Sea.

Otherwise, CIA Director Richard Helms pointed out, the Jewish state would launch a preemptive strike against Egypt that would leave the United States "fully blackballed in the Arab world as Israel's supporter."[49]

Just before the NSC meeting broke up, the president asked Assistant Secretary of State Battle to size up the man in Cairo who had made all the excitement possible. "What," LBJ wondered, "is in Nasser's mind?" Until the Egyptian blockade of the Gulf of Aqaba, Battle replied, Nasser had seemed to be seeking only "a limited propaganda victory." Now that Egypt had closed the Straits of Tiran, however, Battle had to "wonder whether Nasser either has more Soviet support than we know about, or had gone slightly insane." Implying that the best explanation was probably a bit of both, Battle concluded that Nasser's current round of anti-Israeli saber-rattling reflected "his drive to regain leadership in the Arab world, and his need to recoup his position on the world stage."[50]

Was Nasser really a knife-wielding madman bent on castrating Israel and inviting Soviet therapists into the asylum on the eve of the Six-Day War? Was he truly the Santa Ana of the Sinai bent on butchering the Israelis like the Texan patriots who died at the Alamo seventy-five years before Lyndon Johnson was born? Categorical answers to such questions must await the opening of the Egyptian archives, but in the interim there seems to be reasonable doubt on both counts. Although Nasser's public rhetoric had grown ever more anti-Israeli as the decade wore on, down through the spring of 1967 he privately exerted a restraining influence on Palestinian commandos and their Ba'athist patrons in Syria. Although he welcomed the Kremlin's offer of expanded military assistance, Nasser was skeptical about the quality of intelligence he was receiving from Moscow regarding Israel's intentions, and he suspected that the Soviets were manipulating him into defending their left-wing clients in Damascus. And although he insisted that there was no room for compromise on the Straits of Tiran, at the eleventh hour he agreed to send UAR Vice President Zakaria Mohieddin to Washington for secret negotiations to resolve the crisis peacefully.[51]

Yet if Nasser was not crazy, neither was he wise. He failed to realize that when he tweaked the United States for practicing imperialism in Southeast Asia or Southwest Arabia, he confirmed the worst suspicions of those in Washington who saw him as a Kremlin stooge. He failed to understand that the revolutionary fanfare that tickled so many Arab ears would strike most Israelis as the first bars of a funeral dirge for the Jewish state. And he failed to see that despite all the talk about the special relationship between Washington and Tel Aviv, Israel was not America's puppet, and Lyndon Johnson could not prevent Levi Eshkol from striking first.

The longer the Middle East crisis dragged on, however, the less interest there was inside the Johnson administration in preventing an Israeli first strike. When Israeli Foreign Minister Abba Eban visited the White House on May 26 to review American plans for a multilateral "Red Sea regatta" to break the Egyptian blockade, for example, LBJ did not say categorically that the United States would part company with Israel if the Jewish state launched a preemptive war against Egypt. Instead, Johnson cryptically remarked three times: "Israel will not be alone unless it decides to go it alone."[52] Well, if LBJ were here today, we would have to remind him that "no means no," and "maybe means maybe." And given what we know about Lyndon Johnson's temperament, he would probably look us in the eye, utter something unprintable, and then say: "I meant maybe."

LBJ certainly had no illusions that his chat with Eban would restrain Israel for very long. Shortly after the Israeli diplomat left the Oval Office, Johnson convened a late-night debriefing session attended by Walt Rostow, John Roche, and several others. According to Roche, the president sipped "some of that poisonous low-cal Dr. Pepper," waxed comical for a moment, and even "did a takeoff on Eban" agonizing over Israel's options. But when the conversation turned to "what we thought the Israelis were going to do," Roche remembers that LBJ suddenly turned very serious. "They're going to hit [Nasser]," he said. "There's nothing we can do about it."[53]

During the following ten days, the Johnson administration did next to nothing to discourage the Israelis and may actually have encouraged them through the backchannel to hit Nasser hard. Indeed, according to George Ball, who served as undersecretary of state for economic affairs during the Kennedy and Johnson years, "few, either at the State Department, the White House, or on Capitol Hill would have been sorry to see Nasser humiliated or even overthrown." And across the Potomac at the Pentagon, Ball recalled, some Defense Department officials "saw a potential Arab-Israeli war as a heaven-sent opportunity not only to test American vs. Soviet weapons under combat conditions, but also to destroy Soviet influence in the Arab world by demonstrating that nation's inability to protect its Middle East clients."[54]

Ball's remarks do not seem farfetched in light of recent scholarship. In an essay published on the twenty-fifth anniversary of the Six-Day War, William Quandt argued that by the first days of June, 1967, Washington had changed the color of the light it was beaming to Tel Aviv from flashing red to steady yellow. To be sure, Dean Rusk did counsel patience and did emphasize that "the question of who fired first would be significant" when he met with Israeli Ambassador Avraham Harman on June 2. But when Harman arrived at National Airport a few hours later for a flight bound for Tel Aviv, he received a phone call from Abe Fortas, supreme court justice, presidential confidant, and staunch friend of Israel. According to a law clerk who heard only one end of the conversation, Fortas said: "Rusk will fiddle while Israel burns. If you're going to save yourself, do it yourself."[55] Israel did just that three days later.

While Rusk was playing Nero at Foggy Bottom, Walt Rostow was playing Cato in the White House basement. In a memo prepared for LBJ just fifteen hours before the shooting started, Rostow insisted in not so many words that "Nasser delenda est." The Israelis were growing ever more nervous and could not be expected to wait forever while the United States mounted its Red Sea regatta, the Cato of the West Wing pointed out. Equally important, moderates throughout the Muslim world from Beirut to Tehran were growing tired of Nasser's pan-Arab rabble-rousing. "Just beneath the surface is the potentiality for a new phase in the Middle East of moderation; a focusing on economic development; regional collaboration; and an acceptance of Israel as part of the Middle East if a solution to the refugee problem can be found," Rostow told his boss. "But all this depends on Nasser's being cut down to size." Should Nasser succeed in solidifying his radical pan-Arab coalition, Rostow warned, America might in the long run be forced "to maintain Israel as a kind of Hong Kong enclave in the region."[56]

Rostow acknowledged that the Egyptian leader's ultimate objectives remained unclear. "There is considerable legitimate argument as to whether Nasser is now postured as a Hitler, determined at all costs to exploit temporary Arab unity to crush Israel once and for all, or whether he is a shrewd operator, working off a weak base, willing to settle for as much as he can get from this crisis." Nevertheless, the bottom line remained clear. Both American credibility and Israeli national security required that the Straits of Tiran be reopened as soon as possible. "Our interest, and, in fact, the Israeli interest," Rostow pointed out, "is to do this like the sheriff in High Noon." But if Santa Ana and his outlaw band refused to back down, Gary Cooper would have to let his Israeli deputies open fire.[57]

This kind of thinking seems to have guided Lyndon Johnson's policies, and those of his Middle Eastern friends, during the Six-Day War and its immediate aftermath. Almost no one in Israel, of course, doubted that Nasser must be cut down to size, preferably sooner rather than later. Indeed, just two days after the shooting started, a pair of high-ranking Israeli officials whose identities still remain classified three decades later, told U.S. diplomats that the "war has served U.S. interests." Emphasizing that their country's "smashing victory had pricked Nasser's bloated pretensions and undercut Soviet ambitions in the entire area," the two unidentified Israelis insisted that "now was [the] time to begin thinking about [the] shape peace should take." In short, the Jewish state's "stunning military success [was] opening up [a] brave new world for [the] Israelis and ourselves," embassy personnel cabled Foggy Bottom, creating "opportunities for building Middle East stability on more secure foundations." Nor was Rostow wrong to suspect that the Shah of Iran hoped that Nasser would be laid low by Israeli jets and tanks. In fact, during a meeting with Undersecretary of State Averell Harriman in Paris just a few hours after the war erupted, the Shah growled that he "considered the long-range objective of both the United States and Iran to be 'how Nasser could be destroyed.'" Otherwise, "there would be no peace."[58]

But Rostow and his boss seem to have overestimated the pro-Western sentiments of Arab conservatives. Saudi Arabia's newly crowned King Faisal, for example, did not let his nasty skirmish with Nasser in Yemen prevent him from embargoing all oil shipments to the United States and Great Britain in June, 1967, as an act of solidarity with his embattled Egyptian rival. To a very great degree, blood proved thicker than ideology in the Arab world, something that both the Americans and the Israelis would learn the hard way in October, 1973. Lyndon Johnson seems to have been blind to this reality when he invited the Saudi Arabian ambassador and five other Arab diplomats to lunch at the White House four months after the Six-Day War. He tried hard to convince his guests that American policy in the Middle East was not so much pro-Israel as anti-Nasser. Then, somewhere between the salads and the sweets, one of the White House beagles wandered into the Fish Room to beg table scraps. According to one of the Arab diplomats, LBJ called the dog over and began talking to it. "What can I do? One man was so nasty to his neighbor that his neighbor was not able to stand it any more," Johnson drawled. "So his neighbor took hold of him and gave him a good beating. What can I do to him?"[59] For LBJ, the lesson seemed clear. Like ancient Carthage, Nasser's Egypt had finally gotten what it deserved. Although the beagle's thoughts that day went unrecorded, the Arabs would spend the better part of three decades trying to prove Lyndon Johnson wrong.

NOTES

1. Stephen Green, *Taking Sides: America's Secret Relations with a Militant Israel 1948–1967* (Boston: William Morrow, 1984), pp. 180–211; Donald Neff, *Warriors for Jerusalem: Six Days that Changed the Middle East* (New York: Simon & Schuster, 1984), passim; Edward Tivnan, *The Lobby: Jewish Political Power and American Foreign Policy* (New York: Simon & Schuster, 1987), pp. 52–68. For a more polemical and less scholarly account, see George and Douglas Ball, *The Passionate Attachment: America's Involvement with Israel, 1947 to the Present* (New York: W. W. Norton, 1992), pp. 50–66.

2. Steven Spiegel, *The Other Arab-Israeli Conflict: Making America's Middle East Policy from Truman to Reagan* (Chicago: University of Chicago Press, 1985), pp. 118–65; David Schoenbaum, *The United States and the State of Israel* (New York: Oxford University Press, 1993), pp. 148–62; H. W. Brands, *The Wages of Globalism: Lyndon Johnson and the Limits of American Power* (New York: Oxford University Press, 1995), pp. 183–218; Richard B. Parker, *The Politics of Miscalculation in the Middle East* (Bloomington: Indiana University Press, 1993), pp. 3–122.

3. Warren I. Cohen, "Balancing American Interests in the Middle East: Lyndon Baines Johnson vs. Gamal Abdul Nasser," in Warren I. Cohen and Nancy Bernkopf Tucker, eds., *Lyndon Johnson Confronts the World: American Foreign Policy, 1963–68* (New York: Cambridge University Press, 1994), pp. 279–309; Rostow to LBJ, June 4, 1967, 11:30 A.M., *Declassified Documents Reference System 1995* (Woodbridge, Conn.: Research Publications, Inc., 1995), item 1143. (Hereafter DDRS for the appropriate year and item).

4. Battle to DOS, tel. March 4, 1967, in Parker, *Politics of Miscalculation in the Middle East*, pp. 242–45.

5. Lucius Battle, Oral History Interview, Nov. 14, 1968, p. 28, Lyndon B. Johnson Presidential Library, Austin, Tex., (hereafter LBJ Library).

6. For an excellent discussion of America's early hopes for Nasser, see Joel Gordon, *Nasser's Blessed Movement: Egypt's Free Officers and the July Revolution* (New York: Oxford University Press, 1992), pp. 157–74; "Notes on Presidential-Bipartisan Congressional Leaders Meeting," Aug. 12, 1956, U.S. Department of State, *Foreign Relations of the United States, 1955–57*, Vol. 16 (Washington, D.C.: U.S. Government Printing Office, 1990): 188–96 (hereafter *FRUS* for the appropriate year and volume).

7. Ike to Dulles, Dec. 12, 1956, *FRUS 1955–57*, 16: 1296–98.

8. NIE 36.1–57, "The Outlook for Egypt and the Nasser Regime," Nov. 12, 1957, *FRUS 1955–57*, 17: 790–91.

9. Ike to Dulles, Nov. 13, 1957, and Dulles to Ike, Nov. 15, 1957, "Meetings with the President 1957 (1)," Box 5, White House Memoranda Series, John Foster Dulles Papers, Dwight D. Eisenhower Presidential Library, Abilene, Kansas (hereafter DDEL).

10. William J. Burns, *Economic Aid and American Policy toward Egypt, 1955–1981* (Albany, N.Y.: State University of New York Press, 1985), pp. 114–20. On U.S. recognition of the UAR, see Dulles to Ike, Feb. 8, 1958, *FRUS 1958–60*, 13: 421–22; Andrew Goodpaster memcon, Sept. 26, 1960, "United Arab Republic," Box 49, International Series, Ann Whitman Files, DDEL.

11. Komer to JFK, July 30, 1962, *FRUS 1961–63*, 18: 20, source note. For a fuller discussion of the Egyptian-American rapprochement during the early 1960s, see Douglas Little, "The New Frontier on the Nile: JFK, Nasser, and Arab Nationalism," *Journal of American History* 75:2 (Sept., 1988): 501–10.

12. "Vice President's Visit to Iran — Summary Briefing Paper," n.d. (mid-Aug., 1962), "Trip to Middle East 1962," Box 2, Vice Presidential Security File, Lyndon B. Johnson Presidential Library (hereafter VPSF, LBJ Library); Ambassador Julius Holmes (Tehran) to DOS, tels. Aug. 25 and 27, 1962, "Trip to Middle East 1962," Box 2, VPSF, LBJ Library.

13. LBJ to JFK, Sept. 10, 1962, "Middle East Memos," Box 10, VPSF, LBJ Library.

14. Parker T. Hart Oral History Interview, p. 18, JFK Library.

15. McCone memcon, March 26, 1963, *FRUS 1961–63*, 18: 436–37.

16. Little, "New Frontier on the Nile," pp. 510–27.

17. Lyndon B. Johnson, *The Vantage Point: Perspectives on the Presidency, 1963–1969* (New York: Holt, Rinehart & Winston, 1971), pp. 289–90.

18. Komer to McGeorge Bundy, Dec. 3, 1963, "Komer Memos, Vol. 1," Box 6, Name File, NSF, LBJ Library; Komer to McGeorge Bundy, Dec. 3, 1963, *FRUS 1961–63*, 18: 820–21; Badeau to DOS, tel. Jan. 23, 1964, "UAR Cables, Vol. 1," Box 158, Country File, National Security File, LBJ Library (hereafter CO:NSF); Benjamin Read to McGeorge Bundy, Feb. 12, 1964, "UAR Cables, Vol. 1," Box 158, CO:NSF, LBJ Library.

19. Minutes of the 525th NSC Meeting, Apr. 2, 1964, "Vol. 1, Tab 6," Box 1, NSC Meetings, NSF, LBJ Library; Rusk to Badeau, tel. May 5, 1964, "UAR Cables, Vol. 1," Box 158, CO:NSF, LBJ Library; Harriman meeting with LBJ, Apr. 3, 1964, "Memos of Meetings with the President, Vol. 1," Box 19, Files of McGeorge Bundy, NSF, LBJ Library; minutes of the 526th NSC Meeting, Apr. 3, 1964, "Vol. 1, Tab 7," Box 1, NSC Meetings, NSF, LBJ Library; DOS to Badeau, tel. June 5, 1964, "UAR Cables, Vol. 2," Box 159, CO:NSF, LBJ Library.

20. "Major Issues in U.S.-U.A.R. Relations," n.d., attached to Rusk to LBJ, Aug. 21, 1964, "UAR Memos, Vol. 2," Box 159, CO:NSF, LBJ Library.

21. CIA, "Nasir's Arab Policy—The Latest Phase," Aug. 28, 1964, "UAR Memos, Vol. 2," Box 159, CO:NSF, LBJ Library.

22. Embassy Cairo to DOS, tel. Sept. 12, 1964, "UAR Cables, Vol. 2," Box 159, CO:NSF, LBJ Library.

23. Mohamed Heikal, *The Cairo Documents* (Garden City, N.Y.: Doubleday, 1973), pp. 226–27.

24. Battle to DOS, tel. Nov. 19, 1964, "UAR Cables, Vol. 2," Box 159, CO:NSF, LBJ Library.

25. Heikal, *Cairo Documents,* pp. 228–29.

26. Battle to DOS, Dec. 23, 1964, "UAR Cables, Vol. 2," Box 159, CO:NSF, LBJ Library.

27. Heikal, *Cairo Documents,* pp. 229–30.

28. CIA, "Nasir's Port Said Speech," Dec. 24, 1964, attached to Bundy to LBJ, Dec. 24, 1964, "UAR Memos, Vol. 3," Box 159, CO:NSF, LBJ Library. A note from Horace Busby to McGeorge Bundy dated Jan. 2, 1965, reads: "The President read this at the ranch." Ibid.

29. "President's Meeting with Congressional Leaders," Jan. 22, 1965, "Misc. Meetings, Vol. 1," Box 18, McGeorge Bundy Files, NSF, LBJ Library.

30. Heikal, *Cairo Documents,* pp. 348–49.

31. Assistant Secretary of State Phillips Talbot to DOS, tel. Apr. 22, 1965, "UAR Cables, Vol. 4," Box 159, CO:NSF, LBJ Library.

32. Nasser quoted in Benjamin Read to McGeorge Bundy, June 5, 1965, "UAR Cables, Vol. 4," Box 159, CO:NSF, LBJ Library. On FLOSY, see J. B. Kelly, *Arabia, the Gulf, and the West* (New York: Basic Books, 1980), pp. 24–30.

33. "The Protection of American Interests in the Near East," n.d., attached to Rusk to LBJ, Sept. 23, 1965, "UAR Memos, Vol. 4," Box 159, CO:NSF, LBJ Library.

34. DOS memcon, Feb. 23, 1966, "UAR Memos, Vol. 4," Box 159, CO:NSF, LBJ Library.

35. Battle to DOS, tel. May 13, 1966, "UAR Cables, Vol. 4," Box 159, CO:NSF, LBJ Library.
36. CIA, "The Arab Threat to Iran," May 21, 1966, and "Egyptian-Soviet Relations," May 28, 1966, "UAR Memos, Vol. 4," Box 159, CO:NSF, LBJ Library.
37. Battle to DOS, tel. May 25, 1966, "UAR Cables, Vol. 4," CO:NSF, LBJ Library.
38. Rostow to LBJ, June 18, 1966, "UAR Memos, Vol. 4," Box 159, CO:NSF, LBJ Library.
39. Rostow to LBJ, July 23, 1966; Saunders memcon, Aug. 10, 1966; and Howard Wriggins memcon, Aug. 12, 1966, all in "UAR Memos, Vol. 4," Box 159, CO:NSF, LBJ Library.
40. Johnson, *Vantage Point,* p. 288.
41. American Consulate Aden to DOS, Nov. 22, 1966, quoted in Karl Pieragostini, *Britain, Aden and South Arabia: Abandoning Empire* (New York: St. Martin's, 1991), p. 179; Wriggins and Saunders to Rostow, Dec. 1, 1966, "UAR Memos, Vol. 5," Box 159, CO:NSF, LBJ Library. Emphasis in the original.
42. Douglas Little, "Choosing Sides: Lyndon Johnson and the Middle East," in Robert A. Divine, ed., *The Johnson Years, Volume Three: LBJ at Home and Abroad* (Lawrence: University Press of Kansas, 1994), pp. 171–74.
43. "The President's Stake in the Middle East," Saunders to Rostow, May 16, 1967, attached to Walt Rostow to LBJ, May 17, 1967, "Saunders Memos," Box 7, Name File, NSF, LBJ Library.
44. Ibid.
45. Roche to LBJ, May 22, 1967, "Middle East Crisis, Vol. 1," NSC History Files, Box 17, NSF, LBJ Library.
46. "United States Policy and Diplomacy in the Middle East Crisis, May 15–June 10, 1967," Vol. 1, Appendix P, Box 20, NSC History Files: 1967 Middle East Crisis, NSF, LBJ Library, pp. 34–35. (Hereafter NSC History 1967 Middle East Crisis).
47. Merle Miller, *Lyndon: An Oral Biography* (New York: G. P. Putnam's Sons, 1980), pp. 478–79.
48. Walt Rostow to LBJ, "NSC Discussion—South Arabia," May 23, 1967, "Briefing Papers NSC Mtgs," Box 1, Meeting Notes File, LBJ Library.
49. Minutes of the NSC Meeting, May 24, 1967, "Vol. 4, Tab 52, ME Crisis," Box 2, NSC Meeting File, NSF, LBJ Library.
50. Ibid.
51. On Nasser's efforts to restrain Syria and the PLO, see CIA, "Syria: A Center of Instability," Mar. 24, 1967, "Syria, Vol. 1," Box 156, CO:NSF, LBJ Library, and Alan Hart, *Arafat: A Political Biography* (Bloomington: Indiana University Press, 1989), pp. 216–23; Remarks by Salah Baissouny, special assistant to UAR Minister of Foreign Affairs Mahmoud Riad, in Richard Parker, ed., *The Six Day War: A Retrospective* (Gainesville: University of Florida Press, 1996), pp. 41–44; Robert Anderson (Cairo) to LBJ, tel. June 2, 1967, "Middle East Crisis, Vol. 3," Box 18, NSC History Files, NSF, LBJ Library.
52. For the latest sanitized account of this meeting, see DOS memcon, May 26, 1967, *DDRS 1993,* item 546.
53. Miller, *Lyndon,* p. 480.
54. Ball and Ball, *Passionate Attachment,* p. 55.
55. NSC History, "1967 Middle East Crisis," p. 97; William B. Quandt, "Lyndon Johnson and the June 1967 War: What Color Was the Light?" *Middle East Journal* 46 (Spring, 1992): 221.

56. Walt Rostow to LBJ, June 4, 1967, 11:30 A.M., *DDRS 1995,* item 1143.

57. Ibid.

58. Ambassador Walworth Barbour (Tel Aviv) to DOS, tel. June 7, 1967, "Middle East Crisis, Cables, Vol. 4," Box 107, CO:NSF, LBJ Library; NSC History, "1967 Middle East Crisis," p. 115.

59. Little, "Choosing Sides," pp. 179–81; Heikal, *Cairo Documents,* p. 249.

7

Ambivalent Partners

*The Lyndon Johnson Administration
and Its Asian Allies*

ROBERT J. MCMAHON

This essay, in keeping with the "Beyond Vietnam" focus of this collection, explores the complex and troubled relationships that developed during the Johnson years between the United States and some of its *other* Asian allies. When LBJ assumed the presidency, the United States was formally linked, via bilateral or multilateral security pact (or both), to six Asian nations: Japan, South Korea, Taiwan, Pakistan, Thailand, and the Philippines. A number of scholars, including Michael Schaller and Nancy Bernkopf Tucker, have ably examined America's rocky relationships with its Northeast Asian allies during this period. I will concentrate, instead, on the relatively neglected partnerships that obtained between the United States and its South and Southeast Asian allies during LBJ's presidency.

Pakistan, Thailand, and the Philippines were each formally allied to the United States through the Southeast Asia Treaty Organization (SEATO), formed in September, 1954. Two of those nations (Pakistan and the Philippines) were also linked through previously concluded bilateral security agreements. Each of the three had carefully cultivated close ties with the United States, virtually from the inception of the Cold War era, in the hope that concrete security, financial, and political benefits would accrue from formal alignment with the American-led "Free World." Yet each also harbored, from the beginning, doubts and suspicions about the reliability of the United States and concerns about the potential disadvantages of open alignment with the United States.

Theoretically, each partner in an alliance relationship expects a partnership that will prove mutually advantageous, yielding benefits of a roughly comparable nature to both sides. Each invariably calculates as well that the benefits of an alliance—tangible and intangible as they might be—will outweigh any potential costs or risks. It is axiomatic that if basic expectations are not met, if risks appear to outweigh benefits, or if mutuality begins to break down, an alliance will undergo stress and may well atrophy.

This essay will contend that all three of these alliances were severely tested during the Johnson administration, primarily, though not exclusively, through the crucible of the Vietnam War. One alliance—that with Pakistan—wound up completely severed, neither side any longer finding sufficient mutual advantage to justify its continuation. The other two—those with Thailand and the Philippines—temporarily flourished and deepened as the Vietnam War heated up, only to be shaken to their roots following Johnson's decision in March, 1968, to seek a negotiated settlement in Vietnam. That sharp, and wholly unexpected, policy reversal brought old questions to the fore once again about the reliability and staying power of the United States. It impelled as well a searching reexamination in Bangkok and in Manila of the appropriate balance to be sought between the benefits and the risks of alignment.

The search for allies forms a major theme of U.S. foreign policy throughout the early Cold War era. In the late 1940s and early and mid-1950s, the United States cemented security ties with a host of nations in Europe, Latin America, the Middle East, and the Asia-Pacific region. The Dwight D. Eisenhower administration, in particular, placed great weight on the importance of bilateral and multilateral security pacts. Convinced that fiscal realities imposed limitations on Washington's capabilities, Eisenhower and Secretary of State John Foster Dulles assiduously cultivated allies and sought to construct a series of regional alliance systems. More alliances, they were convinced, served several U.S. foreign policy goals simultaneously. They enabled the United States to encircle the Soviet Union with nations formally committed to the West; they provided for the utilization of local manpower should a global or regional conflict erupt, thus promising to save American lives; they offered potential deterrent power by erecting an American security shield that would presumably discourage Soviet or Chinese aggression against any state aligned with the United States; and they provided a psychological boost to nations already inclined to find common cause with the West. Dulles often remarked that nations needed to stand up and be counted. For him, as for most other U.S. statesmen of his generation, the Cold War involved issues of enormous historical and moral weight; fence-sitting, for them, was simply not a tolerable option.

In this sense, Pakistan, Thailand, and the Philippines passed Dulles's test. They stood up to be counted, winning considerable favor from U.S. policy makers for so doing. Of course, they did so for their own purposes and not for America's—as most U.S. officials, consummate realists that they were, recognized from the outset. Pakistan, which signed a mutual security pact with the

United States early in 1954, sought a patron who would provide protection principally against India, its chief rival on the subcontinent. Thailand and the Philippines also felt highly vulnerable in the early postwar era, a vulnerability exacerbated by the spread of colonial conflicts in Indochina, Indonesia, and Malaya and the emergence of a revolutionary, communist regime in China. The United States appeared to both nations as the most dependable guarantor of their survival in a highly fluid, unpredictable, and dangerous security environment. When, following the French collapse in Indochina early in 1954, the United States cast about for some form of multilateral security arrangement for Southeast Asia, Pakistan, Thailand, and the Philippines eagerly joined— seeking, in each case, to deepen a formal relationship with a superpower patron willing, or so it seemed, to provide much-needed military and economic assistance *and* protection against external threats.[1]

Lyndon B. Johnson inherited, as had John F. Kennedy before him, not only the alliances forged by White House predecessors but the Cold War geopolitical vision that had brought them to life. The new chief executive also fell heir to a series of nettlesome disputes that had recently rocked U.S. relations with many of its alliance partners—including SEATO allies Pakistan, Thailand, and the Philippines. As Johnson inched ever closer to open involvement in Vietnam during his first year and a half in office, he looked increasingly to America's allies for succor and support. SEATO's three Asian member states were thus assuming increased importance to the Johnson administration at the very moment when each was questioning the dependability of its more powerful partner.

Pakistan: From Alienated Ally to Ex-Ally

With JFK's strong personal backing, his administration had engineered a major shift in America's South Asia priorities between 1961 and 1963. The Sino-Indian War of October, 1962, proved the catalytic event; the Kennedy administration saw that border conflict as the historic opportunity to draw nonaligned India closer to the West that it had been seeking. Convinced that India represented a political and strategic asset of potentially enormous value to the United States, Kennedy had hurriedly dispatched emergency military aid to it while holding out the prospect for a generous, long-term military assistance agreement. The initiative had stalled, however, largely because of Pakistan's vehement opposition.

The administration attempted to ease Indo-Pakistani bitterness and hostility by helping to mediate an amicable resolution of the emotionally charged dispute over the disposition of the state of Kashmir. The endeavor had failed, and Pakistan had countered the American tilt toward its fractious neighbor by establishing close diplomatic ties with China. Kennedy delayed a final decision on the proposed Indo-American military connection because of a hesitance about further alienating Pakistan. Not only was Pakistan formally allied to the West through SEATO, the Central Treaty Organization, and a bilateral security pact with the United States, but it was the site of highly valued intelligence-collection facilities.[2]

From the earliest days of his presidency, Johnson made clear to the Pakistanis that he shared Kennedy's strong distaste for the newly emergent Sino-Pakistani entente. During a White House meeting with Pakistani Foreign Minister Zulfikar Ali Bhutto, immediately following Kennedy's funeral, LBJ forcefully warned Bhutto that any further demonstrations of friendship between Pakistan and China could jeopardize congressional support for future U.S. military and economic aid.[3] In a subsequent letter to Pakistani President Mohammed Ayub Khan, a man whom Johnson not only liked personally but had treated two years earlier to a lavish barbecue at his Texas ranch, the president reiterated those concerns. Pakistan's developing ties to China, LBJ wrote, "undermine our efforts to uphold our common security interests in the face of an aggressive nation which has clearly and most explicitly announced its unswerving hostility to the Free World." He appealed to Ayub to recognize that "Pakistan's interests are best served by doing everything possible to strengthen, not weaken, its ties with the Free World."[4]

Plainly, a gaping chasm separated the world views of American and Pakistani leaders. Pakistan's overture toward China derived not from any ideological affinity for its communist neighbor; instead, it represented diplomatic pragmatism of the highest order. Obsessed with the potential danger posed to their nation's security by a larger and more powerful India, Pakistani policy makers believed that an entente with China provided a greater degree of protection than their Western alliances alone could offer. Born of small-power insecurity conjoined with a deepening skepticism about the reliability of its principal ally, Pakistan's opening toward China serves as a classic case of geopolitical expediency overcoming ideological dissonance.

From Washington's perspective, however, the opening stood as an egregious provocation. It violated the bedrock assumptions undergirding all of America's Cold War alliances. Further, it conferred a degree of respectability on what American policy makers contemptuously regarded as an outlaw state. The Kennedy administration's military commitment to India, after all, was driven primarily by American concern about the threat China posed to the noncommunist nations of South and Southeast Asia. In the view of American national security planners, China had become a near-demonic force in world affairs; the Sino-Soviet split, they were convinced, had just emboldened Beijing's leaders, making them more, rather than less, aggressive, adventuristic, and unpredictable. Kennedy's fixation with India's importance to the United States flowed largely from his belief that India could help contain an expansionist China. Pakistan's China gambit infuriated Johnson, as it had Kennedy, because it threatened to undermine that fundamental goal of U.S. diplomacy.

But LBJ's appeals to Bhutto and Ayub had little effect on the direction of Pakistani policy. When the United States offered India a multiyear military assistance pact in mid-1964, Pakistan exploded in an angry wave of anti-American demonstrations. The knowledge that the Johnson administration was deliberately delaying future military aid commitments to Pakistan as a crude form of punishment for its China policy just added to the intensity of the protests. In a curt letter to LBJ on July 7, 1964, Ayub said that Pakistan might now have to reappraise its commitments to SEATO and CENTO. Subsequent criticisms by Ayub of U.S. policy in Vietnam, his absolute refusal even to consider sending token troop commitments there, despite U.S. entreaties, and the continuing exchange of high-level visits with the Chinese further incensed Johnson.[5]

Infuriated with the "disloyalty" of his ally, Johnson directed that U.S. relations with Pakistan should be correct but aloof. That remained LBJ's approach right up to the watershed Indo-Pakistani War in the fall of 1965. He kept up the pressure on Ayub, evidently calculating that with sufficient pressure Pakistan would abandon its flirtation with China and return to the American fold. "We may lose Pakistan," influential National Security Council aide Robert Komer had advised the president, "unless we can convince Ayub that he can't have his cake and eat it too. Pakistan's still desperate need for US aid gives us real leverage."[6]

But that strategy, which led LBJ to cancel abruptly Ayub's scheduled state visit to the United States early in 1965 and shortly thereafter to postpone the annual meeting of the Pakistan aid consortium, proved disastrously counterproductive. Pakistani rage with the United States just boiled over in the wake of those heavy-handed actions, making the Pakistani-American alliance moribund even before the outbreak of the 1965 war.

That conflict simply put the final nail in the coffin. When Ayub came to visit Johnson in Washington in December, 1965, both leaders recognized that the alliance, for all intents and purposes, was now over. The only question remaining for Johnson was: what could be salvaged from the wreckage? As subsequent events would make painfully obvious: not much.

Thailand and the Philippines: Harnessing Regional Allies

The deepening American involvement in Indochina during the early and mid-1960s bore direct and immediate consequences for Thailand and the Philippines. The importance of both of those nations to the United States grew substantially during this period for two basic reasons. First, Thailand and the Philippines each provided the United States with vital military facilities, facilities whose value increased in direct proportion to the intensification of the U.S. combat role in the region. Second, Johnson considered it politically imperative to demonstrate that strong allied support existed for America's Vietnam commitments, especially among SEATO member states. To that end, LBJ pressured the governments in Manila and Bangkok to contribute not only unqualified, public support for U.S. actions in Vietnam but also token numbers of troops to what he invariably depicted as a collective struggle against external aggression. For their part, Thai and Filipino leaders learned quickly that America's need for military installations and diplomatic backing brought a commensurate gain in their bargaining leverage. U.S. escalation in Vietnam led to a reversal in the traditional relationship between patron and client. The Johnson administration wound up needing Thailand and the Philippines every bit as much as those countries needed the United States, a state of affairs that political authorities in Bangkok and Manila did everything within their power to capitalize upon.

When Kennedy entered office in January, 1961, that sense of mutual dependence was not yet much in evidence. Quite to the contrary, growing differences over bilateral and regional security issues were creating serious alliance strains with both Thailand and the Philippines. The Kennedy administration's much-ballyhooed opening toward the nonaligned nations did not play any better in Bangkok or Manila than it did in Karachi, Seoul, or Taipei. What advantages were they gaining from open alignment with the United States, those Asian allies grumbled, when Washington was preparing to reward India, Indonesia, Egypt, and other fence-straddlers with economic and military largesse? Throughout the early months of the Kennedy administration, disgruntled politicians and diplomats in Thailand and the Philippines hurled charges of inconstancy and unreliability at their American ally with disturbing regularity—in much the same way as did their counterparts in Pakistan. Filipinos and Thais complained openly that SEATO was providing precious little real protection. They also blamed SEATO—and the Kennedy administration—for pursuing a policy of vacillation and retreat in Laos that jeopardized their own security interests.

Speaking to an American reporter in May, 1961, Philippine President Carlos Garcia declared that the United States had to stand firm against communist expansion in Asia "before it's too late." He urged the United States to "put out the fires" in Laos and Vietnam "now before they get too large." Nagging bilateral disputes concerning the Philippine sugar quota and longstanding Filipino damage claims stemming from World War II served to further roil the waters.[7]

American observers were temporarily relieved with the election in November, 1961, of Diosdado Macapagal as Garcia's successor. They expected that the new president—described by one U.S. expert as "pro-American to the point where it is a source of some embarrassment to us"—would move quickly to close the breach. Instead, he opened it still further. In response to the Kennedy administration's brushing aside of his request for additional economic assistance and congressional rejection of a compensation package for Filipino war damage claimants, Macapagal shocked Washington officialdom by canceling a scheduled visit to the United States. "It seems the United States treats her friends more shabbily than those who are not with her," the Philippine president charged in a statement issued to the press.[8] "The feeling of resentment among our people and the attitude of the U.S. Congress," he subsequently wrote Kennedy, "negate the atmosphere of good will upon which my state visit to your country was predicated."[9]

As always, when problems muddied relations with its former colony, the United States focused first and foremost on the security of its invaluable military base sites. Macapagal brought that issue to the surface when he told a reporter that a continued deterioration of U.S.-Philippine relations could endanger American base rights in his country. However empty that threat might have been, it certainly caught the attention of U.S. diplomatic and defense officials. They moved quickly to heal the wound. Philippine bases were far too critical to the overall U.S. defense posture in the Pacific to allow them to be jeopardized by minor irritants. The Kennedy administration, consequently, made a concerted effort to reassure the Filipinos of its intentions and its commitment. JFK even twisted some arms in Congress to gain passage of a generous Philippine war damage bill that he signed in August, 1962. Those efforts, though they helped alleviate some of the more pronounced strains in U.S.-Philippine relations, did little to erase the underlying—and largely accurate—suspicion from which they sprang: namely, that the United States took the Philippines for granted and paid little heed to Philippine interests and concerns.[10]

Thailand's complaints about U.S. policy at the start of the Kennedy administration proved even harsher and more frequent than those being issued from the Philippines. The success of communist insurgencies in neighboring Laos and nearby South Vietnam heightened the historic Thai sense of vulnerability. It was that sense of vulnerability, of course, that had impelled the Bangkok government to cast its fate with the United States a decade earlier and that had made it so eager a signatory to the SEATO pact. As the Pathet Lao insurgency to the north gained strength, the faith of Thai leaders in the ability of the United States to guarantee their security weakened. In a series of personal letters to

JFK and in several face-to-face meetings with U.S. representatives, Prime Minister Sarit Thanarat and Foreign Minister Thanat Khoman laid bare their concerns. The deterioration of the situation in Laos directly threatened Thailand's security, they stressed. Yet SEATO, saddled not only with unwieldy procedural mechanisms but, in Britain and France, with two members adamantly opposed to military intervention in Laos, afforded little hope of positive action. Sarit, in exasperation, told the CIA representative in Bangkok, "We are not threatening to get of SEATO, we *are* getting out."[11] Underlying that persistent focus on SEATO's inadequacies lay a far broader concern: in a crisis, could Thailand truly count on the United States? That question became increasingly urgent with the Kennedy administration's push for the neutralization of Laos, a policy choice anathema to the ardently anticommunist Thais and one they equated with appeasement.

From the first, the Kennedy administration recognized that Thai dissatisfaction posed a potentially grave threat to the U.S. position throughout the region. Ambassador Kenneth T. Young hardly exaggerated when he called Thailand "an unofficial and disguised base of operations for the United States in Southeast Asia." The government of Thailand, Young added, "is allowing us to carry on an increasing number of operations in and out of Thailand which we could not conduct from any other piece of real estate in Asia. If we lose this base of operations we will have to retreat to the island chain and depend solely on sea and air power."[12] All contingency planning for direct U.S. military intervention in either Laos or South Vietnam was predicated on a friendly Thailand providing liberal access to military bases and intelligence facilities located on its soil. Thailand, in short, was America's indispensable ally on mainland Southeast Asia. "The principal purpose of SEATO," Secretary of State Dean Rusk pointed out during closed hearings of the Senate Foreign Relations Committee early in 1964, "was that it offered protection to Thailand. The others are connected to us in other respects, but Thailand was the central member."[13]

The Kennedy administration labored to reassure Thai leaders about the depth and reliability of the U.S. commitment, much as it was doing with their Filipino counterparts. In several personal messages, Kennedy made clear that Washington continued to place a high value on its ties with Bangkok; U.S. officials insisted that any Pathet Lao or North Vietnamese air strikes against Thai territory would bring forth a direct and immediate U.S. military response. A joint communiqué, following a meeting between Secretary of State Rusk and Foreign Minister Thanat in 1962, restated the U.S. commitment to Thailand's security embodied in SEATO. Those efforts did not fully succeed, however, in curbing what one U.S. observer described as the "morbid fears gripping the Thais."[14] American planners, consequently, debated another tack as well: the emplacement of a small contingent of U.S. combat troops in Thailand to serve as a tripwire that might serve to deter any hostile action against Thailand while simultaneously signaling to the Thais the seriousness of the U.S. commitment.[15]

The sudden unraveling of the Laotian cease-fire in the spring of 1962 and the subsequent Pathet Lao seizure of the town of Nam Tha in northwestern Laos provided the United States with both the opportunity and the perceived need to implement such a plan. When some 5,000 Royal Lao troops fled across the Mekong River into Thailand after the fall of Nam Tha, Thailand responded with alarm and looked to the United States for help. After a series of intensive meetings with his top national security advisers, Kennedy authorized, with Sarit's approval, the immediate dispatch of 1,800 U.S. ground forces to Thailand, together with an Air Force fighter squadron and a Marine air squadron.[16]

The dispatch of U.S. troops at the height of the Nam Tha crisis opened a new chapter in Thai-American relations. However trivial the precipitating episode might seem in retrospect, the Kennedy administration's swift and decisive response earned it considerable respect among Thai elites, easing doubts about the credibility of American promises. "This action," remarked one high-ranking Thai official approvingly, "shows that SEATO is no 'paper tiger.'"[17]

With his dramatic escalation of the U.S. military commitment to the Saigon regime in 1964 and 1965, Lyndon Johnson certainly went a long way toward easing any lingering doubts about U.S. resolve—in both Thailand and the Philippines. LBJ's decision to embroil the United States in a major land war on the Southeast Asian mainland enhanced, in turn, the value of each of those SEATO allies to the United States. Thailand and the Philippines, each of which provided military facilities essential for the swift movement of troops and the necessary projection of U.S. air and naval power throughout the region, became irreplaceable props behind the U.S. war effort. In July, 1965, the State Department alerted U.S. diplomats in Manila that they should prepare President Macapagal for the "greatly increased use" of U.S. bases; shortly thereafter, the Pentagon pushed for a blanket approval of U.S. overflights of Philippine territory.[18] Also in the summer of 1965, coincident with the arrival of large numbers of U.S. combat units in South Vietnam, the joint chiefs of staff called attention to the necessity for "a suitable build-up in Thailand to enable the expeditious deployment there of major US forces." Specifically, the chiefs recommended the immediate development of additional logistic support bases, the construction of new airfields, the improvement of existing air bases so as to increase their capacity, and "measures to increase the readiness of Thai armed forces."[19] Approximately half of the bombing raids conducted by the United States against North Vietnam during the 1965–68 period were, in fact, launched from U.S.-controlled air bases in Thailand.

Johnson also personally pressed first the Filipinos and later the Thais to contribute troops to the struggle in Vietnam. At a White House meeting at the end of 1964, Defense Secretary Robert S. McNamara observed candidly that a few thousand troops from such countries as the Philippines, Australia, and Britain did "not make much diff[erence] militarily, but much politically." If the Philippines committed a contingent of troops to Vietnam, American representatives made clear, the United States was "prepared to pick up the tab."[20] No one could anticipate, at this early stage, how many other payments would be needed to ensure continued Filipino and Thai support.

In Vietnam's Shadow

The intensification of the Vietnam War during the mid- and late 1960s left a profound imprint throughout all of Southeast Asia. Outside of Indochina, no countries became as deeply embroiled in the conflict as Thailand and the Philippines. Essential props of the American war effort, Thailand and the Philippines provided the United States with crucial air, naval, and logistics bases, unswerving political support, and token contingents of troops. The Indochina conflict also brought both nations enhanced stature and influence, increased aid dollars, and a boom in GI-related local businesses.

Throughout the course of the war, Thailand served as a crucial forward base for U.S. military and intelligence operations across Indochina. Thailand made its air bases available for U.S. bombing missions against Pathet Lao and North Vietnamese targets within technically neutral Laos, beginning in the early 1960s and continuing with increasing intensity through the mid- and late 1960s. Without Thai support, the United States simply could not have carried on its covert war in Laos. In addition, the Bangkok regime actively supported the U.S. bombing of North Vietnam. Many works on the Vietnam War fail even to mention Thailand's role. Yet, as noted above, about half of all American bombing missions flown over North Vietnam from the initial sorties of February, 1965, through the end of the Johnson administration took off from airfields in Thailand.[21]

Not surprisingly, the Chinese and North Vietnamese, from the first, paid close attention to the Thai role. Both communist powers, in fact, regularly denounced Thailand as an American surrogate and accomplice. On April 25, 1965, an official statement issued by the North Vietnamese Foreign Ministry repudiated the Thais for "their complicity in the United States aggressive war in South Vietnam and for having let the United States use bases on Thailand territory to attack the Democratic Republic of Vietnam."[22] Despite those protests, Thailand refused to shift course. Prime Minister Thanom Kittikachorn, Foreign Minister Thanat Khoman, and their chief associates in the military-dominated regime were convinced that Thai security—and, not coincidentally, the preservation of their own grip on power within Thailand—necessitated firm alignment with the United States and a strong commitment to the American-led war against communist expansion in Indochina. Chinese and North Vietnamese support for a burgeoning communist insurgency within northeastern Thailand just buttressed that conviction.

Initially, the Bangkok government sought to shroud its role in secrecy. Thai officials scrupulously avoided any public mention of the growing American military presence within their country. But, as *New York Times* columnist C. L. Sulzberger observed in April, 1966, it was "one of Asia's worst kept secrets." Assistant Secretary of State William Bundy acknowledged as much during an executive session of the Senate Foreign Relations Committee. "It is a matter of common knowledge," he conceded, "known to any reporter who visits Thailand." The Thais preferred, nonetheless, to avoid public revelation of their role in the bombing of North Vietnam and Laos because they did not want to expose "themselves to unnecessary additional abuse and exacerbation of the situation from Radio Peiping and Radio Hanoi." The United States, Bundy explained, has "had to go along with their basic desire not to publicize those operations."[23]

After several U.S. newspaper articles called attention to the growing ties of intimacy between Washington and Bangkok, Prime Minister Thanom broke his government's official silence. On August 10, 1966, the field marshal opened the newly constructed, $140 million air base at Sattahip with formal ceremonies. The new air base, the seventh constructed within Thailand since the early 1960s, featured an impressive, 11,500-foot concrete runway. The lengthy runway had been built so that the base could accommodate B-52 bombers, the largest in the American fleet. Up to then, U.S. B-52s had operated from Guam, some 2,550 air miles from Saigon; the new Thai military installation, from which the huge bombers began operating against guerrilla strongholds within South Vietnam in March, 1967, was a mere 125 air miles from Saigon.[24]

The opening of the sprawling Sattahip-U Thapao base complex, which included, along with the fully equipped airfield, a new, deep harbor port and a large ammunition depot, testified powerfully to America's growing reliance on Thailand. By the end of 1967, 35,000 U.S. troops were serving there, most of them stationed at one of the seven air bases constructed from scratch or expanded by the United States within the past several years. That was more than twice as many soldiers as had been present in South Vietnam when Johnson assumed office. "We are running a major war effort in Thailand," marveled Senator Stuart Symington in March, 1966.[25]

The hundreds of millions of dollars that the Johnson administration had poured into Thailand during that time certainly seemed a sound investment. When LBJ saw political advantages to be reaped from the presence of "many flags" in South Vietnam, he naturally turned again to his Thai friends. And they came through once again, dispatching a 2,300-man combat force in January, 1967, and supplementing that force with another 10,000 men at the end of the year.[26] Thai and American interests, cemented by common security concerns and lubricated by Washington's willingness to pay liberally for what it needed, appeared to be running along parallel tracks. "The people of America," declared a grateful U.S. Ambassador Graham Martin immediately after the Sattahip festivities, "do not fully understand the extent of the cooperation between the two countries."[27]

The same observation could doubtless have been made about Filipino-American cooperation during the war. The mammoth air and naval installations at Clark Field and Subic Bay had, by the mid-1960s, become indispensable to U.S. military operations and troop movements throughout the region. "The bases," observed National Security Council staffer Marshall Wright, "are central to our operations in Viet Nam and our longer range military effectiveness in Southeast Asia."[28] The United States had always insisted upon its right to use those facilities as it saw fit. Political leaders in Manila, consequently, could not capitalize on the sudden increase in the bases' value as easily as had their counterparts in Bangkok. Johnson's interest in foreign troop commitments to Vietnam proved another matter. President Macapagal pledged late in 1965 to send a 2,000-man engineer battalion to Vietnam, only to have nationalist opposition in the Philippine Senate block the legislation needed to authorize the commitment. With the election of the ambitious Ferdinand Marcos to the presidency in November, 1965, the very man who as leader of the Senate had led the opposition to the Macapagal troop proposal, the Johnson administration had to start from ground zero.

U.S. officials discovered that in Marcos they were dealing with a tough, relentlessly self-interested bargainer. After intense pressure from the Johnson White House, punctuated by special appeals from such high-level visitors as Vice President Hubert Humphrey and Ambassador-at-Large Averell Harriman, Marcos finally relented. But he extracted a substantial quid pro quo for the troop commitment, gaining an additional $80 million in U.S. economic aid in return for the long-promised battalion of combat engineers as well as a U.S. subsidy for the cost of the troops. Jack Valenti, one of Johnson's top political advisers, asked with resignation: "What is too high a cost for the presence of 2,500 Philippine fighting men in Viet Nam?"[29] Senator J. William Fulbright, the powerful chairman of the Senate Foreign Relations Committee and an increasingly outspoken critic of the Vietnam War, proved considerably less enthusiastic about the Philippine commitment. "This is a new policy for this country to hire mercenaries to fight our wars, isn't it?" he sarcastically asked a Johnson administration representative.[30]

In September, 1966, at almost the exact same time that the Philippine engineers were disembarking for Vietnam, Marcos was departing Manila for his first state visit to the United States. The Filipino leader's knack for telling his listeners what they wanted to hear was fully in display throughout the two-week trip. During a formal reception at the White House, Marcos lavishly praised Johnson for his wisdom, courage, and leadership. "The compulsion of the timorous you have discarded," proclaimed the Philippine visitor; "the importunings of friends you have rejected. But staying close to the image that you knew of America and your vision of what is America, you have insured the security of my part of the world." In a seventy-minute speech before Congress the next day, Marcos saluted the United States for its decision to stand tall against communist aggression in Southeast Asia and urged Americans to remain intensively involved in the defense and economic affairs of Asia.[31] It was music to the notoriously vain Johnson's ears, even if Marcos's fawning rhetoric could not entirely disguise the blatantly self-interested agenda that lay behind it.

A Wavering Commitment?

From the beginning, one of the stated goals of American intervention in Vietnam was to bolster the noncommunist states of the region by reassuring them about the strength, resolution, and beneficence of the United States. But that goal appeared little closer to realization during Johnson's final two years in office than did the goal of military victory in Vietnam. Even Thailand and the Philippines, probably the most loyal of America's Asian allies, quietly expressed resentment at the arrogance and self-interestedness of their superpower patron and felt deep unease about the presence of a half-million foreign troops in Vietnam. Nationalism remained a potent force in an area just emerging from centuries of colonial oppression; and regionalism—the search for Asian solutions to Asian problems—remained a powerful dream.

Even the Thai elite, who had embraced the anticommunist cause—and the United States—as unequivocally as any other ruling faction within Southeast Asia, dreamed of a future free of external interference. Thai Foreign Minister Thanat, though a rabid backer of the U.S. war effort in Vietnam, told the foreign ministers of Malaysia and the Philippines in August, 1966, that it was time "to take our destiny into our hands instead of letting others from far away mold it at their whim." In April, 1967, Thanat confidently predicted that the nations of Southeast Asia would move "fairly rapidly" toward regional cooperation in the economic, cultural, and political spheres, free from the "dictation" of the great powers. He continued to emphasize the need for victory in Vietnam, a struggle whose outcome the Thai diplomat considered essential to his nation's security. Yet peace, when it came, Thanat insisted, must be "an Asian peace"— a peace that would spur regional progress, bring an end to Western interference, and lead to the removal of all foreign troops.[32]

The Filipino elite displayed an equally ambivalent attitude toward the United States. Filipinos had come to rely on the protection their superpower ally afforded them and certainly welcomed the infusion of dollars that extensive American aid programs and the presence of 40,000 U.S. military personnel generated. Yet, like the Thais, they resented the dependence fostered by a relationship among unequals, a dependency complicated in the Philippine case by the powerful legacy of American colonialism. "Although there is a strong residue of affection for the U.S. among the masses," noted the NSC's Marshall Wright in August, 1967, "ultranationalism is rampant in the elite." The United States, and the American Embassy in particular, he added, "are the natural focus for ultranationalist suspicions and hostilities."[33] Filipino leaders, too, longed for a Southeast Asia in which Southeast Asians could mold their own destiny.

On August 7, 1967, Thailand, the Philippines, Malaysia, Indonesia, and Singapore formed a new regional grouping, the Association of Southeast Asian Nations (ASEAN), in an effort to bring that dream closer to reality. The primary purposes of ASEAN, according to its founding charter, were nothing less than the "promotion of regional peace and stability," the avoidance of "self-defeating and wasteful" interstate conflicts in the area, the promotion of regional economic, social, and cultural cooperation, and the establishment of a framework for regional order. With the Vietnam War then at its height, few observers paid much attention to the ASEAN initiative or to the lofty goals articulated by its founders.[34] Yet this halting step toward regional cooperation tapped a deep root. In the long run, ASEAN would prove far more dynamic and durable than anyone at the time could have imagined.

Johnson's decision, in the wake of the watershed Tet offensive of January and February, 1968, to curtail U.S. bombing raids against North Vietnam and to enter into formal negotiations with Hanoi looking toward a negotiated settlement rocked U.S.-Thai and U.S.-Filipino relations, giving an additional boost to the regional trend that ASEAN symbolized. The U.S. policy shift plainly carried momentous consequences for America's Asian allies. Thailand and the Philippines shared with the United States a genuine fear of the threat posed by China to the region's security and, more broadly, by communist expansion and locally based insurgent movements. Yet, now, the United States was beginning to extricate itself from Vietnam while moving to limit its commitments throughout the region—or so it seemed. Leading officials in the Philippines and Thailand, much like their counterparts in South Vietnam and Laos, found this new policy direction highly worrisome. Presented to them as a fait accompli, Johnson's announcement of a partial bombing halt and his call for a negotiated settlement with Hanoi seemed to presage American withdrawal from the region and abandonment of its friends.

Within a week of Johnson's March 31 speech announcing that policy shift, Philippine President Marcos expressed concern publicly that the United States was beginning to pull out of Asia. If that occurred, he warned solemnly, Manila might need to reach an accommodation with Beijing. Earlier, Marcos had warned that the loss of South Vietnam to the communists would push the nonaligned countries of the region into China's arms. "Probably all the countries in Asia and the leaders of Asia would start reassessing their positions," he said.[35]

Thai Foreign Minister Thanat voiced similar fears. Thais, he exclaimed after Johnson's surprise announcement of the U.S. bombing halt and renewed commitment to negotiations with North Vietnam, suddenly found themselves "in much great danger." They needed, consequently, to bring pressure on Washington to prevent it from "compromising with the Communists in any way that would be tantamount to capitulation." Complained Thanat on another occasion: "How can you expect others to have faith in you, if you have no faith in yourselves?" The Thais, who had chosen to trust their fate to the United States as much as any other Southeast Asian people, felt the ground shifting ominously beneath them. "The impact of the Vietnam war is total," observed a Thai political science professor in April, 1968. "It relates directly to our security, it has altered our way of life and swollen our economy. It should not surprise anyone that we are vitally concerned about what happens there." In early May, Premier Thanom traveled to Washington in a frustrating attempt to find out exactly what the new U.S. position portended for his country.[36]

The visit solved little. Realizing that the Thais were "uneasy about the constancy of the U.S. commitment to the defense of Thailand in particular and Southeast Asia in general," as the State Department delicately phrased it, Johnson and other top officials sought to reassure Thanom that the United States fully intended to stand by its commitments. He remained skeptical. The United States continued to rely on Thailand as a staging area for bombing and intelligence operations across the Indochina peninsula right up to the end of the Johnson administration—and thereafter. For its part, Thailand continued to benefit from the American alliance, and especially from the infusion of dollars into the Thai economy that it made possible. Yet, by 1968, fundamental changes in the alliance were underway that neither side could ignore. "More and more senior Thai Army officers lean toward the idea of lessening Thailand's dependence on the United States," noted a realistic CIA intelligence report of December, 1968. "All current military policy and planning," it added, was now "based upon the assumption that Thailand cannot depend upon the Southeast Asia Treaty Organization and that the United States may withdraw from Southeast Asia."[37] Significantly, U.S. analysts realized that some Thai civilian and military officials were beginning to consider détente with China as a hedge against a future American withdrawal from the region.

The critical reactions in the Philippines and Thailand to the American policy shift in Vietnam did not exactly catch the Johnson administration by surprise. The United States had, after all, consistently justified its military intervention in Vietnam by emphasizing the need to bolster Southeast Asia's noncommunist states, demonstrate to them America's credibility and dependability, and prevent any potential regional dominoes from toppling. It was easily predictable, if no less problematic for being so, that the nations in whose names the United States was making its stand in Indochina would protest at the first hint of a diminished American commitment. Top administration officials responded simply by denying that any fundamental change in U.S. policy was taking place. But that was a ploy whose utter transparency was as evident in Asian capitals as it was in Washington.

The anguished, if anticipated, reaction from such key regional allies as Thailand and the Philippines (joined, of course, by South Vietnam) helps explain why Johnson never completed the policy reorientation he set in motion. Acute financial and diplomatic pressures, rippling domestic unrest, and the doubts of some of his closest advisers had turned LBJ around, impelling him to limit U.S. troop commitments while pressing for a peace settlement. But this proud, strong-willed politician, nearing the end of over three stormy decades in public life, refused to tolerate even the thought of defeat of Vietnam. Nor would he countenance any action that might erode the very international credibility that he had, from the first, sought to preserve by his Vietnam decisions.

Several broad conclusions can be drawn from this brief survey of U.S. relations with Pakistan, Thailand, and the Philippines during the 1963–68 period. First, alliance dissatisfactions, rooted in unfulfilled expectations, were present on both sides of the alliance divide in all three cases. Second, there should be nothing surprising about this state of affairs because tensions are endemic to alliance relationships—especially so in the case of alliances among unequals. Third, those ever-present tensions became unusually acute during this period in large part because it was a time of great international crisis and internal stress.

Finally, quid pro quos form the coin of the realm in alliance relationships. The failure of either partner, or both, to satisfy the expectations of the other will inevitably generate severe strains in an alliance, a phenomenon manifested in all three of these cases.

LBJ inherited a deteriorating partnership with Pakistan upon his ascension to the White House and quickly managed to make it worse. On his watch, the Pakistani-American alliance dissolved because neither side any longer could justify its continuance; the parallel interests that had brought it about no longer existed. Johnson inherited an improving relationship with both Thailand and the Philippines when he assumed office, an improvement brought about by America's Vietnam-induced politico-military needs and the benefits it was willing to dispense to meet those needs. A sort of golden era ensued, based on an unusual mutuality of interests. But it proved as short lived as it was artificial. Following his decision, early in 1968, to shift course in Vietnam, a new crisis of faith erupted. As Johnson left office, America's relationships with Thailand and the Philippines once again echoed with charges of bad faith and inconstancy. Johnson had proved no more adept at solving the alliance conundrum in Asia than had his predecessors—or would his successors.

NOTES

1. Gary R. Hess, "The American Search for Stability in Southeast Asia: The SEATO Structure of Containment," in *The Great Powers in East Asia, 1953–1960,* Warren I. Cohen and Akira Iriye, eds. (New York: Columbia University Press, 1990), pp. 272–95.
2. Robert J. McMahon, *The Cold War on the Periphery: The United States, India, and Pakistan* (New York: Columbia University Press, 1994).
3. Secretary of State Dean Rusk to the Embassy in Pakistan, Dec. 2, 1963, NSC History of South Asia, National Security File (NSF), Lyndon B. Johnson Library (LBJ Library), Austin, Tex.; Robert Komer to Johnson, Sept. 9, 1965, ibid.; George W. Ball, *The Past Has Another Pattern: Memoirs* (New York: Norton, 1982), p. 314.
4. Johnson to Ayub, Dec. 9, 1963, NSC History of South Asia, NSF, LBJ Library.
5. Under Secretary of State George Ball to Johnson, July 5, 1964, ibid.; Rusk to Ambassador Walter McConaughy, July 29, 1964, ibid.; CIA Special Report, "Pakistan and the Free World Alliance," July 10, 1964, NSF, Pakistan, Cables, vol. I, LBJ Library.
6. Komer to Johnson, Apr. 16, 1965, NSC History of South Asia, NSF, LBJ Library. For a fuller account of U.S. relations with Pakistan during the Johnson administration, see Robert J. McMahon, "Toward Disillusionment and Disengagement in South Asia," in *Lyndon Johnson Confronts the World: American Foreign Policy, 1963–1968,* Warren I. Cohen and Nancy Bernkopf Tucker, eds. (New York: Cambridge University Press, 1994), pp. 135–71.

7. Rusk to Kennedy, Feb. 24, 1961, *Foreign Relations of the United States* (hereafter cited as *FRUS*), 1961–1963, 23: 841; memorandum from Lucius Battle to McGeorge Bundy, July 13, 1961, ibid., pp. 770–73; *New York Times,* May 11, 1961, p. 1, and May 13, 1961, p. 2.

8. Robert H. Johnson (NSC) to Walt Rostow, July 14, 1961, *FRUS,* 1961–1963, 23: 775–76.

9. *New York Times,* May 11, 1962, p. 3; Macapagal to Kennedy, quoted in H. W. Brands, *Bound to Empire: The United States and the Philippines* (New York: Oxford University Press, 1992), p. 278.

10. William E. Stevenson (U.S. ambassador in the Philippines), to Roger Hilsman, May 6, 1963, *FRUS,* 1961–1963, 23: 818–21.

11. Memorandum, Feb. 26, 1962, ibid., p. 915.

12. Young to Maxwell Taylor, Oct. 27, 1961, ibid., pp. 28–29.

13. Rusk comments, Mar. 3, 1964, *Executive Sessions of the Senate Foreign Relations Committee,* 1964, Historical Series, 88th Cong., 2nd sess. (Washington, D.C.: U.S. Government Printing Office, 1988), 16: 139–40 (hereafter cited as *Executive Sessions*).

14. Memorandum from Robert Johnson to Rostow, June 26, 1961, *FRUS,* 1961–1963, 23: 870.

15. Rostow to Kennedy, Oct. 2, 1961, ibid., pp. 885–86.

16. Ibid., pp. 926–39; Timothy Castle, *At War in the Shadow of Vietnam: U.S. Military Aid to the Royal Lao Government, 1955–1975* (New York: Columbia University Press, 1993), pp. 45–46. See also Roger Warner, *Shooting at the Moon: The Story of America's Clandestine War in Laos* (South Royalton, Vt.: Steerforth Press, 1996).

17. *New York Times,* June 8, 1962, p. 3.

18. Summary of discussions at Honolulu Conference, Oct. 8–9, 1962, *FRUS,* 1961–1963, 23: 973–74; Brands, *Bound to Empire,* pp. 281–82.

19. Joint Chiefs of Staff Paper, Aug. 27, 1965, *FRUS,* 1964–1968, 3: 363.

20. Memorandum of White House meeting, Dec. 1, 1964, ibid., 1: 967.

21. *New York Times,* July 11, 1966, p. 3.

22. Ibid., Apr. 26, 1965, p. 3

23. Ibid., Apr. 15, 1966, p. 38. Bundy comments, Sept. 20, 1966, Senate Foreign Relations Committee, *Executive Sessions,* 1966, 18: 946.

24. See, for example, *New York Times,* Dec. 12, 1965, p. 4; Apr. 15, 1966, p. 38; July 11, 1966, p. 3; Mar. 23, 1967, p. 1; Apr. 8, 1967, p. 3; and Aug. 11, 1966, p. 2.

25. Symington comments, Mar. 4, 1966, Senate Foreign Relations Committee, *Executive Sessions,* 1966, 18: 589.

26. W. Scott Thompson, *Unequal Partners: Philippine and Thai Relations with the United States, 1965–1975* (Lexington, Mass.: D. C. Heath, 1975), pp. 83–86; *New York Times,* Apr. 16, 1967, IV, p. 4 and Nov. 10, 1967, p. 1. See also Robert M. Blackburn, *Mercenaries and Lyndon Johnson's "More Flags": The Hiring of Korean, Filipino and Thai Soldiers in the Vietnam War* (Jefferson, N.C.: McFarland, 1994).

27. *New York Times,* Aug. 11, 1966, p. 2. See also *United States Security Agreements: Kingdom of Thailand,* Hearings before the Subcommittee on United States Security Agreements and Commitments Abroad of the Committee on Foreign Relations, U.S. Senate, 91st Cong., 1st sess., Part 3, Nov. 10–18, 1969 (Washington, D.C.: U.S. Government Printing Office, 1970).

28. Memorandum from Marshall Wright to Rostow, Aug. 2, 1967, NSF, Philippines, Memos (2), vol. IV, Box 279, LBJ Library.

29. Quoted in Raymond Bonner, *Waltzing with a Dictator: The Marcoses and the Making of American Policy toward the Philippines* (New York: Times Books, 1987), p. 49. See also Stanley Karnow, *In Our Image: America's Empire in the Philippines* (New York: Ballantine, 1989), pp. 375–77.

30. Fulbright comments, Feb. 23, 1966, Senate Foreign Relations Committee, *Executive Sessions,* 1966, 18: 280.

31. *New York Times,* Sept. 15, 1966, pp. 1, 15, and Sept. 16, 1966, pp. 1, 3.

32. Ibid., Oct. 29, 1966, p. 10, and Apr. 12, 1967, p. 6.

33. Wright to Rostow, Aug. 2, 1967, NSF, Philippines, Memos (2), vol. IV, Box 279, LBJ Library.

34. Michael Leifer, *ASEAN and the Security of South-East Asia* (London: Routledge, 1989), pp. 19–21.

35. *New York Times,* Jan. 7, 1968, p. 14, and Apr. 6, 1968, p. 6.

36. Ibid., Feb. 7, 1968, p. 13; Mar. 23, 1968, p. 2; Apr. 14, 1968, p. 1; and May 8, 1968, p. 5.

37. Scope Paper for Thanom visit, May, 1968, NSF, Thailand, PM Thanom Visit (1), Box 285, LBJ Library; CIA Intelligence Information Cable, Dec. 4, 1968, NSF, Thailand, Memos, vol. VIII, Box 284, LBJ Library.